A Better Bible Study Method – Book Two

Right in the Sight of the LORD

God's Word Can Teach Us

How to Know the Truth

J. Phillips

Find this book series and links to free Bible study tools at:
www.ABetterBibleStudyMethod.com (ABBSM.com)

Right in the Sight of the LORD, A Better Bible Study Method – Book Two
© 2020 by J. Phillips

The website for the Better Bible Study Method book series is: www.ABetterBibleStudyMethod.com – or – ABBSM.com

Send all correspondence to:
ABetterBibleStudyMethod.com
P.O. Box 885, Lockport, IL 60441
Phone: (770) 842-6370

ISBN13: 978-0-9702687-8-5
Library of Congress Control Number: 2019937604

Scripture references are from the Holy Bible, King James Version.

Some of this work appeared in a prior edition under another title. Portions of that book are included herein along with new research and more examples to show scripture's teaching leads people to grow in grace and knowledge by challenging them with the truth.

Right in the Sight of the LORD

Table of Contents

Preface		4
Introduction		5
Chapter 1	Founded Upon God's Word	7
Case Study	The Case of David's Turn	17
Chapter 2	Right in the Sight of the LORD	31
Case Study	The Case of John's Question	43
Chapter 3	The Religious Environment	53
Chapter 4	Learning from God's Word	71
Case Study	The Case of The Eleven	89
Chapter 5	Build on a Firm Foundation	97
Chapter 6	A Change for the Better	109
Case Study	The Case of Jesus Wept	123
Chapter 7	According to the Scriptures	131
Chapter 8	The Love of the Truth	151
Case Study	The Case of God's Gift	167
Chapter 9	The Law of Liberty	179
Chapter 10	In Conclusion	193
Postscript		232
Index		233

Note: The disciple whom Jesus loved was the anonymous author of the fourth gospel in our Bible and the term fourth gospel is used in this book to identify quotations from his work. Visit TDWJL.com for biblical evidence on the identity of this unnamed gospel author.

Preface

"Whom the LORD loveth he correcteth" (Prv 3:12).

"Reproofs of instruction *are* the way of life" (Prv 6:23).

"The fear of the LORD *is* a fountain of life" (Prv 14:27).

"Teach me thy way, O LORD; I will walk in thy truth" (Ps 86:11).

"O LORD: give me understanding according to thy word" (Ps 119:169).

"The fear of the LORD *is* the instruction of wisdom; and before honor *is* humility" (Prv 15:33).

"Give unto the LORD the glory due unto his name" (Ps 96:8).

"Thou hast magnified thy word above all thy name" (Ps 138:2).

"The word of our God shall stand forever" (Isa 40:8).

"The entrance of thy words giveth light" (Ps 119:130).

"All scripture *is* given by inspiration of God" (2Ti 3:16).

"He that is faithful in that which is least is faithful also in much: and he that is unjust in the least is unjust also in much" (Lk 16:10).

"A little leaven leaveneth the whole lump" (Gal 5:9).

"Cease, my son, to hear the instruction *that causeth* to err from the words of knowledge" (Prv 19:27).

"Wherewithal shall a young man cleanse his way? by taking heed *thereto* according to thy word" (Ps 119:9).

"The fear of man bringeth a snare: but whoso putteth his trust in the LORD shall be safe" (Prv 29:25).

"The fear of the LORD *is* the beginning of wisdom" (Ps 111:10).

"The LORD *is* nigh unto all them that call upon him, to all that call upon him in truth" (Ps 145:18).

Introduction

"Faith *cometh* by hearing, and hearing by the word of God" (Rom 10:17). This teaches a progression that results in faith. It begins with God's word producing hearing, then this hearing produces faith. This book focuses on the first step in this process and shows it is possible to get better at hearing God's word.

If we desire to please God and know "without faith it is impossible to please *him*" (Heb 11:6), then we should welcome every opportunity to increase our faith. Since the word of God produces the hearing that produces faith, we should spend time thinking on God's word and do what we can to improve our understanding of it.

People often come to opposite conclusions about what the Bible is saying. The hearing produced by God's word would surely not lead to contrary beliefs. So, if we are confronted by contrary ideas, we can know that one or both of them arise from an inaccurate understanding of scripture because both cannot be true.

How should we go about deciding what is true on biblical matters? We should do so according to the scriptures. Proverbs 30:5 tells us, "every word of God *is* pure: he *is* a shield unto them that put their trust in him." The evidence herein will show how God's word can correct mistakes in our understanding or prevent them from occurring in the first place. For instance, the following example shows how terms used in scripture can be easily misunderstood if they are not defined according to a biblical standard.

Word pictures are figures of speech that briefly convey a complex idea. One used by Jesus was that of drinking a man's blood, such as when he said, "whoso eateth my flesh, and drinketh my blood, hath eternal life; and I will raise him up at the last day" (Fourth gospel 6:54). Drinking his blood is not about the oral intake of a red liquid (Jesus' hemoglobin) and God's word had already established this by scripture's use of this term. As the following example shows, a straightforward reading of scripture can open our eyes to the truth like nothing else. When David was in the cave of Adullam and the city of Bethlehem was in Philistine hands, three of his mighty men put their lives at risk on a covert mission to satisfy David's longing:

"David *was* then in the hold, and the Philistines' garrison *was* then at Bethlehem. And David longed, and said, Oh that one would give me drink of the water of the well of Bethlehem, that *is* at the gate! And the three brake through the host of the Philistines, and drew water out of the well of Bethlehem, that *was* by the gate, and took *it,* and brought *it* to David: but David would not drink *of* it, but poured it out to the LORD, And said, My God forbid it me, that I should do this thing: shall I drink the blood of these men that have put their lives in jeopardy? For with *the jeopardy of* their lives they brought it. Therefore, he would not drink it" (1Chr 11:16-19).

Here, David taught a lesson about the value of life to his men and his words also give us the key to the word picture that was used by Jesus. The Bible has the keys to the word pictures that we find in scripture and, when we learn this, we discover one of the ways God's word teaches men how to properly understand scripture. As he poured out the water to the LORD, David said, "shall I drink the blood of these men that have put their lives in jeopardy?" (1Chr 11:19) "Drink the blood" is not a physical description. It portrays a willingness to accept a man laying down his life on your behalf!

Jesus laid down his life for his friends and when they accept this, they drink his blood. As this example shows, it is important to view the words of scripture according to the standard of scripture, and it will be shown how holding to God's word as our measure of truth can correct errors that result from false assumptions. [Some think Jesus' use of this word picture caused many of his disciples to forsake him and, later, we will see if scripture supports this idea.]

"*It is* better to trust in the LORD than to put confidence in man" (Ps 118:8). Therefore, scripture will be the only source cited herein. Since we all make mistakes, we should be humble enough to put our beliefs to the test of scripture and invite biblical correction.

Results speak for themselves, and this book uses an approach to scripture that will prove to be a reliable way to distinguish truth from error. So, if the evidence-based Bible study method that will be modeled in the case studies can lead to a better understanding of God's word, then it makes sense for us to keep on using it.

Chapter 1 – Founded Upon God's Word

This chapter begins to show how the counsel of scripture teaches us a better bible study method. God's counsel can help us to identify faulty views that result from our blind spots and teach us how to view scripture from the right perspective.

Growth Requires Change

"Trust in the LORD with all thine heart; and lean not unto thine own understanding" (Prv 3:5). This warns against allowing assumptions to prejudice our view of scripture since there may be a difference between what the Bible says and what people think it means. But in God's word, we have a reliable standard we can use to validate our understanding of scripture, and admonitions like Proverbs 3:5 should guide our approach to scripture. The words "lean not unto thine own understanding" also counsel us against relying on the teachings of men, for why would we rely on the understanding of men who should not even be leaning on their own understanding? Proverbs 3:6 goes on to say, "in all thy ways acknowledge him, and he shall direct thy paths," and God, through his word, will be the authority who directs us throughout the examples in this book.

"All scripture *is* given by inspiration of God, and *is* profitable for doctrine, for reproof, for correction, for instruction in righteousness" (2Ti 3:16). This profit comes at a cost. Growth requires change and change can be uncomfortable, so people may resist change for this reason alone. If it turns out something we believe does not line up with scripture, then our judgment is called into question by the process of correction. But we do not like having our judgment called into question. So, we must be conscious of the tug of war which will tend to go on between pride and humility, because pride will naturally incline us toward resisting correction.

How to Find Right Answers

Teachers can give students the right answers, but they help them grow by showing them *how to derive the answer*. God's word can do both. It can move us from error to truth on an issue and it also teaches us how to find the right answers, as will be shown.

Paul and Timothy wrote, "we dare not... compare ourselves with some that commend themselves: but they <u>measuring themselves by themselves, and comparing themselves among themselves</u>, are not wise" (2Cor 10:12). Even so, looking at what others believe and conforming to groupthink is a common practice.

Many fall prey to the notion that a given belief must be right if it is believed by a majority. But this is not reliable, for men can hold a common belief and still be wrong, even if they are highly trained.

Good investigators weigh the evidence themselves. They do not rely on others to tell them what to think. Likewise, our conclusions on biblical issues should be dictated by the evidence that is found in God's word, not on what others have already concluded it says.

A Consistent Regard for Scripture

Some think the Old Testament part of our Bible has little to say to us today. But this was the only scripture that existed in Jesus' day, and the New Testament tells us this part of scripture is for us also.

- "Whatsoever things were written aforetime were written for our learning" (Rom 15:4).
- "Now all these things happened unto them for examples and they are written for our admonition" (1Cor 10:11).

The Old Testament has things to teach us, and it also provides us with part of the context of New Testament events. It is easy for us to misconstrue God's word if it is taken out of context, as we saw when the term "drink my blood" was considered earlier.

Paul said he believed "all things which are written in the law and in the prophets" (Acts 24:14). Teaching people to trust what is written in God's word is what Jesus and the apostles did each time they cited scripture!

Terms such as "it is written," and "all things must be fulfilled, which were written in the law of Moses, and in the prophets, and in the psalms" (Mt 2:5, Lk 24:4, et al.) taught people to respect the authority of the Old Testament. So, we need to value *all* of God's word.

Prove All Things

"Prove all things; hold fast that which is good" (1Th 5:21) urges us to put every idea to the test. The Bereans "received the word with all readiness of mind and searched the scriptures daily, whether those things were so" (Acts 17:11), and we can do likewise. If an idea we thought was true ends up failing the test of scripture, is this a problem, or a blessing that comes to those who prove all things? To those who love the truth, the answer is evident.

It is important to speak the word of God faithfully (cf. Jer 23:28), but many do not do so. For example, if people simply say, *'the truth will set you free'* they take Jesus' words out of context. How so? First, this was said to people who believed on Jesus. Second, this was part of a qualified statement. Here are his words in context:

> "Then said Jesus **to those Jews which believed on him**, If **ye** continue in my word, *then* are **ye** my disciples indeed; and **ye** shall know the truth, and the truth shall make **you** free" (Fourth gospel 8:31-32).

"If ye continue in my word" is a condition; therefore, "the truth shall make you free" only applied to those who continue in Jesus' word. To say, "the truth shall make you free" as if this unconditionally applies to anyone, does not present God's word faithfully, and as the reader will see, failing to do this causes many problems.

Scripture encourages proper judgment, and asking questions is part of the process that people use to distinguish truth from error. Some say it is not good to ask too many questions, but as will be shown in a moment, scripture does not back up this claim.

Since scripture says, "*it is* better to trust in the LORD than to put confidence in man" (Ps 118:8), it is important to know if a teaching is of God or of men. The case studies herein will show how this can be done. If people stopped adopting the beliefs of other men, would this undermine the authority of scripture? No, the opposite is what happens. People grow in grace and knowledge when they stop putting confidence in the teachings of men and, instead, rely on the words of scripture as their measure of truth.

Ask Good Questions

Scripture does not warn against asking too many questions. Rather, it focuses on the *kind* of questions we ask. It says to avoid foolish and unprofitable questions.

Paul told Timothy to "follow righteousness, faith, charity [love], peace, with them that call on the Lord out of a pure heart" (2Ti 2:22). Then he said, "but foolish and unlearned questions avoid" (2Ti 2:23). In Titus 3:9, we find similar counsel: "avoid foolish questions, and genealogies, and contentions, and strivings about the law; for they are unprofitable and vain." People do not turn from the truth because they ask too many questions about the Bible but because they adopt beliefs that turn them from the teachings of scripture. Problems arise when people question the authority of God's word. But questioning whether a teaching or idea is in line with scripture does not dishonor God, because upholding the word of God as the standard of truth is precisely what scripture urges us to do!

Check for Blind Spots

We tend to make assumptions about what we read in the Bible. This often leads to a flawed view of God's word. For an example, consider this report:

> "there stood by the cross of Jesus his mother, and his mother's sister, Mary the *wife* of Cleophas, and Mary Magdalene. When Jesus therefore saw his mother, and the disciple standing by, whom he loved, he saith unto his mother, Woman, behold thy son! Then saith he to the disciple, Behold thy mother! And from that hour that disciple took her unto his own *home*" (Fourth gospel 19:25-28).

Did he want this disciple to adopt his mother and care for her from then on? No. While Mary's four other sons (cf. Mt 13:55) were not on the scene, they were not going to abandon their mother because their brother Jesus was killed. Therefore, Mary would not need a caretaker for the remainder of her life. So, Jesus must have had something else in mind. Is there a way we can determine what he meant when he spoke those words from the cross? Yes, there is.

Jesus said many things during his ministry and at times his words were misunderstood. Therefore, this shows that <u>what people think Jesus' words meant may not equate to what he actually meant</u>. While this could be true of any passage, let us focus on the words spoken by Jesus in the passage above.

"When Jesus therefore saw his mother, and the disciple standing by, whom he loved, he saith unto his mother, Woman, behold thy son! Then saith he to the disciple, Behold thy mother!" How can we know for sure what was in his mind when he said this? We can let scripture teach us to see Jesus' words from *his* point of view.

He knew he would rise from the dead on the third day! On multiple occasions Jesus taught his disciples, he would rise from the dead on "the third day" (Mt 16:21, et al.), yet they did not take this to heart.

But this must be considered because it gives context to the words Jesus spoke from the cross. Taking account of what Jesus knew enables us to see his words from his point of view. When Jesus was dying, he knew his mother's grief would be turned into joy in less than 72 hours, so he was giving the disciple "whom he loved" a *temporary* assignment! He was to comfort Mary during her time of grief, and this did not require her to move in with this disciple. [Note: the disciple whom Jesus loved was not the Apostle John, as many assume. For the biblical proof on this see TDWJL.com.]

When Mary, Jesus' brothers, and the disciples learned about his resurrection, it would change everything for them. Mary was not going to be left destitute, and Jesus surely knew this. In Acts 1:14, we are told, the apostles "continued with one accord in prayer and supplication, with the women, and Mary the mother of Jesus, and with his brethren." God added "about three thousand souls" (Acts 2:41) to their number just ten days later. Acts 2:44-46 also tells us:

"all that believed were together, and had all things common; And sold their possessions and goods, and parted them to all *men*, as every man had need. And they, continuing daily with one accord in the temple, and breaking bread from house to house, did eat their meat with gladness and singleness of heart."

Here again, we see how scripture can correct beliefs that come from a rush to judgment. We have blind spots when we are not considering all of the data the Bible has to offer. Another example of a blind spot involves John the Baptist, and later it will be shown how scripture can correct us there too.

Practicing Due Diligence

Above, when we took the time to weigh Jesus' words, we could understand what he meant. It is possible to gain this kind of insight from a quick read through scripture, but this is more likely to occur when we meditate on God's word.

One sermon a week is not the same as consuming daily bread! The more we read the Bible and think on what it says, the better equipped we will be to understand it. Paul's admonition to Timothy indicates "rightly dividing the word of truth" (2Ti 2:15) follows from a diligent focus on God's word. For an example of the kind of things that can be missed in a cursory reading of scripture, consider what we are told about the events on the day of Pentecost:

"there came a sound from heaven as of a rushing mighty wind, and it filled all the house where they [120 disciples (cf. Acts 1:15)] were sitting. And there appeared unto them cloven tongues like as of fire, and it sat upon each of them. And they were all filled with the Holy Ghost, and began to speak with other tongues, as the Spirit gave them utterance. And there were dwelling at Jerusalem Jews, devout men, out of every nation under heaven. Now when this was noised abroad, the multitude came together, and were confounded, because that every man heard them speak in his own language. And they were all amazed and marveled, saying one to another, Behold, are not all these which speak Galileans? And how hear we every man in our own tongue, wherein we were born? … we do hear them speak in our tongues the wonderful works of God. And they were all amazed, and were in doubt, saying one to another, What meaneth this?" (Acts 2:2-8 & 11-12)

Pentecost was one of the annual feasts of the LORD, so this is why these "devout men" from "every nation" were there in Jerusalem.

These men went to look into rumors of the disciples speaking in "other tongues" and they heard the disciples speaking in their own languages. They wondered how this could be since they could tell the disciples were Galileans. Nevertheless, they understood what the disciples had said, and they declared, "we do hear them speak in our tongues the wonderful works of God." However, when they said this, it caused a division:

> "Others mocking said, These men are full of new wine. But Peter, standing up with the eleven, lifted up his voice, and said unto them, Ye men of Judaea, and all ye that dwell at Jerusalem, be this known unto you, and hearken to my words: For these are not drunken, as ye suppose, seeing it is *but* the third hour of the day" (Acts 2:12-15).

Who was accused of being drunk? Some say the disciples, but if this idea is put to the test of scripture what happens? The disciples did not slur their words or talk nonsense. Those who heard them in their own languages were "amazed," and devout men would not be mocking after they heard about "the wonderful works of God." So, what conclusion is demanded by the data? Well, who accused who of being drunk? The evidence indicates this dispute occurred between two groups (identified by the terms "they" and "others").

"Devout men" in Jerusalem heard about the disciples speaking in "other tongues." When they looked into it, "every man heard them speak in his own language." It says, "**they** were all amazed and marveled" and said to each other, "how hear **we** every man in our own tongue, wherein we were born?" and then they testified, "**we** do hear them speak in our tongues the wonderful works of God." But when they declared this, they were mocked by "others!" Why? Because their claim would seem insane to men from their nations who also spoke those same languages but heard no such thing. Those who claimed to hear about God's works were the ones who were accused of being drunk, and Peter spoke up to defend them against this charge. He asked everyone to listen to him and said:

> "Ye men of Judaea, and all ye that dwell at Jerusalem, be this known unto you, and hearken to my words: For **these** are not drunken, as ye suppose... " (Acts 2:14-15).

13

At that point, Peter spoke in a language that was understood by the whole crowd, and they did not think *he* was drunk because they listened to everything he said. Also, notice Peter did not say *'we'* are not drunk, for the accusation was not directed against him and the disciples who spoke in other tongues. It was against those who claimed to hear the disciples in their own native languages! Still, the accusation made no sense, as he showed when he said it was only "the third hour of the day."

We are not told what the mockers thought of the disciples who spoke in other tongues. Regardless, one cannot assume mockers and "devout men" are equally able to hear God's truth, for scripture repeatedly teaches that not everyone has ears to hear (Rv 2:7, et al.). Moreover, blessings are often linked to conditions. On the night before Jesus was crucified, one of his disciples asked, "Lord, how is it that thou wilt manifest thyself unto us, and not unto the world?" (Fourth gospel 14:22) If he would "manifest" himself to his followers, but he would not do this for "the world," this involves discrimination. In his reply, Jesus said, "If a man love me, he will keep my words: and my Father will love him, and we will come unto him, and make our abode with him" (Fourth gospel 14:23). So, this blessing is only for those who keep the words of Jesus because of their love for him.

Biblical Correction is a Blessing

A misunderstanding here or there is not an indicator. But a pattern of misjudging scripture indicates something is definitely wrong. This need not be discouraging, for scripture contains the remedy. An evidence-based Bible study method will consistently lead us to a correct understanding of scripture, if we submit to the authority of God and welcome the correction we receive from his word, both on individual topics and on how we assess truth. In Luke 5:30-39, men who resisted Jesus' teachings confronted him. He told them, "new wine must be put into new bottles" (Lk 5:38). Here he taught the importance of compatibility. Beliefs must be compatible with the thinking process that a person uses when they are choosing what to believe. The practice of consistently relying on God's word is compatible with scripture and this is what is taught in this book. Trusting in our beliefs or in the teachings of men causes us to lose the benefits that come with thinking that adheres to God's counsel.

A person does not need to be a scholar to understand God's word, but proper understanding does require respect for God's authority. Jesus once asked a group of men, "how can ye believe, which receive honor one of another, and seek not the honor that *cometh from God only*?" (Fourth gospel 5:44) If this taught a principle that was not only true for people in his day, then we must think about how it applies to us. If belief in Jesus is founded on seeking "the honor that *cometh* from God only," then we must also do this. Herein, the principle he taught will be applied to the study of scripture.

In the same context, Jesus said, "I receive not honor from men" (Fourth gospel 5:41). Should we be following his lead? We are honored when men invite us into their group. We like it when people want to associate with us. We take confidence in knowing others agree with us. Social media leads many to seek the affirmation of others. Seeking the approval of men can lead us to avoid doing what is right in God's eyes (because people tend to conform to the views of those who they associate with.) This is the danger of receiving "honor one of another." It gets people to adopt a standard that honors men rather than God. In verses like, "set your affection on things above, not on things on the earth" (Col 3:2) we find additional counsel on this topic that can also help to keep our eyes focused on God's authority when it comes to our approach to scripture.

Some Final Words Before Proceeding

"Thy word *is* a lamp unto my feet, and a light unto my path" (Ps 119:105). This pictures one of the ways God's word can direct us if we let it teach us where to stand on an issue and where to go with a thought.

Five biblical case studies will be used to show how the testimony of scripture can teach people a right understanding of God's word. Each case study is set up as an exercise that will allow the reader to get a sense of how much they might benefit from the approach that is being presented. Of course, this book cannot possibly deal with every item in every passage. Nevertheless, the evidence that is presented will advance the cause of truth. While many common questions will be addressed, others will remain unanswered and new ones will be raised for the reader to answer.

Double quotation marks will be reserved for scripture quotes only, and God's word will be the only authority cited. This format will enable the scripture citations to stand out. But it also means that, at times, single quotation marks will be used at points where one might typically expect to find double quotation marks being used. The King James Version (KJV) will be referenced, so some words or spellings that are in the biblical quotations may be unfamiliar. Even so, those who use other Bible translations will still be able to follow all the points of evidence.

Note: When words in a Bible quotation are in italics, it is because this is how the words appear in the KJV. Also, the abbreviation cf. is used to reference verses that can provide further <u>confirmation</u> on the point being deliberated at the time.

Hopefully, the passages already discussed have offered insights that will motivate you to want more. The same strategy employed in the case studies that are interspersed between the chapters, will also be used to weigh the evidence on all the topics that will be considered, and it will help to answer questions such as these:

- James 2:26 says "faith without works is dead," but what does this mean and how is belief different from faith?
- What about people who have never heard about Jesus?
- Do men get into the kingdom of God by being born again?
- Why was Abel's offering accepted, while Cain's was not?
- The last book of the Bible mentions a great white throne, but who sat on the other great white throne in scripture?
- What was Nicodemus seeking when he met with Jesus?
- Did the woman who spoke with Jesus at Jacob's well have a good reputation among her fellow Samaritans?
- Where do antichrists come from?

If we are shown biblical evidence that can lead us to the truth on these issues and others, then, at that point, it is up to us to go where the evidence in the word of God leads. "Whatsoever ye do, do *it* heartily, as to the Lord, and not unto men" (Col 3:23). Since this was written to the "faithful brethren in Christ" (Col 1:2), this counsel would surely apply to our study of God's word also. Thus, our eyes need to be on the Lord and not on men if we want to do right.

Case Study: The Case of David's Turn

David Turned Aside

When the prophet Samuel said, "the LORD hath sought him a man after his own heart" (1Sa 13:14), those words referred to David. This was cited when the apostle Paul said God spoke this about David: "I have found David the *son* of Jesse, a man after mine own heart" (Acts 13:22).

Besides being called a man after God's own heart, 1 Kings 15:5 says, "David did *that which was* right in the eyes of the LORD, and turned not aside from any *thing* that he commanded him all the days of his life, save only in the matter of Uriah the Hittite."

Unlike any other thing in David's life, the matter of Uriah the Hittite is singled out as the only time when David turned aside from the LORD's commandment. Scripture lets us know why this is so, but only if we consider all of the evidence that it presents.

2 Samuel 11:1-12:15 gives us the report of this episode. You can test your current practice by doing what you normally do when you look at a passage. Read those verses and jot down your thoughts on what they teach. Then return to this study and see if scripture can teach us how to get more out of what we read.

The Case of David's Turn

David Takes Uriah's Wife

Here is how scripture introduces us to this episode:

"at the time when kings go forth *to battle*... David sent Joab, and his servants with him, and all Israel... But David tarried still at Jerusalem. And it came to pass in an evening, that David arose from off his bed, and walked upon the roof of the king's house: and from the roof he saw a woman washing herself; and the woman *was* very beautiful to look upon. And David sent and enquired after the woman. And *one* said, *Is* not this Bathsheba, the daughter of Eliam, the wife of Uriah the Hittite? And David sent messengers, and took her; and she came in unto him, and he lay with her; for she was purified from her uncleanness: and she returned unto her house. And the woman conceived, and sent and told David, and said, I *am* with child" (2Sa 11:1-5).

When David acted on his lustful thoughts and "enquired after the woman," "*one* said, *Is* not this Bathsheba, the daughter of Eliam, the wife of Uriah the Hittite?" If we assume David wanted to know the identity of a beautiful stranger, then this report about her will be seen in this light. However, we need to consider all of the data in scripture regarding this episode, including how David schemed to avoid having to deal with the unexpected result of the night he spent with her after he found out Bathsheba was pregnant.

What Happened Next?

"And David sent to Joab, *saying*, Send me Uriah the Hittite. And Joab sent Uriah to David. And when Uriah was come unto him, David demanded *of him* how Joab did, and how the people did, and how the war prospered. And David said to Uriah, Go down to thy house, and wash thy feet. And Uriah departed out of the king's house, and there followed him a mess *of meat* from the king. But Uriah slept at the door of the king's house with all the servants of his lord, and went not down to his house" (2Sa 11:6-9).

If Uriah was off at war, he could not be the father of the child his wife was carrying. David needed Uriah to spend a night at home so Uriah would think the child was his. But this plan did not work because of Uriah's affinity for his fellow soldiers:

"when they had told David, saying, Uriah went not down unto his house, David said unto Uriah, Camest thou not from *thy* journey? Why *then* didst thou not go down unto thine house? And Uriah said unto David, The ark, and Israel, and Judah, abide in tents; and my lord Joab, and the servants of my lord, are encamped in the open fields; shall I then go into mine house, to eat and to drink, and to lie with my wife? *As* thou livest and *as* thy soul liveth, I will not do this thing" (2Sa 11:10-11).

Uriah did not go home that night. So, David had him stay another night, hoping to weaken Uriah's resolve by getting him drunk:

"David said to Uriah, Tarry here today also, and tomorrow I will let thee depart. So, Uriah abode in Jerusalem that day, and the morrow. And when David had called him, he did eat and drink before him; and he made him drunk: and at evening he went out to lie on his bed with the servants of his lord, but went not down to his house" (2Sa 11:12-13).

Then David turned to desperate measures. He had Uriah killed in a way that would make it seem as if he died as a casualty of war:

"David wrote a letter to Joab, and sent *it* by the hand of Uriah. And he wrote in the letter, saying, Set ye Uriah in the forefront of the hottest battle, and retire ye from him, that he may be smitten, and die. And it came to pass, when Joab observed the city, that he assigned Uriah unto a place... and there fell *some* of the people of the servants of David; and Uriah the Hittite died also" (2Sa 11:14-17).

David had spilled innocent blood, but not only Uriah's, for others of "the servants of David" were killed along with Uriah. When news of this reached David, he instructed the messenger to "say unto Joab, Let not this thing displease thee, for the sword devoureth one as well as another" (2Sa 11:25).

Second Samuel, Chapter 11, closes with these words:

"And when the wife of Uriah heard that Uriah her husband was dead, she mourned for her husband. And when the mourning was past, David sent and fetched her to his house, and she became his wife, and bare him a son. But the thing that David had done displeased the LORD" (2Sa 11:26-27).

At this point, David probably thought he had gotten away with it. However, the LORD was not going to leave it there.

The Truth Comes Out

The following passage tells us what happened next:

"The LORD sent Nathan unto David. And he came unto him, and said unto him, There were two men in one city; the one rich, and the other poor. The rich *man* had exceeding many flocks and herds: But the poor *man* had nothing, save one little ewe lamb, which he had bought and nourished up: and it grew up together with him, and with his children; it did eat of his own meat, and drank of his own cup, and lay in his bosom, and was unto him as a daughter. And there came a traveler unto the rich man, and he spared to take of his own flock and of his own herd, to dress for the wayfaring man that was come unto him; but took the poor man's lamb, and dressed it for the man that was come to him. And David's anger was greatly kindled against the man; and he said to Nathan, As the LORD liveth, the man that hath done this *thing* shall surely die: And he shall restore the lamb fourfold, because he did this thing, and because he had no pity" (2Sa 12:1-6).

Taking Nathan's words in physical terms led David to misconstrue the word picture. This led him to unwittingly pronounce judgment on his own behavior. As David declared the penalty, he was blind to his hypocrisy.

Moments later, he learned he had judged himself, when Nathan explained the parable, as 2 Samuel 12:7-10 reports:

"Nathan said to David, Thou *art* the man. Thus saith the LORD God of Israel, I anointed thee king over Israel, and I delivered thee out of the hand of Saul; And I gave thee thy master's house, and thy master's wives into thy bosom, and gave thee the house of Israel and of Judah; and if *that had been* too little, I would moreover have given unto thee such and such things. Wherefore hast thou despised the commandment of the LORD, to do evil in his sight? Thou hast killed Uriah the Hittite with the sword, and hast taken his wife *to be* thy wife, and hast slain him with the sword of the children of Ammon. Now therefore the sword shall never depart from thine house; because thou hast despised me, and hast taken the wife of Uriah the Hittite to be thy wife."

No doubt, David was surprised to hear "thou *art* the man" and the words, "thus saith the LORD God of Israel" were even weightier. But this parable also has an added lesson for us.

Nathan's Parable

"Every word of God *is* pure: he *is* a shield unto them that put their trust in him" (Prv 30:5). As will be shown, looking to "every word of God" in this instance can keep us from missing what is hidden in plain sight. The rich man with many flocks and herds took the poor man's lamb. Does this line up with what occurred? Yes. David had multiple wives and concubines and he probably could have had his pick of almost any unmarried woman in the nation. Yet, he took Uriah's wife. So, there is a parallel between the parable and reality on those points. But if we merely identify the rich man, the poor man, and the poor man's lamb, then we have not considered all the evidence.

Who is the traveler? If every word of God is worthy of attention, then we also need to take note of the parable's fourth character.

If our approach to scripture led us to overlook this figure, then this lets us know something needs to change. Those who think their process of assessing biblical truth works fine may say the traveler is irrelevant, so they can avoid having to deal with this character. But does scripture suggest he is irrelevant?

Attention to Detail

Several things call our attention to the importance of the traveler. For example, he is referred to three times. He is called a traveler, the wayfaring man, and the man that was come to him. One key factor links those terms. What they have in common is they all speak of the one who came to the rich man. Beyond his being mentioned three times, there is something else about this figure that should grab our attention.

Scripture lets us know the trouble between the two men in one city began when the traveler came unto the rich man. Why did his coming cause the rich man to take the poor man's lamb, and how would this help people identify the figures in the parable?

Weighing the attributes that are tied to each character is how we can determine who those characters represent. This lets scripture define the terms. In the case of Nathan's parable, the following details were included:

A. the rich man had exceeding many flocks and herds,
B. the poor man had nothing, save one little ewe lamb, and
C. the rich man took the poor man's lamb.

The parable is followed by Nathan's rebuke of David for taking Uriah's wife, so it is easy to see a parallel between David's actions and the parable. But the parable involved more than those three points noted above. When a traveler came to the rich man, he did not "take of his own flock and of his own herd, to dress for the wayfaring man that was come unto him; but took the poor man's lamb, and dressed it for the man that was come to him" (2Sa 12:4). The rich man did take the lamb, but it was *taken for* and *served to* the man that was come to him; it was not served to the rich man. If the poor man pictured Uriah and the lamb portrayed Bathsheba, what must we conclude?

The rich man took the poor man's lamb, so this would be picturing David since he took Uriah's wife. Yet, this lamb was taken for and served to the wayfaring man. Thus, the question this presents is, who got the lamb?

The LORD also sent David this rebuke: "thou hast despised me, and hast taken the wife of Uriah the Hittite to be thy wife" (2Sa 12:10). David took Uriah's wife and he took her for himself. In the parable, the wayfaring man got the lamb, and in reality, David got Uriah's wife. So, the traveler was David himself! The rich man and the traveler both portrayed him – one pictured him before his lust for Bathsheba and the other pictured him after he gave into it!

Not everyone overlooks the traveler. Some who notice him say, *'Satan is the traveler.'* Others try to deal with this figure by saying, *'the traveler is sin.'* But, Nathan did not mention Satan, the devil, or demons. Also, a concept (sin) did not get Bathsheba pregnant; David did.

An Assumption and an Opportunity

Jesus said, "with what measure ye mete, it shall be measured to you again" (Mt 7:2). Notice how this principle applies in this instance. If we think each figure must represent a different person, then we cannot help but see the parable in this way. If an assumption is not true, it has the same effect as any prejudice. Our conclusions will not be justified by the evidence if we use a false balance to weigh the data. Although it may *seem* reasonable to assume each character must depict a different person, the word of God is not our measure when our assumptions dictate our view of scripture.

If God's word showed a one-to-one correspondence between the parable and reality, then we would have biblical justification for this idea and we would not need to make an assumption. Since Nathan's parable used multiple characters to represent different aspects of one person, then this technique may also have been used in other Bible parables! Thus, the biblical correction from this aspect of Nathan's parable could open our eyes to things we have overlooked in other parables.

A one-to-one assumption does not automatically mean we have misunderstood other parables. However, this possibility is there, so it would be good for us to reconsider other parables in scripture now that we know different elements in a parable can correspond to different aspects of a single individual, group, or thing.

Picture It This Way

Seeing David as the rich man and the wayfaring man may cause some to bristle because it says, "there came a traveler unto the rich man." Twice more it says he was come to the rich man. Is it reasonable to speak of a man coming to himself? The Bible does:

- "when he came to himself, he said, How many hired servants of my father's have bread enough and to spare, and I perish with hunger" (Lk 15:17),
- "when Peter was come to himself, he said, Now I know of a surety, that the Lord hath sent his angel, and hath delivered me out of the hand of Herod" (Acts 12:11).

The first verse is from the parable of the prodigal son. The second is from the time Peter was set free from prison. Both cases are portraying a moment of internal dialogue; a man talking to himself. Also, the Hebrew word translated as "came" in 2 Samuel 12:4 was used of the coming of feelings like fear, pride, shame, and desire (cf. Prv 1:27, et al.). The words "come" and "came" do refer to physical travel and arrival, but this is not the only way they are used. Thus, according to scripture, a man *can* "come to himself." The question for us is, does this picture the kind of self-talk that was going on in David's mind when he chose to lust after Uriah's wife?

Consider what Jesus said on this subject: "whosoever looketh on a woman to lust after her hath committed adultery with her already in his heart" (Mt 5:28). Some say this means thinking about adultery is the same as doing it. However, Jesus did not say that.

He used the word "already" to highlight a sequence. Before a man can look "on a woman to lust after her," he must have "committed adultery with her already in his heart." Thoughts always precede the behaviors they produce, and Jesus applied this principle to instances of lust.

The act of looking to lust comes second, adultery in the heart comes first. James 1:14 tells us, "every man is tempted, when he is drawn away of his own lust, and enticed." Therefore, this must have also happened when David pursued Bathsheba.

David turned and traveled away from the LORD when he sold himself on the idea of going after Uriah's wife. No one else talked him into it. He had that conversation with himself and convinced himself to do it. David was a man after God's own heart (cf. 1Sa 13:14, Acts 13:22-23). So, for him to do what he did to Uriah, he first had to turn away from God! The LORD's rebuke of David was, **"thou hast despised me**, and hast taken the wife of Uriah the Hittite to be thy wife"** (2Sa 12:10). Note the sequence of those words. Is it correct to say that before David went after Uriah's wife, he first had to ignore the LORD's authority and despise the counsel of the LORD that is provided in scripture?

David committed adultery with Bathsheba in his heart prior to their physical union. The words of Jesus indicate this took place before David looked on her to lust after her (cf. Mt 5:28). For David to commit adultery in his heart, he had to turn away from the light of scripture and the commandment that said, "thou shalt not commit adultery" (Ex 20:14). He was rightly portrayed as a traveler because he moved away from being a man after God's own heart. He had the same body, but at that point, there was a man of a different character residing therein.

The Other David

The rebuke was not so much against an act of lust as it was against David's turn – because in turning aside from the LORD's commandment, he turned his back on the LORD. David did not see it when he began to lust after Bathsheba, but that choice put him in opposition to the LORD. Stories and movies will use images of a person speaking good advice in their right ear, while whispering contrary advice in their left ear. This portrays someone weighing the right choice versus the wrong one.

David elected to cater to the lusts of "the wayfaring man that was come unto him" (2Sa 12:4). But he had to first disregard what he knew to be right. Scripture says, "the fear of man bringeth a snare: but whoso putteth his trust in the LORD shall be safe" (Prv 29:25). After David found out Bathsheba was pregnant, his actions were motivated by a fear of man, for if the fear of God had been the basis of David's actions, he would not have done what he did.

The principle "a little leaven leaveneth the whole lump" (Gal 5:9) is easy to see in this episode. When David chose to go against part of God's law, all of God's word was made of no effect unto him! Because he was no longer under God's authority, even murder seemed acceptable to him.

"Purge out therefore the old leaven" (1Cor 5:7) is the advice we find in scripture. This is what David needed to do (by repenting of his disrespect for the LORD).

The Background on David's Turn

The LORD's rebuke was a lesson in humility for David and it is also a lesson for us. What it can teach us about being diligent in holding fast to God's word should motivate us to do better.

David disregarded the authority of God. Whenever people choose to disregard what is said in scripture, they take a step down that same path.

It is a mistake to think of David's turn as a momentary slip-up because scripture lets us know this was not the case. Why did he move so fast to get rid of Uriah? The fear of embarrassment for being caught in one act of adultery would not have been enough to drive him to spill innocent blood in arranging the death of Uriah.

Given David's military experience prior to that point, he must have known his directive would result in other men being killed along with Uriah. Should we assume the possibility of being labeled an adulterer would provide a sufficient motive for David to kill Uriah and sacrifice other lives in the process?

No doubt, David did not want his union with Uriah's wife to become public knowledge. Nevertheless, his coveting of the wife of Uriah went far beyond the sin of adultery.

Adultery is wrong, but the consequences are compounded when a man does it with the wife of a brother, friend, or man of renown. Such things cause people to take a different view of the offense and David knew he had stepped over this line.

Who Was Uriah?

Uriah's name appears 22 times in the verses on David's adultery, his murder of Uriah, and the LORD's rebuke of David via Nathan. Besides this, only three other Old Testament verses mention him. One is 1 Kings 15:5, where it refers to David turning aside from the commandment of the LORD "in the matter of Uriah the Hittite." The other two verses where Uriah is named give us details that can open our eyes and help us to see just how far David had fallen in this episode. They are 2 Samuel 23:39 and 1 Chronicles 11:41.

Taken out of context, those verses tell us little since they merely have Uriah's name included in a list of names. However, his name takes on great significance when those verses are read in context, because they are found in passages which tell us about David's mighty men (cf. 2Sa 23:8-39, 1Chr 11:11-47). In both passages, some men are called more honorable. But just being included in the list surely set those men apart from all the other men in Israel.

Of all those in the armies, few had their names noted in scripture with this noteworthy designation. In the list of David's mighty men, one name truly jumps off the page – Uriah the Hittite. The idea of *'Uriah the mighty'* may seem very strange, however, it is biblical. His reputation is further confirmed when the term "the valiant men of the armies" (1Chr 11:26) is applied to a group of men that includes Uriah the Hittite.

Half the Facts Versus Have the Facts

If we only consider 2 Samuel 11 & 12, our view of these events will be based on incomplete data. Think of the difference between a General taking the wife of a foot soldier or the wife of a war hero.

If the army learned David had betrayed one of his mighty men, it would create a much bigger problem for him than if he had chosen to commit adultery with another woman. He had a strong motive to move quickly against this potential threat to his reputation and possibly his reign. Just as Medal of Honor winners are esteemed in America, it is very likely the mighty men and the valiant men of the armies were esteemed in their day.

Knowing who Uriah was explains a lot of things. The palace was surely in the good part of town, and Uriah lived within eyeshot of the palace with a relatively unobstructed view (cf. 2Sa 11:2).

War heroes are often rewarded for their exploits, and a king would want men like this living near him (since they would act as a rapid protection force for the king). There were only a handful of men who made the mighty men list and this tells us David knew Uriah. Besides this, Uriah and Bathsheba also lived in his neighborhood! So, this raises a question. Was David aware of the wife of Uriah *before* the night of their adulterous union?

We are told, "It came to pass in an evening, that David arose from off his bed, and walked upon the roof of the king's house: and from the roof he saw a woman washing herself; and the woman *was* very beautiful" (2Sa 11:2). Reading this in isolation may lead people to picture David accidentally laying his eyes on Uriah's wife and being suddenly so smitten by her beauty that it drove him to one bad spur-of-the-moment decision. But is this conclusion justified? Not if one considers all the facts.

David was a man of war. Yet, at the time of David's affair with Bathsheba, we are told, "at the time when kings go forth *to battle*," David "tarried still at Jerusalem" (2Sa 11:1). Why did he act un-kingly and send his men off to war while he stayed home? If David knew Uriah's wife, he also knew staying behind would provide him with a window of opportunity when Uriah would be away. Was it simply a coincidence that this was when David took Bathsheba?

When he "sent and enquired after the woman" he was not seeking details on a stranger. The response was, "*is* not this Bathsheba, the daughter of Eliam, the wife of Uriah the Hittite?" This was not a report of information. It was a rhetorical question to warn David against pursuing this well-known woman. Why was her marriage cited last and why was Bathsheba's father Eliam mentioned first? It might be because he too was a man of renown, who was also known to David. Like Uriah, Eliam was one of David's mighty men! 2 Samuel 23:8 tells us, "these *be* the names of the mighty men whom David had" and in the middle of the list is "Eliam the son of Ahithophel the Gilonite" (2Sa 23:34).

Who was Bathsheba?

So, David messed with the wife of one of his mighty men and defiled the daughter of another of his mighty men in the same act. But there is even more.

Eliam was the son of Ahithophel. Ahithophel is mentioned 20 times in the Bible. Consider two notable facts about Ahithophel:

- "Ahithophel was "David's counselor" (2Sa 15:12),
- "The counsel of Ahithophel, which he counseled in those days, *was* as if a man had enquired at the oracle of God: so *was* all the counsel of Ahithophel both with David and with Absalom" (2Sa 16:23).

The object of David's lust was the wife of one of his mighty men, the daughter of another of his mighty men, and the granddaughter of his counselor. Her links to all these close relationships to David prove the odds of her being unknown to David before the night of their adulterous union are slim to none!

David did not have Uriah killed merely to avoid a public relations problem or a soiled reputation from being labeled an adulterer. Bathsheba had family ties to three men who were close to David, notable, and very influential. Thus, her pregnancy presented an extremely complex problem for David and scripture indicates he did everything possible to ensure this could not happen. How so? Because it says, "she came in unto him, and **he lay with her**; **for she was purified from her uncleanness**" (2Sa 11:4). Two verses before this it says he saw her "washing herself," which indicates this was the washing of purification that a Hebrew woman would do following her menstrual period. No doubt, this bit of knowledge made David think Bathsheba could not get pregnant on that night. He was wrong, however.

As with all of scripture, the passages on David's turn have much to say and there is much we have not considered. David's Psalms, what happened in his life after Nathan rebuked him, how the son of David and Bathsheba fits in the lineage of Jesus, and other items linked to this episode are left for your further consideration.

The Conclusion of the Case of David's Turn

The LORD used Nathan's parable to teach David, and the LORD can still use this parable to teach people today.

The importance of the traveler was not lost on David because Nathan said David was "the man." David did not have to wonder which man Nathan was equating him to, for David knew he had taken Uriah's wife and he had given her to himself.

The LORD had richly blessed him, but he became a wayfaring man when he chose to despise the commandment of the LORD. If this can happen to someone like David, we all need to be on guard.

The end of the Case of David's Turn

Chapter 2 – Right in the Sight of the LORD

The results of reasoning among men and reasoning with God will be contrasted in this chapter. We will also consider why a woman who asked Jesus for living water is often derided in churches today even though she was respected in her day.

The Bible's Counsel on Reasoning

"Every way of a man *is* right in his own eyes" (Prv 21:2). Using this wrong standard lets men tell themselves they are in the right even when they are doing "evil in the sight of the LORD" (1Ki 11:6, et al.). Scripture says, "the way of a fool *is* right in his own eyes: but he that hearkeneth unto counsel *is* wise" (Prv 12:15). But all counsel is not equal. Men took counsel among themselves when a sick man was carried to Jesus by his friends and here is what happened:

"When Jesus saw their faith, he said unto the sick of the palsy, Son, thy sins be forgiven thee. But there were certain of the scribes sitting there, and <u>reasoning in their hearts</u>, Why doth this *man* thus speak blasphemies? who can forgive sins but God only? And immediately when Jesus perceived in his spirit that <u>they so reasoned within themselves</u>, he said unto them, Why <u>reason ye these things in your hearts</u>? Whether is it easier to say to the sick of the palsy, *Thy* sins be forgiven thee; or to say, Arise, and take up thy bed, and walk?" (Mk 2:5-9)

Their reasoning was proven wrong when Jesus healed the man (cf. Mk 2:11-12). Elsewhere, Jesus told a parable about self-reasoning:

"The ground of a certain rich man brought forth plentifully: And <u>he thought within himself</u>, saying, What shall I do, because I have no room where to bestow my fruits? And he said, This will I do: I will pull down my barns, and build greater; and there will I bestow all my fruits and my goods. And I will say to my soul, Soul, thou hast much goods laid up for many years; take thine ease, eat, drink, *and* be merry. But God said unto him, *Thou* fool, this night thy soul shall be required of thee" (Lk 12:16-20).

In scripture, group reasoning among scholars fared no better:

"the chief priests and the scribes came upon *him* [Jesus] with the elders, And spake unto him, saying, Tell us, by what authority doest thou these things? or who is he that gave thee this authority? And he answered and said unto them, I will also ask you one thing; and answer me: The baptism of John, was it from heaven, or of men? And they reasoned with themselves, saying, If we shall say, From heaven; he will say, Why then believed ye him not? But and if we say, Of men; all the people will stone us: for they be persuaded that John was a prophet. And they answered, that they could not tell whence *it was*" (Lk 20:1-7).

Reasoning among themselves also did not help the disciples:

"Jesus said unto them [his disciples], Take heed and beware of the leaven of the Pharisees and of the Sadducees. And they reasoned among themselves, saying, *It is* because we have taken no bread. *Which* when Jesus perceived, he said unto them, O ye of little faith, why reason ye among yourselves, because ye have brought no bread?" (Mt 16:6-8)

The parable of a son sent to get the fruits of his father's vineyard from his workers ends this way, "when the husbandmen saw him [the son], they reasoned among themselves, saying, This is the heir: come, let us kill him, that the inheritance may be ours" (Lk 20:14). So, reasoning together does not guarantee a rational result.

Reasoning is Better When God is Included

If the individual and/or the collective reasoning of men cannot be counted on to lead people to judge rightly, then we cannot assume any individual or group can be trusted to tell people how to view God's word. So, we need a way to validate the reasoning of men (including our own). Scripture gives us a right standard and verses like "prove all things; hold fast that which is good" and "judge not according to the appearance, but judge righteous judgment" (1Th 5:21 & Fourth gospel 7:24) are calling on us to be critical thinkers and diligent truth seekers.

Reasoning is necessary to make judgments and weigh evidence, but how can we avoid errors in reasoning like those noted above? In the first chapter of Isaiah, the LORD's people "rebelled against" him (v. 2) and he called them a "sinful nation, a people laden with iniquity, a seed of evildoers" (v. 4). This was his counsel for them – "wash you, make you clean; put away the evil of your doings from before mine eyes; cease to do evil" (v. 16). He then said, "**let us reason together, saith the** LORD: though your sins be as scarlet, they shall be as white as snow" (v. 18). So, when the LORD's people needed correction, his counsel for them was to reason together with him! If God's view of what is right is the basis of our judgment, then the LORD is included in our reasoning.

As we would expect, the words "let us reason together, saith the LORD" are a perfect fit with passages like, "*it is* better to trust in the LORD than to put confidence in man" and "trust in the LORD with all thine heart; and lean not unto thine own understanding" (Ps 118:8, Prv 3:5).

Reasoning According to the Scriptures

When we are not diligent to include the LORD in our reasoning, misunderstandings of God's word will occur. We will now look at some examples to see how reasoning together with the LORD can correct faulty views or keep them from happening in the first place. First, we will consider Jesus' conversation with a woman he met at Jacob's well. If we reason according to scripture, how will we view her reputation and character? Here is the passage:

"Jesus therefore, being wearied with *his* journey, sat thus on the well: *and* it was about the sixth hour. There cometh a woman of Samaria to draw water: Jesus saith unto her, Give me to drink. (For his disciples were gone away unto the city to buy meat.) Then saith the woman of Samaria unto him, How is it that thou, being a Jew, askest drink of me, which am a woman of Samaria? for the Jews have no dealings with the Samaritans. Jesus answered and said unto her, If thou knewest the gift of God, and who it is that saith to thee, Give me to drink; thou wouldest have asked of him, and he would have given thee living water. The woman saith unto him, Sir, thou hast nothing to draw with, and the well is deep: from whence then hast thou that living water? Art thou greater than our father Jacob, which gave us the well, and drank thereof himself, and his children, and his cattle? Jesus answered and said unto her, Whosoever drinketh of this water shall thirst again: But whosoever drinketh of the water that I shall give him shall never thirst; but the water that I shall give him shall be in him a well of water springing up into everlasting life. The woman saith unto him, Sir, give me this water, that I thirst not, neither come hither to draw. Jesus saith unto her, Go, call thy husband, and come hither. The woman answered and said, I have no husband. Jesus said unto her, Thou hast well said, I have no husband: For thou hast had five husbands; and he whom thou now hast is not thy husband: in that saidst thou truly. The woman saith unto him, Sir, I perceive that thou art a prophet. Our fathers worshipped in this mountain; and ye say, that in Jerusalem is the place where men ought to worship. Jesus saith unto her, Woman, believe me, the hour cometh, when ye shall neither in this mountain, nor yet at Jerusalem, worship the Father. Ye worship ye know not what: we know what we worship: for salvation is of the Jews. But the hour cometh, and now is, when the true worshippers shall worship the Father in spirit and in truth: for the Father seeketh such to worship him. God *is* a Spirit: and they that worship him must worship *him* in spirit and in truth. The woman saith unto him, I know that Messiah cometh, which is called Christ: when he is come, he will tell us all things. Jesus saith unto her, I that speak unto thee am *he*. And upon this came his disciples, and marveled that he talked with the woman: yet no man said, What seekest thou? or, Why talkest thou with her? The woman then left her water pot, and went her way into the city, and saith to the men, Come, see a man, which told me all things that ever I did: is not this the Christ? Then they went out of the city, and came unto him" (Fourth gospel 4:6-30).

What do we know about the woman from this passage? There are people who view her in a bad light after they read these verses. We will discuss why they come to this conclusion, but we will also reason together with scripture and see why scripture demands a different conclusion.

Jesus said, "thou hast had five husbands; and he whom thou now hast is not thy husband." If we rush to judgment, we may conclude he was citing problems in her relations with men. But just because we cannot see how his words could mean something else, it is not a justification for us leaning on our understanding. Blind spots can lead to accidents on the road and, in the same way, blind spots lead to mistakes in our reasoning. This is why we need to allow scripture to guide our thinking. Those who think this woman had a low moral character tend to say things like:

- *'she was a serial adulterer,'*
- *'she had a problem with commitment,'*
- *'she had a reputation for being the town floozy,'*
- *'she was now in a relationship with a live-in lover,'* etc.

Those who reason within themselves and conclude this is what he meant, view other things in the passage in this light. Some say, *'She was alone at the well because people in the town would not associate with her.'* Others say, *'When he put the spotlight on her personal life, she changed the subject.'* Are such ideas justified?

The Evidence of Her Character

"The woman then left her water pot, and went her way into the city, and saith to the men, Come, see a man, which told me all things that ever I did: is not this the Christ? Then they went out of the city, and came unto him" (Fourth gospel 4:28-30).

If a town drunk said he had a cure for cancer, who would listen? An outrageous claim that would be ridiculed or rejected if it comes from a person of low moral character will carry weight if it is made by someone who is respected.

If she had a bad reputation, those in her city would have been inclined to doubt her word on most anything, let alone a claim to have met the Christ. Yet, when she invited the men of her city to meet the Christ, "they went out of the city, and came unto him" (Fourth gospel 4:30). She invited people who knew her to meet a man who she thought was the Christ and they did not ridicule her, they jumped into action!

This does not suggest the men in her city saw her as immoral or as a shunned outcast. If people infer such things from the words Jesus spoke about the five husbands in her past, this shapes how they see her from then on. It also leads them to overlook facts that argue against their view, like how the men reacted when she said she had met the Christ, and to overlook what was explicitly said later in the passage about their response to her claim:

"many of the Samaritans of that city believed on him for the saying of the woman, which testified, He told me all that ever I did. So, when the Samaritans were come unto him, they besought him that he would tarry with them: and he abode there two days. And many more believed because of his own word; And said unto the woman, Now we believe, not because of thy saying: for we have heard *him* ourselves, and know that this is indeed the Christ, the Savior of the world" (Fourth gospel 4:39-42).

Many believed based on her witness! So, her word carried weight. Others did not believe until they heard Jesus for themselves, yet they still went out at her word; then later, after hearing Jesus, they came to the same conclusion about him.

What Did She Know and When Did She Know It?

He told her, "if thou knewest the gift of God, and who it is that saith to thee, Give me to drink; thou wouldest have asked of him, and he would have given thee living water" (Fourth gospel 4:10). So, a lack of knowledge is what kept her from recognizing him at that point.

She also thought he was speaking about physical water at first. But she grasped the spiritual nature of his words moments later when the following part of their conversation took place:

"Whosoever drinketh of this water [from Jacob's well] shall thirst again: But whosoever drinketh of the water that I shall give him shall never thirst; but the water that I shall give him shall be in him a well of water springing up into everlasting life. The woman saith unto him, **Sir**, **give me this water**, that I thirst not, neither come hither to draw" (Fourth gospel 4:13-15).

Jesus said he would give her living water if she asked. She did, and then he said, "go, call thy husband, and come hither." Why? He was talking about spiritual matters before her request. Did he suddenly stop doing this and start talking about physical matters and her relations with men? No, for here is what happened next:

> "The woman answered and said, I have no husband. Jesus said unto her, Thou hast well said, I have no husband: For thou hast had five husbands; and he whom thou now hast is not thy husband: in that saidst thou truly. The woman saith unto him, Sir, I perceive that thou art a prophet. Our fathers worshipped in this mountain; and ye say, that in Jerusalem is the place where men ought to worship. Jesus saith unto her, Woman, believe me, the hour cometh, when ye shall neither in this mountain, nor yet at Jerusalem, worship the Father. Ye worship ye know not what: we know what we worship: for salvation is of the Jews. But the hour cometh, and now is, when the true worshippers shall worship the Father in spirit and in truth: for the Father seeketh such to worship him. God *is* a Spirit: and they that worship him must worship *him* in spirit and in truth. The woman saith unto him, I know that Messiah cometh, which is called Christ: when he is come, he will tell us all things. Jesus saith unto her, I that speak unto thee am *he*" (Fourth gospel 4:17-26).

Jesus' disciples arrived at this point and the conversation ended. When he said she spoke truly, she said, "I perceive that thou art a prophet." Everything said after this involved spiritual matters. Some have said she wanted to change the subject to get the focus off her personal life when she called him a prophet. If this is true, it worked, because the remainder of their conversation was about spiritual things.

They were discussing spiritual matters before Jesus said, "go, call thy husband" and after he told her she spoke truly. If we reason according to scripture, then the phrase "five husbands" has to be weighed in light of his focus on spiritual issues. But before looking at this, we will consider a perspective that is sometimes needed to rightly divide God's word. Then this principle will be applied to help us see what the term "five husbands" meant.

Word Pictures versus Physical References

If someone says, *'it was raining cats and dogs,'* it is relatively easy to figure out this is not talking about animals falling from the sky. This word picture sometimes refers to a heavy downpour of water, but it is also used in other ways. If a wife calls her husband at work and asks him about his day, if he says, *'it is raining cats and dogs'* she will not assume a cloudburst has occurred. Given the context, she knows this means his day has been frantic and problems are raining down on him.

English uses word pictures, but they are misunderstood when a physical meaning is attached to the words. Other languages also use word pictures. The phrase "drink the blood" did not refer to the oral intake of a liquid, as was shown earlier. To say this must refer to sipping a liquid *'because scripture means what it says,'* is to misconstrue the words. [Scripture does mean what it says! Yet some people will use statements like this to imply scripture means what *they say* it says.]

Reasoning according to scripture lets God's word be the measure of truth. If we think scripture must be as we see it, then we make our view that measure. We can think we *know* something is true and still be wrong. Saul of Tarsus thought he knew God's word, but his view led him to persecute Jesus' followers (cf. Acts 22:4).

As noted above, Jesus' words indicate a lack of knowledge is what kept the woman from responding to him correctly. So, rather than assume she lived an immoral life because he said, "thou hast had five husbands; and he whom thou now hast is not thy husband," why not look to see if we could have missed something?

Jesus was not teaching cannibalism when he said, "my flesh is meat indeed, and my blood is drink indeed" (Fourth gospel 6:55), and anyone who would define his words in physical terms is doing an injustice to the text. Yet, many do not see how viewing the phrase "five husbands" in physical terms does injustice to the text.

But her response to Jesus' words should grab our attention, for it shows she understood his words reflected her spiritual ignorance:

"I perceive that thou art a prophet. Our fathers worshipped in this mountain; and ye say, that in Jerusalem is the place where men ought to worship" (Fourth gospel 4:19-20).

Right in the middle of their spiritual discussion, Jesus contrasted historical fact (the prior "five husbands") with her present reality ("he whom thou now hast is not thy husband"). This led her to call him a prophet and to contrast Samaritan and Jewish views on the proper worship place. How do her words follow from what he said?

A woman could marry seven men under the law of Moses (cf. Mk 12:23), so why not five? Jesus did not mention divorce, adultery, or fornication, yet many *infer* these things because "five husbands" were in her past. Does scripture justify this inference? If not, then do the words, "he whom thou now hast is not thy husband" imply she was immoral and had 'a live-in lover'? If this is what we think, then we will view her in that light. But what if we are wrong?

Seeing word pictures in physical terms is an easy mistake to make since they use images from the natural world. The woman herself made this mistake twice. At first, she figured his talk about water meant liquid H_2O. Likewise, when he said, "call thy husband," she said she was not married to a man. Yet, shortly thereafter she concluded he was a prophet – because he did what the prophets of God did throughout Israel's history and throughout scripture.

One of the things prophets did was call people back to God, and they often used word pictures in the process. This occurred when the prophet Nathan rebuked David in 2 Samuel 12:1-3:

"the LORD sent Nathan unto David. And he came unto him, and said unto him, There were two men in one city; the one rich, and the other poor. The rich *man* had exceeding many flocks and herds: But the poor *man* had nothing, save one little ewe lamb."

Viewing this in terms of two men and one animal will lead one to miss the truth the words conveyed. Likewise, Jesus' words on her marital status, past and present, presented a word picture, and it was not talking about her sexual relations with men.

A Spiritual Challenge

Jesus highlighted her *spiritual* status when he said, "thou hast had five husbands; and he whom thou now hast is not thy husband." To help her see she was not as loyal to God as she thought, Jesus cited Samaritan history and her current condition. Amazingly, she immediately recognized this, and this led her to conclude he was a prophet! The remainder of her words show she wanted to know how to worship God properly.

She contrasted the practice of the Samaritans (her "fathers") and the teaching of the Jews on the issue of the right worship location. Once she knew Jesus was a prophet, she sought his counsel on this spiritual dilemma. She thought she had to choose to follow either Samaritan or Jewish tradition. But if people pick between the contrary opinions of men, they lack a way to confirm the truth. God's word gives people the way to answer such questions, and we see this in Jesus' response to her. We will come back to this after we take a moment to consider the history of the Samaritans, so we can understand the word picture that was used by Jesus.

Who Were the Samaritans?

The Samaritans were not Gentiles (Mt 10:5), yet they were not Jews. The northern kingdom of Israel had acquired Samaria (1Kgs 16:24) and came to be called by this name. Israel lost control of the area when they were forcibly relocated to Assyria (2Kgs 17:23). The king of Assyria brought in foreigners to populate the land of the former kingdom of Israel: "the king of Assyria brought *men* from Babylon, and from Cuthah, and from Ava, and from Hamath, and from Sepharvaim, and placed *them* in the cities of Samaria instead of the children of Israel" (2Kgs 17:24).

Later, the king of Assyria moved a priest of Israel back to the land to teach those foreigners "the manner of the God of the land" (2Kgs 17:27). He "taught them how they should fear the LORD" (v. 28). Even so, it says, "every nation made gods of their own, and put *them* in the houses of the high places which the Samaritans had made" (v. 29). They learned the truth but still held onto error and, as a result, "they feared the LORD, and served their own gods" (2Kgs 17:33).

It was a mix of truth and error from then on. "These nations feared the LORD, and served their graven images, both their children, and their children's children: as did their fathers, so do they unto this day" (2Kgs 17:41). Yet, even before they got there, both Samaria and Jerusalem were rebuked by the LORD who said, "with their idols have they committed adultery" (Eze 23:37). It was not between men and women, this was against the LORD, who was their husband: "thy Maker *is* thine husband; the LORD of hosts *is* his name" (Isa 54:4). He was pictured as a husband way back in Egypt. The LORD said this about the Exodus, "I took them by the hand to bring them out of the land of Egypt; which my covenant they brake, although I was a husband unto them, saith the LORD" (Jer 31:32).

Samaria and Jerusalem were "adulteresses" (Eze 23:45). The LORD even gave Israel "a bill of divorce" (Jer 3:8). So, without a doubt, God's word did use marital terms to portray spiritual relations.

Five Husbands?

Marriage portrayed the bond between a people and their God(s). So, this is why the woman knew Jesus' reference to five husbands in her past referred to the worship of God – because five groups replaced Israel in Samaria and all five worshipped their own gods! They were "from **Babylon**, and from **Cuthah**, and from **Ava**, and from **Hamath**, and from **Sepharvaim**" (2Kgs 17:24), and each group "made gods of their own, and put *them* in the houses of the high places which the Samaritans had made" (2Kgs 17:29).

Jesus cited her history. She judged him to be a prophet because he gave a reproof and used word pictures, as God's prophets did. Beyond her troubled roots, Jesus noted, "he whom thou now hast is not thy husband" (Fourth gospel 4:18). So, if she was not married to the ideas of her past, who did she have at that time and why was he not her husband? She believed God was her God, but she was not married to him. Jesus told her, "ye worship ye know not what" (Fourth gospel 4:22), and we cannot marry someone we do not know. She was spiritually confused. For example, thinking she must pick between the traditions of the Samaritans and the Jews (regarding the proper place to worship God) kept her from worshiping God "in spirit and in truth" (Fourth gospel 4:24), as Jesus said must be done.

She asked, "art thou greater than our father Jacob, which gave us the well?" (Fourth gospel 4:12) Thus, she identified with Jacob and, thereby, with the God of Abraham, Isaac, and Jacob. Yet, she also said, "our fathers worshipped in this mountain; and ye say, that in Jerusalem is the place where men ought to worship" (Fourth gospel 4:20). So, on this, she identified with the tradition of the Samaritans over that of the Jews. However, she must have had her doubts on this spiritual dilemma, since the first thing she did when she knew she was talking with a prophet was ask about this issue.

Living Water

Jesus indicated she would respond to the truth if she knew it (cf. Fourth gospel 4:10). Not surprisingly, therefore, she responded rightly when she learned the truth from him during their talk.

He indicated he could give her living water. She came to believe he could do it. We know this because moments later she did what he told her to do, she asked for it! She said, "give me this water".

Jesus told his disciples "other sheep I have, which are not of this fold: them also I must bring, and they shall hear my voice; and there shall be one fold, and one shepherd" (Fourth gospel 10:15). Did this Samaritan woman hear his voice? Consider this exchange:

"The woman saith unto him, I know that Messiah cometh, which is called Christ: when he is come, he will tell us all things. Jesus saith unto her, I that speak unto thee am *he*" (Fourth gospel 4:25-26).

Did she believe him? Yes. The return of the disciples interrupted their interaction at that point, but she staked her reputation on him. She witnessed to the men of her city, "come, see a man, which told me all things that ever I did: is not this the Christ?" She could say this because he had given her living water and she drank it!

[Later on, we will look at what scripture means by the word faith. If a biblical definition of faith is applied, it proves this woman acted in faith. Therefore, the rewards that come along with acting in faith would also apply to her.]

Case Study: The Case of John's Question

Reasonable Doubt?

The Bible has much to say about John the Baptist, starting with the miracle of his birth (Lk 1:5-25, 36-44, & 57-80). He was also related to Jesus, for John's mother was a cousin of the mother of Jesus (cf. Lk 1:36).

At one point, John was put in prison by Herod. While he was there, he sent two of his disciples to ask Jesus, "art thou he that should come, or do we look for another?" (Mt 11:2-3, Lk 7:19)

What are we to make of this question? Here are some of the ways people will typically try to explain John's question:

A. *'he had a moment of doubt, but he was despondent since he was in prison at the time, so this is understandable,'*
B. *'he was perplexed and/or frustrated because Jesus had not yet overthrown the Romans as John had expected,'*
C. *'he knew Jesus was the Christ, but he asked the question so his disciples would know it.'*

Now is the time to get your Bible and investigate John's question. After you jot down your thoughts, return to this case study and compare your notes to the evidence scripture presents, to see if it shows us a better way to gain insight on John's question.

The Case of John's Question

Doubting John?

The tendency to want fast answers can lead us to settle for ideas that sound reasonable but are not actually in line with the Bible. This is one reason why we need to see if our beliefs can stand up to biblical scrutiny.

Many rush to judgment and assume John was asking if Jesus was the Christ. John did not use that word, and they cite no evidence to show this was the point of his question. Nonetheless, *since they are unable to see how his question could refer to anything else*, they fall into the trap of leaning on their own understanding.

John baptized Jesus and "saw the Spirit descending from heaven like a dove, and it abode upon" Jesus (Fourth gospel 1:32). He declared Jesus to be "the Lamb of God" (Fourth gospel 1:29). He was "filled with the Holy Ghost, even from his mother's womb" (Lk 1:15). His mother surely told him about his own miracle birth, along with all she knew about Jesus' birth (from her cousin Mary). So, those who say John was asking if Jesus was the Christ have to downplay this evidence in order to hold their view of John's question.

Since John was in prison when he asked it, some say, *'he was depressed and had a moment of doubt like we all do.'* But would being in prison always lead a man of God to feel dejected? No. When Paul and Silas were in prison, they "prayed, and sang praises unto God" (Acts 16:25). While this does not prove John was not despondent when he asked his question, it does show it is wrong to infer he was demoralized just because he was in prison at the time. Moreover, his execution came as a surprise (cf. Mt 14:6-10, Mk 6:20-27). Thus, it is incorrect to suggest John was distressed because he was facing death.

John said, "one mightier than I cometh, the latchet of whose shoes I am not worthy to unloose" (Lk 3:16). Did he do an about-face and decide he was worthy to question Jesus' credentials? No, but we need to trust scripture to show us how to see John's question from his point of view if we are to understand his purpose for asking it.

The Context of the Question

In Matthew 11, John's question is found in this context:

"it came to pass, when Jesus had made an end of commanding his twelve disciples, he departed thence to teach and to preach in their cities. Now when John had heard in the prison the works of Christ, he sent two of his disciples, And said unto him, Art thou he that should come, or do we look for another?" (Mt 11:1-3)

Hearing about the works of Christ provoked John's question, and hearing this would not have frustrated John or lead him to doubt Jesus *was* the Christ. So, why did he ask if Jesus was "he that should come?" Luke7:11-10 gives us some additional details:

"he [Jesus] went into a city called Nain; and many of his disciples went with him, and much people. Now when he came nigh to the gate of the city, behold, there was a dead man carried out, the only son of his mother, and she was a widow: and much people of the city was with her. And when the Lord saw her, he had compassion on her, and said unto her, Weep not. And he came and touched the bier: and they that bare *him* stood still. And he said, Young man, I say unto thee, Arise. And he that was dead sat up, and began to speak. And he delivered him to his mother. And there came a fear on all: and they glorified God, saying, That a great prophet is risen up among us; and, That God hath visited his people. And this rumor of him went forth throughout all Judea, and throughout all the region round about. And the disciples of John showed him of all these things. And John calling *unto him* two of his disciples sent *them* to Jesus, saying, Art thou he that should come or look we for another?"

"The disciples of John showed him of all these things" (Lk 7:18), and hearing about Jesus raising a dead man and the crowd's reaction to this miracle would not cause John to doubt or be impatient.

Furthermore, John's disciples told him this news. So, the question was not asked for their benefit since they knew about "the works of Christ" before John did.

Of course, a person might doubt a report of Jesus raising a man from the dead. But if the person believed the report, it would not lead that person to doubt Jesus. When the religious leaders heard about Jesus raising Lazarus from the dead they did not doubt him, they plotted to kill him (Fourth gospel 11:43-53). When John heard about Jesus raising someone from the dead and the crowd's reaction to this miracle, it led him to ask Jesus a question.

Our Assumptions Versus Scripture

After Jesus sent the two disciples back to John with his reply, he publicly declared, "among those that are born of women there is not a greater prophet than John the Baptist" (Lk 7:28). These words do not suggest Jesus thought John's question indicated doubt, impatience, or a weak moment on John's part. Jesus criticized his disciples in their moments "of little faith" (Mt 6:30, 8:26, 14:31, & 16:8), but he said no such words about John.

Jesus did tell John's disciples, "blessed is *he*, whosoever shall not be offended in me" (Mt 11:6 & Lk 7:23). We will look at this statement a bit later. For now, however, realize that to assume this justifies the doubting John viewpoint, one must ignore two key things:

A. the news that prompted John to ask the question, and
B. the high regard for John that was expressed by Jesus right after he sent his response to John.

Besides hearing about a miracle, John was also told: "there came a fear on all: and they glorified God, saying, That a great prophet is risen up among us; and, That God hath visited his people" (Lk 7:16), for his disciples told him "all these things" (Lk 7:18). Why would this news cause John to ask Jesus a question?

We view things in the Bible through the lens of our beliefs. Since we assume our beliefs are correct, we see John's question from our perspective. Yet, we do not see things in the way the men of that era did. The people in John's day had a different perspective. John knew more about Jesus than most people in his day, but we have the Bible and it tells us things he did not know. So, if we are to understand his question, we must see it from his point of view.

Did John ask, *'Was I wrong?'* or *'Are you really the Lamb of God?'* No. He asked if Jesus was "he that should come" (Mt 11:3, Lk 7:19). John did not ask if Jesus was the Messiah, and we twist his words when we infer he was asking this. In that era, "the people were in expectation, and all men mused in their hearts of John, whether he were the Christ, or not" (Lk 3:15-19). Even so, "the Christ" was not the only one they were expecting.

After Jesus raised the young man in the casket, all the people said a "great prophet" had risen among them (Lk 7:16). This caused John to wonder if Jesus was "he that should come." Why? Scripture has the answer, for it teaches us the people were looking for someone other than the Christ! They were also waiting for...

The Prophet

In John's day, there was still an unfulfilled prophecy that had been delivered by Moses, about one who would be "like unto" Moses (Dt 18:15). So, we should not be surprised to learn that the Jews of John's day were expectantly awaiting this prophet.

Moses said, "the Lord thy God will raise up unto thee a Prophet from the midst of thee, of thy brethren, like unto me" (Dt 18:15). A few verses later this prophecy was highlighted again when the Lord told Moses, "I will raise them up a Prophet from among their brethren, like unto thee, and will put my words in his mouth; and he shall speak unto them all that I shall command him" (Dt 18:18). Would the fulfillment of this prophecy have been high on the list of the expectations of Abraham's descendants? No doubt.

But it may surprise some to learn the people in John's day thought the prophecies of the Christ and that prophet had to be fulfilled by two different people! We cannot make sense of John's question until we realize this was *his* perspective.

At the time of Jesus' ministry, God's faithful did not view Jesus as we do now. Like others in his day, John believed the prophet "like unto" Moses would be a separate person from the Christ. At least he thought this until he heard a report that led him to wonder if Jesus could also be the prophet "like unto" Moses.

Scripture says, "all men mused in their hearts of John, whether he were the Christ, or not" (Lk 3:15). Yet, scripture shows us they also considered other possibilities as to who John might be:

"the Jews sent priests and Levites from Jerusalem to ask him, Who art thou? And he confessed, and denied not; but confessed, I am not the Christ. And they asked him, What then? Art thou Elias [Elijah]? And he saith, I am not. Art thou that prophet? And he answered, No" (Fourth gospel 1:19-21).

There were three options in their view, "the Christ," "Elias [Elijah]," or "that prophet." So, these three were seen as distinct individuals in that era. The questions they asked of John prove they thought "the Christ" and "that prophet" referred to two people.

The Pharisees also asked John: "why baptizest thou then, if thou be not that Christ, nor Elias, neither that prophet?" (Fourth gospel 1:25) He told the first group he was none of these three, and everything suggests he also assumed "the Christ" and "that prophet" would be different men.

John was a prophet and a cousin of Jesus, yet his knowledge of Jesus was lacking. Twice he said, "I knew him not" (Fourth gospel 1:31 & 33), so for him to learn something new about Jesus is no surprise.

Division Caused by Jesus

Opinions about Jesus were often split and contentious, just as he indicated they would be, for he said, "suppose ye that I am come to give peace on earth? I tell you, Nay; but rather division" (Lk 12:51). Once it says, "there was a division among the people because of him" (Fourth gospel 7:43) and this happened at other times also.

Jesus asked his disciples, "whom say the people that I am?" (Lk 9:18) They replied, "John the Baptist; but some say, Elias [Elijah]; and others say, that one of the old prophets is risen again" (Lk 9:19). What is missing from this list? It should arrest our attention that "the Christ" did not even show up on this list! When the Pharisees inquired of John, "the Christ" topped their list of speculations as to whom John might be. This was not the case with Jesus.

However, this idea did come up. At one point, "many of the people believed on him, and said, When Christ cometh, will he do more miracles than these which this *man* hath done?" (Fourth gospel 7:31)

The debates about Jesus were fueled by men who sowed doubts about him. When a group of Pharisees said, "this man is not of God, because he keepeth not the sabbath day. Others said, How can a man that is a sinner do such miracles? And there was a division among them" (Fourth gospel 9:16). At a different time, "many of them [the Jews] said, He hath a devil, and is mad; why hear ye him? Others said, These are not the words of him that hath a devil. Can a devil open the eyes of the blind?" (Fourth gospel 10:20-21)

The Prophet *and* the Christ

Jesus came on the scene when the people were looking for Elijah, the Christ, and the prophet like Moses. Twice in scripture, we see where some saw Jesus as a possible candidate for the prophet like Moses. After he fed five thousand men with five barley loaves, and two small fishes we are told, "then those men, when they had seen the miracle that Jesus did, said, This is of a truth that prophet that should come into the world" (Fourth gospel 6:14).

On another occasion, the possibility of Jesus being this prophet was raised by people who heard him teach:

"In the last day, that great *day* of the feast, Jesus stood and cried, saying, If any man thirst, let him come unto me, and drink. He that believeth on me, as the scripture hath said, out of his belly shall flow rivers of living water. (But this spake he of the Spirit, which they that believe on him should receive: for the Holy Ghost was not yet *given*; because that Jesus was not yet glorified.) Many of the people therefore, when they heard this saying, said, Of a truth this is the Prophet. Others said, This is the Christ. But some said, Shall Christ come out of Galilee?" (Fourth gospel 7:37-41)

The Prophet? The Christ? Some people thought one thing, some believed another. John's question appears to be the first time anyone wondered if those two terms might refer to one person!

In Acts 3, Peter spoke to the people in the temple and said they "killed the Prince of life, whom God hath raised from the dead" (Acts 3:15). In this context he went on to say:

> "Repent ye therefore, and be converted, that your sins may be blotted out, when the times of refreshing shall come from the presence of the Lord; And he shall send Jesus Christ, which before was preached unto you: Whom the heaven must receive until the times of restitution of all things, which God hath spoken by the mouth of all his holy prophets since the world began. For Moses truly said unto the fathers, A prophet shall the Lord your God raise up unto you of your brethren, like unto me; him shall ye hear in all things whatsoever he shall say unto you. And it shall come to pass, *that* every soul, which will not hear that prophet, shall be destroyed from among the people. Yea, and all the prophets from Samuel and those that follow after, as many as have spoken, have likewise foretold of these days" (Acts 3:22-24).

Here we see, the prophecy regarding the prophet like Moses was speaking about the risen Jesus. "Foretold of these days" refers to the time after Jesus rose from the dead. Thus, the resurrection is the key! This prophecy had remained unfulfilled since Moses' day, and it could only be fulfilled after Jesus was raised. The idea of Jesus being both the Prophet and the Christ does show up after his resurrection, but John died before this. So, his question must be viewed in light of the data that shows the people of his day assumed the Prophet and the Christ would be different men.

Men who thought Jesus was the Christ, as John surely did, would be unlikely to think Jesus might also fulfill the prophecy about the Prophet like Moses. However, since among those born of women there is no greater prophet than John, he would have been more likely than most to be open to correction.

Jesus Responds to John's Question

After John's disciples posed his question to Jesus it says, "in that same hour he cured many of *their* infirmities and plagues, and of evil spirits; and unto many *that were* blind he gave sight" (Lk 7:21).

This was not done to prove Jesus could do miracles since he had raised a man from the dead. Jesus then told John's disciples:

"tell John what things ye have seen and heard; how that the blind see, the lame walk, the lepers are cleansed, the deaf hear, the dead are raised, to the poor the gospel is preached. And blessed is *he*, whosoever shall not be offended in me" (Lk 7:22-23).

When John got this report, he likely recalled passages such as Isaiah 35:5, "then the eyes of the blind shall be opened, and the ears of the deaf shall be unstopped." Does scripture ever suggest miracles would only be associated with Jesus' role as the Christ?

"To him [Jesus] give all the prophets witness" (Acts 10:43). So, his reply to John had to take account of all of God's word. He would not only be the Christ, nor would he be only the Prophet.

For example, he would also become "a high priest after the order of Melchisedec" (Heb 5:10). Even so, Jesus could not merely discuss the idea of fulfilling multiple roles. Why? Because a prophecy must be fulfilled – and many prophecies, like the one about the prophet like Moses, would not be fulfilled until Jesus rose from the dead.

His reply to John ended with, "blessed is *he*, whosoever shall not be offended in me" (Lk 7:23). So, he pronounced a blessing on John and all who do this! [Compare this to the blessings Jesus listed in Matthew 5:3-11.] It was not said as a warning to a doubting John as some mistakenly conclude. Scripture says, "blessed *is* the man that walketh not in the counsel of the ungodly, nor standeth in the way of sinners, nor sitteth in the seat of the scornful" and "blessed *is* the man that endureth temptation" (Ps 1:1, Jas 1:2). Does the record in the Bible indicate this is what John did? Yes, it does.

The Conclusion to the Case of John's Question

John said, "I am not the Christ, but that I am sent before him" (Fourth gospel 3:28) and nothing suggests John ever had doubts about this. As with all the other biblical evidence, this shows scripture always argued against assuming John was asking if Jesus was the Christ.

In context, John's question makes sense if he wanted to know if Jesus would also fulfill the role of "the prophet" (Fourth gospel 7:40), i.e., in addition to being the Christ.

When people tell us John was doubting if Jesus was the Christ, then this is likely to influence our view unless we put it to the test. From then on, what we heard could prejudice our views, until we take the time to weigh the words of scripture.

But as this case study shows, "rightly dividing the word of truth" (2Ti 2:15) allows scripture to lead us to the correct understanding.

The end of the Case of John's Question

Chapter 3 – The Religious Environment

What is the kingdom of God? Why do men resist it? Who was Nicodemus, and why could he not see it? How can we rightly understand phrases like born again or born of water? In this chapter, scripture will shed light on these issues and more.

Of the Truth

Jesus said, "**every one that is of the truth heareth my voice**" (Fourth gospel 18:37). So, the religious leaders who resisted him were not "of the truth," and this had been revealed before Jesus arrived on the scene, as their response to John the Baptist proves.

"The Pharisees and lawyers rejected the counsel of God against themselves, being not baptized of him [John]" (Lk 7:30). John was "sent from God" (Fourth gospel 1:6), yet the leaders would not submit to his message. Furthermore, Jesus compared his own reception to the reception of John the Baptist:

"whereunto shall I liken this generation? It is like unto children sitting in the markets, and calling unto their fellows, And saying, We have piped unto you, and ye have not danced; we have mourned unto you, and ye have not lamented. For John came neither eating nor drinking, and they say, He hath a devil. The Son of man came eating and drinking, and they say, Behold a man gluttonous, and a winebibber, a friend of publicans and sinners. But wisdom is justified of her children" (Mt 11:16-19).

[Note: the phrase "Son of man" refers to Jesus himself (cf. Mt 8:20).]

God's authority was being rejected. It did not matter if it came via John or Jesus. Those who resist the truth are not inclined to be truthful, so they will not admit they do not want the truth. Instead, when they reject the truth, they give themselves reasons as to why they are right to do so. The process of self-justification is what was being pictured by Jesus in the passage above. When the truth is rejected any reason will do. The justification does not need to make sense, but it will always be portrayed as a *righteous* excuse.

Justified of Her Children?

Paul called Timothy his "beloved son" (1Cor 4:17). This did not refer to physical lineage, for Paul was "a Jew" (Acts 21:39) and Timothy's father was "a Greek" (Acts 16:1). It was a picture of how Timothy came to believe in Jesus and Paul made this clear when he said Timothy was his "son in the faith" (1Ti 1:2) (i.e., the word of God gave new life to Timothy and Paul had delivered this lifegiving seed). Similarly, Paul called Titus his "own son after the common faith" (Titus 1:4). He also called the brethren in Corinth "my beloved sons" (1Cor 4:14) and said, "though ye have ten thousand instructors in Christ, yet *have ye* not many fathers: for in Christ Jesus I have begotten you through the gospel" (v. 15). What is the difference between an instructor in Christ and a father? One has information to share about Christ, the other produces children.

The picture here is men are "begotten" by the things they believe! This idea is also seen in Jesus' rebuke of the missionary work of the scribes and Pharisees. He told them, "ye compass sea and land to make one proselyte [convert], and when he is made, ye make him twofold more the child of hell than yourselves" (Mt 23:15).

When ideas are believed they produce behaviors that follow from those ideas. Those missionaries were children of hell, so this is all they could produce. If a child of hell teaches others to believe as he does, those who are begotten by those ideas will find it *twice* as hard to break free from the bondage of those beliefs. Why? Because they will have to acknowledge their own blindness and the blindness of the people whom they had put confidence in – and doing both of these things is doubly hard. Jesus could say, "wisdom is justified of her children" because people are a product of the ideas they believe and self-justification knows no limits.

Notice what Jesus said right before he said those words:

"whereunto shall I liken this generation? It is like unto children sitting in the markets, and calling unto their fellows, and saying, we have piped unto you, and ye have not danced; we have mourned unto you, and ye have not lamented" (Mt 11:16-17).

Both John and Jesus taught ideas that challenged the teachings of their generation. So, men in that generation found reasons to justify disrespecting them, as Jesus went on to note:

"For John **came neither eating nor drinking**, and they say, He hath a devil. The Son of man **came eating and drinking**, and they say, Behold a man gluttonous, and a winebibber, a friend of publicans and sinners. But wisdom is justified of her children" (Mt 11:18-19).

John and Jesus both rebuked the religious groups of their day for not honoring God's authority. That is not two different messages. It is the same message, delivered by two different messengers. Those who they criticized could either admit the error of their ways or find a reason for rejecting the message. But eating and drinking do not determine if a message is true or not. Thus, the excuses were bogus. Moreover, since the purpose was to justify rejecting Jesus and John, it did not matter if the reasons for doing so were total opposites. When the intent is to avoid the truth, any reason will do, it does not have to make sense.

The purpose of attacking the messenger is to avoid having to deal with the message, so even contrary objections could be used as the basis for attacking the messenger's character. The goal was to find a righteous-sounding excuse for dismissing God's authority (as this was the foundation of the message of Jesus and John).

"*There is* no wisdom nor understanding nor counsel against the LORD" (Prv 21:30). When people are opposing the LORD, this reveals they lack wisdom, understanding, and counsel. So, why did Jesus use the word "wisdom" about the people who opposed him and John? Because like other gifts including life, wisdom can be used for good or ill. Many people will read a positive connotation into the word "wisdom," but scripture lets us know not to do so.

"The wisdom of this world is foolishness with God" (1Cor 3:19), thus, such wisdom is not good. Wisdom must be judged according to God's perspective. Those who use the measure of this world will come to one conclusion, while those who judge according to what is right in the sight of God, will see things very differently.

Consider the words "wisdom is justified of her children" (Mt 11:19). Here is an example of how we can benefit when we stop and ask, how does it follow? Jesus noted the contradictory reasoning that was used to denigrate himself and John (both of whom were sent by God). At that point, he said, "wisdom is justified of her children." How would this follow? We can see how this follows when we let God's word show us how to identify those children and the wisdom that begat them. It was *not* the wisdom of God; it was the wisdom of the world because their foolish excuses make this clear.

Religious Leaders Versus God's Counsel

The message of John was called "the counsel of God" by Jesus. He said those who were baptized by John "justified God" (Lk 7:29), and said, "the Pharisees and lawyers rejected the counsel of God against themselves, being not baptized of him [John]" (Lk 7:30).

Jesus used the words "hypocrite," "hypocrites," and "hypocrisy" about members of the educated religious elite in many verses (Mt 16:3, et al.). Their practice of promoting the teachings of men made the word of God void (cf. Mk 7:13) and Jesus rebuked this practice. His many miracles did not change men who were inclined to resist God's truth. Conversely, if a *lack* of miracles was a just cause for doubting someone, this argument would have been raised against John the Baptist, for "John did no miracle" (Fourth gospel 10:41).

What did the scholars do after eyewitnesses told them Jesus had raised Lazarus from the dead? The chief priests and Pharisees met and said, "what do we? for this man doeth many miracles" (Fourth gospel 11:47). They knew of the many miracles he had done. Did this change them? No. "From that day forth they took counsel together for to put him to death" (Fourth gospel 11:53). What led them to react this way? "Men loved darkness rather than light, because their deeds were evil" (Fourth gospel 3:19).

Trying to kill Jesus was surely evil. But what about other people in that era? What about those who rejected the counsel of God or those who spread the rumor that claimed John had a devil (Mt 11:18) and gossiped about Jesus by saying he was gluttonous, and a winebibber? (Mt 11:19) They were denying God's authority.

Scripture had warned them to "keep thy foot when thou goest to the house of God, and be more ready to hear, than to give the sacrifice of fools: for they consider not that they do evil" (Ecc 5:1). Fools do not see they do evil when *they* give a sacrifice to God.

The leaders of that day did not want to hear, but they still offered sacrifices to God. When men think sacrificing without repentance will work, their standard of right and wrong is not scripture, it is their own opinion. Such blindness is why many men could not see the kingdom of God, even as it was being brought near to them.

Missing the Kingdom of God

Jesus once appointed seventy "and sent them two and two before his face into every city and place, whither he himself would come" (Lk 10:1). He told them:

"into whatsoever city ye enter, and they receive you, eat such things as are set before you: And heal the sick that are therein, and say unto them, The kingdom of God is come nigh unto you. But into whatsoever city ye enter, and they receive you not, go your ways out into the streets of the same, and say, Even the very dust of your city, which cleaveth on us, we do wipe off against you: notwithstanding be ye sure of this, that the kingdom of God is come nigh unto you" (Lk 10:8-11).

Notice, their message brought the kingdom of God near to people, whether the messengers were received or not. When Jesus sent out the twelve, he told them something similar; "as ye go, preach, saying, The kingdom of heaven is at hand" (Mt 10:7). The message of God and miracles give people a taste of his kingdom because he is represented in both of these. Yet, while physical eyes can see a miracle, insight is needed for one to receive the message. The Pharisees could not see the kingdom and Jesus had to tell them, "the kingdom of God cometh not with observation" (Lk 17:20).

Once a scribe responded to Jesus by citing scripture. Jesus said he was "not far from the kingdom of God" (Mk 12:34). What brought him near to God's kingdom was the truth, not a miracle or a sign.

When Jesus sent out the seventy, he told them, "he that heareth you heareth me; and he that despiseth you despiseth me; and he that despiseth me despiseth him that sent me" (Lk 10:16). He also applied this principle when he sent out the twelve. He told them, "he that receiveth you receiveth me, and he that receiveth me receiveth him that sent me" (Mt 10:40). Moreover, he later told his disciples, "he that receiveth whomsoever I send receiveth me; and he that receiveth me receiveth him that sent me" (Fourth gospel 13:20). In each of these statements, Jesus taught the principle of delegated authority.

A failure to hear the message of the disciples was not merely about rejecting them. It is about rejecting Jesus and the one who sent him. Rejecting the witness of God's messengers led people to miss the kingdom of God and people did this to Jesus himself as occurred in this notable episode:

"he [Jesus] was casting out a devil, and it was dumb. And it came to pass, when the devil was gone out, the dumb spake; and the people wondered. But some of them said, He casteth out devils through Beelzebub the chief of the devils. And others, tempting *him*, sought of him a sign from heaven. But he, knowing their thoughts, said unto them, Every kingdom divided against itself is brought to desolation; and a house *divided* against a house falleth. If Satan also be divided against himself, how shall his kingdom stand? because ye say that I cast out devils through Beelzebub. And if I by Beelzebub cast out devils, by whom do your sons cast *them* out? therefore shall they be your judges. But if I with the finger of God cast out devils, no doubt the kingdom of God is come upon you" (Lk 11:14-20).

God's authority was behind what happened, thus, a manifestation of God's kingdom had occurred. But instead of acknowledging this and submitting to God's authority, those men justified themselves with excuses for not doing so. Some called Jesus' good deed evil by saying he did it through the power of Beelzebub. Others asked him for "a sign from heaven," which was a slam on Jesus because this implied they knew how to recognize "a sign from heaven" and what he had done did not qualify in their eyes.

A man who asks for a sign but shuts his eyes when God gives it is divided against himself. Jesus knew their thoughts, so he taught a lesson on why mutually exclusive efforts must always end up in self-destruction. He asked a question that put them on the spot:

"If Satan also be divided against himself, how shall his kingdom stand? because ye say that I cast out devils through Beelzebub. And if I by Beelzebub cast out devils, **by whom do your sons cast** them **out**? therefore shall they be your judges" (Lk 11:18-19).

They admitted Jesus had "cast out devils," but to avoid having to submit to the truth of what this meant, they said he did it "through Beelzebub." However, he did not let them get off that easily and he asked, "if I by Beelzebub cast out devils, by whom do your sons cast them out?"

Did they raise sons who would be walking in the power of God? Certainly not. This is what Jesus exposed with his question. If they or their sons had cast out devils, they would have thrown that in Jesus' face. Jesus learned from his Father and did cast out devils. Their sons learned from them and had no power. Therefore, the answer that should have pricked their conscience was "by" no one! Their sons did not cast out any devils. This is why Jesus was able to cite their sons as evidence against them – "therefore shall they be your judges" (Lk 11:19).

When people resist the truth, they judge it to be not of God. Thus, they resist his authority. "Judge not according to the appearance, but judge righteous judgment" (Fourth gospel 7:24) was Jesus' counsel regarding making right judgments. To judge rightly, our measure needs to be what is right in the sight of the LORD and not merely our own opinion. Human judgments are affected by many things and appearance is a judgment call, for it depends on how a person or thing is perceived. If we judge according to the appearance, our own opinion is our standard of judgment.

In the episode above, those who saw Jesus cast out devils did not "judge righteous judgment." Jesus said, "the kingdom of God" had come upon them, but those accusers could not see it.

Nicodemus

Another who could not see the kingdom of God was Nicodemus, even though what he said to Jesus shows he presumptuously thought he could. He was a top religious leader, as was noted in the passage that tells us of the night he went to speak with Jesus:

"[1]There was a man of the Pharisees, named Nicodemus, a ruler of the Jews: [2]The same came to Jesus by night, and said unto him, Rabbi, we know that thou art a teacher come from God: for no man can do these miracles that thou doest, except God be with him. [3]Jesus answered and said unto him, Verily, verily, I say unto thee, Except a man be born again, he cannot see the kingdom of God. [4]Nicodemus saith unto him, How can a man be born when he is old? can he enter the second time into his mother's womb, and be born? [5]Jesus answered, Verily, verily, I say unto thee, Except a man be born of water and *of* the Spirit, he cannot enter into the kingdom of God. [6]That which is born of the flesh is flesh; and that which is born of the Spirit is spirit. [7]Marvel not that I said unto thee, Ye must be born again. [8]The wind bloweth where it listeth, and thou hearest the sound thereof, but canst not tell whence it cometh, and whither it goeth: so is every one that is born of the Spirit. [9]Nicodemus answered and said unto him, How can these things be? [10]Jesus answered and said unto him, Art thou a master of Israel, and knowest not these things? [11]Verily, verily, I say unto thee, We speak that we do know, and testify that we have seen; and ye receive not our witness. [12]If I have told you earthly things, and ye believe not, how shall ye believe, if I tell you *of* heavenly things?" (Fourth gospel 3:1-12)

Was Nicodemus on a quest for truth when he went to meet Jesus? If we assume this was his motive, we will see the passage from this perspective and we may make inferences based on this view.

For example, because it says he went "by night," many insist he did this so his fellow religious leaders would not know about his meeting with Jesus, and they feel free to infer this even though scripture never said any such thing. Is this inference justified?

Hear the Words of Jesus

All inferences rely on assumptions. If one of them is wrong, then the inference will be too. What if instead of making inferences, our practice was to conform our view to the data we see in scripture? What would be the result? Is the view of Nicodemus coming as an honest truth-seeker contrary to the evidence? Yes! For starters, consider what Jesus said to him: "we speak that we do know, and testify that we have seen; and **ye receive not our witness**" (v. 11). Since Nicodemus did not receive the "witness" of Jesus, what was he seeking on that night?

Consider two statements of Jesus: "my sheep hear my voice, and I know them, and they follow me" (Fourth gospel 10:27) and "he that is of God heareth God's words" (Fourth gospel 8:47). Do these words describe Nicodemus? No, for he would not receive the "witness" of Jesus. Also, Jesus told him, "if I have told you earthly things, and ye believe not... " (Fourth gospel 3:12), so Nicodemus did not even believe the things Jesus told him on that night. But to grasp the depth of his resistance to the truth, it is important to realize the witness he rejected was not limited to the words he heard Jesus speak on that night.

Nicodemus referred to miracles Jesus had done. Miracles would also bear profound witness to Jesus' authority. So, what miracles did Nicodemus have in mind when he mentioned Jesus' miracles?

What Provoked Nicodemus' Visit?

Nicodemus said, "Rabbi, we know that thou art a teacher come from God: for no man can do these miracles that thou doest, except God be with him" (Fourth gospel 3:2). This has to be viewed in light of the details that are recorded at the end of the prior chapter:

> "when he [Jesus] was in Jerusalem at the Passover, in the feast *day*, many believed in his name, when they saw the miracles which he did. But Jesus did not commit himself unto them, because he knew all *men*, And needed not that any should testify of man: for he knew what was in man" (Fourth gospel 2:23-25).

Those miracles caused many to believe in Jesus' name, but not Nicodemus! He claimed to know God was with Jesus because of the miracles, yet Jesus' words show Nicodemus did not receive the witness of those miracles.

Prior to doing those miracles, Jesus cast the merchants out of the temple (Fourth gospel 2:13-22). This disturbed the religious status quo, much like John the Baptist had done. John was also sent by God, and his witness was also rejected by the Pharisees (cf. Lk 7:30), and Nicodemus was a Pharisee. But miracles would make it harder to deal with Jesus because John did no miracles (cf. Fourth gospel 10:31). Jesus' deeds and teachings were making the religious leaders look bad. If they could not convince Jesus to play ball with them, they would either have to discredit him or get rid of him.

Who Was Nicodemus Speaking For?

In the KJV, the words "thee," "thou," "thy," and "thine" are all singular. "Ye," "you," "your," and "yours" are plural. This was done to allow Bible readers to distinguish between the singular and plural pronouns that were used when the scriptures were written in Hebrew and Greek. These distinctions are in God's word but are ignored by translations of the Bible which use a single word ("you") to translate both the singular and the plural pronouns. However, the conversation in question provides a good example of why these distinctions are important.

When Jesus said, "ye receive not our witness" he was not only speaking against Nicodemus and the word "ye" lets us see this. Who did Jesus include along with Nicodemus in this indictment? Nicodemus was not there on his own behalf. He claimed to speak for his fellow religious leaders. He said, "we know that thou art a teacher come from God: for no man can do these miracles that thou doest, except God be with him" (Fourth gospel 3:2).

Nicodemus was speaking for a group and he claimed they knew that Jesus had "come from God." But Jesus explicitly rejected this claim of knowledge when he said, "except a man be born again, he cannot see the kingdom of God" (Fourth gospel 3:3). Ask yourself, how does this follow?

When sequential statements seem unconnected, it is good to ask, how does it follow? This causes us to look to scripture to help us understand what was being said. Jesus' reply should prompt us to wonder, how is Jesus' statement a fitting response to the claim Nicodemus had made on behalf of the Pharisees?

How Does It Follow?

Jesus' reply to "we know that thou art a teacher come from God" was "except a man be born again, he cannot see the kingdom of God." So, how does it follow? It follows because he was refuting their claim! Nicodemus boldly claimed he and his group perceived the authority of God in the works of Jesus. The response of Jesus proved their claim was false. Those men could not possibly see what they claimed to see, because they had not met the condition ("except a man be born again").

Fleshly eyes do not give us the ability to see the kingdom of God. Jesus noted the difference between eyesight and perceiving truth when he said, "by hearing ye shall hear, and shall not understand; and seeing ye shall see, and shall not perceive" (Mt 13:14). So, what kind of sight was Jesus referring to in his reply to Nicodemus?

"We know that thou art a teacher come from God" is a claim of insight. Nicodemus asserted he and his fellow Pharisees knew this based on their assessment of Jesus' miracles. But their claim to perceive the hand of God at work is at odds with Jesus' words, "ye receive not our witness".

Notice the Words of Nicodemus

Nicodemus' words are similar to this – "Master, we know that thou sayest and teachest rightly, neither acceptest thou the person *of any*, but teachest the way of God truly" (Lk 20:21). Yet, this statement was not spoken in truth. Here is the context:

"the chief priests and the scribes... sent forth spies, which should feign themselves just men, that they might take hold of his [Jesus'] words, that so they might deliver him unto the power and authority of the governor" (Lk 20:19-20).

Those spies spoke nice words to Jesus, but had an ulterior motive for saying them. Since Nicodemus was representing other leaders when he met with Jesus, is it possible he had an ulterior motive? The religious leaders rejected John the Baptist before Jesus and just prior to Nicodemus' visit, Jesus threw the merchants out of the temple. This made those leaders look bad because they had not done this. For Nicodemus to say the Pharisees believed Jesus was "a teacher come from God" was dishonest. Jesus said a man "cannot see the kingdom of God" unless he is "born again." So, this is a necessary condition for a man to see the kingdom of God. To counter Jesus, Nicodemus said, "how can a man be born when he is old? can he enter the second time into his mother's womb, and be born?" (Fourth gospel 3:4) What are we to make of his question?

Nicodemus did not stick to Jesus' words; he put it in his own words and, in doing so, he mischaracterized what Jesus said. His phrase "the second time" translates a Greek word which means second. But in the phrase "born again," Jesus used a different Greek word with a different meaning. When Nicodemus changed Jesus' word, Nicodemus linked the term "born again" to a man's physical birth (i.e., another of the same kind). However, a different *kind* of birth is what was indicated by Jesus' words.

How to Verify the Meaning of a Word

Our English Bible is a translation of the Hebrew and Greek words used by the writers of scripture. Their use of words can keep our understanding of scripture on track if we will look at other verses where they used the same word and we let their word choices teach us how to view the words. This may sound difficult, but it is surprisingly easy thanks to a tool called Strong's Concordance, that assigned numbers to each of the Greek and Hebrew words. This lets us see how those words were translated and it tells us every verse where the original Hebrew or Greek word was used. The Strong's numbers show when one English word was used to translate multiple original words or when multiple English words were used to translate a single original Hebrew or Greek word. The word numbers also let us confirm the meaning of the words in our English Bible since these word numbers allow us to find all the other verses where the same Hebrew or Greek word appears.

Looking to see how the writers of scripture used a word can help us to confirm their intended use of a word. Free online tools make it very easy to correlate their words using these word numbers. [The format G#### will be used to make it easy for the reader to follow the Strong's number of the Greek word being discussed.]

From Above

Greek word number G509 was used in the term born "again G509" and this talks about the source or start of a thing. This indicates another *source* of birth and the term "from above" that translates this word elsewhere helps to show this.

We find this word a few verses later in the phrase "he that cometh from above G509" (Fourth gospel 3:31). Moreover, Jesus told Pilate, "thou couldest have no power at all against me, except it were given thee from above G509" (Fourth gospel 19:11).

It was also translated this way three times in the Book of James:

- "every good gift and every perfect gift is from above G509" (Jas 1:17),
- "if ye have bitter envying and strife in your hearts, glory not, and lie not against the truth. This wisdom descendeth not from above G509" (Jas 3:14-15),
- "the wisdom that is from above G509 is first pure, then peaceable, gentle, *and* easy to be intreated, full of mercy and good fruits, without partiality, and without hypocrisy" (Jas 3:17).

Adam's descendants have all been born physically. Thus, being born "again G509" would be a subsequent birth. But in substituting a word that *only* means second for a word that refers to beginning or source, Nicodemus discounted the idea of another *type* of birth. He implied Jesus was talking about a second physical birth, but since scripture teaches resurrection, not reincarnation, he should have known better. On the other hand, Jesus' words perfectly fit with the idea of a resurrection. Also, as will be shown, Nicodemus should have already known people had to be born from above to see the kingdom of God because scripture taught this all along.

Two Distinct Conditions

Being able to see a walled city like Jericho did not mean you could enter it. Those are two different thresholds. Seeing a kingdom or a city does not guarantee entry. Jesus' reply to Nicodemus shows being born again is not the ultimate goal, because he also said, "except a man be born of water and *of* the Spirit, he cannot enter into the kingdom of God" (Fourth gospel 3:5). The contrast of "see" and "enter" shows us Jesus spoke of two things. The first is required to see the kingdom of God, but the second is needed to enter it. "Every word of God is pure" (Prv 30:5). This is why we need to heed the word choices in scripture.

The following gives us Jesus' response to Nicodemus' question:

"Verily, verily, I say unto thee, Except a man be born of water and *of* the Spirit, he cannot enter into the kingdom of God. That which is born of the flesh is flesh; and that which is born of the Spirit is spirit. Marvel not that I said unto thee, Ye must be born again. The wind bloweth where it listeth, and thou hearest the sound thereof, but canst not tell whence it cometh, and whither it goeth: so is every one that is born of the Spirit" (Fourth gospel 3:5-8).

This prompted Nicodemus to ask, "how can these things be?" (v. 9) Jesus then marveled at the ignorance of this esteemed teacher:

"Art thou a master of Israel, and knowest not these things? Verily, verily, I say unto thee, We speak that we do know, and testify that we have seen; and ye receive not our witness. If I have told you earthly things, and ye believe not, how shall ye believe, if I tell you *of* heavenly things? (Fourth gospel 3:10-12).

This was a striking rebuke of Nicodemus. It noted his ignorance, and this episode also provides us with an important lesson.

In our day, Nicodemus would be called a scholar. He was deemed a master of Israel, which suggests he had been studying for many years. He undoubtedly knew the words of scripture. But knowing the words is not the same as knowing what the words mean.

Jesus' words prove a person who knew scripture should have known this. Yet, Nicodemus was blind to the fact "these things" were taught in God's word. What were those things? They were the things Jesus had said to him earlier in their conversation:

- "Except a man be born again, he cannot see the kingdom of God" (Fourth gospel 3:3),
- "Except a man be born of water and *of* the Spirit, he cannot enter into the kingdom of God. That which is born of the flesh is flesh; and that which is born of the Spirit is spirit. Marvel not that I said unto thee, Ye must be born again. The wind bloweth where it listeth, and thou hearest the sound thereof, but canst not tell whence it cometh, and whither it goeth: so is every one that is born of the Spirit" (Fourth gospel 3:5-8).

If Nicodemus could know these things, this tells us we can look to the Old Testament to learn more about these topics (cf. Eze 36:25 & 37:9, et al.). We know "born again" or "born of water and *of* the Spirit" are ideas that were taught in the Old Testament, for Jesus' words show this is so. Moreover, he told Nicodemus, "if I have told you earthly things, and ye believe not, how shall ye believe, if I tell you *of* heavenly things?" (Fourth gospel 3:12) What does this teach us?

His words teach us a principle. Those who will not believe when the truth is revealed about things that can be seen, are unable to believe the truth about things that cannot be seen and that cannot be perceived without a foundation of truth.

Also, Jesus said he told Nicodemus "earthly things." On that night, he told him about being "born again" and being "born of water and *of* the Spirit," so these topics are in the category of earthly things.

A Kingdom Founded on Truth

After Jesus rose from the dead, over the next forty days he taught the disciples about "the things pertaining to the kingdom of God" (Acts 1:3). If the focus of Jesus in the days following his resurrection was teaching about "the kingdom of God," then this subject is worthy of our attention.

God is "a God of truth" (Dt 32:4) and this quality is linked to God throughout scripture (Gen 24:27, Ex 34:6, Ps 31:5, Isa 65:16, et al.). Therefore, it follows that the kingdom of God must be founded on the truth (and people cannot both resist the truth and see things according to God's perspective at the same time).

Paul told the Thessalonians, "when ye received the word of God which ye heard of us, ye received it not as the word of men, but as it is in truth, the word of God, which effectually worketh also in you that believe" (1Th 2:13). Nicodemus lied to Jesus, for he and his fellow leaders did not receive Jesus' words as the word of God. They could not see the kingdom of God because regard for the kingdom and respect for the king's authority go hand in hand. While they claimed to "know G1492" Jesus came from God, Jesus used the same Greek word to refute their claim and tell them why they could not "see G1492 the kingdom of God" (cf. Fourth gospel 3:2 & 3).

Jesus told the Jewish leaders who had rigged a trial against him, "hereafter shall ye see the Son of man sitting on the right hand of power, and coming in the clouds of heaven" (Mt 26:64). Since they were not born again, they could not see the kingdom of God, yet they could see these things. What is the difference? It depends on how we perceive things. If we submit to God's authority, we will see his judgment as righteous. Those who resist it, will judge God with a false standard and they will experience a different outcome. [This explains why different Greek words were used in the terms "see G3700 the Son of man" and "see G1492 the kingdom of God" (cf. Mt 26:64 & Fourth gospel 3:3). To investigate the word pictures "sitting on the right hand of power" and "coming in the clouds of heaven," the reader should search for other passages that use these terms.]

Born of Water

What did Jesus mean by "born of water and of the Spirit?" Some people assume "born of water" refers to physical birth, because the sac in the womb breaks in the birth process. Yet, the Bible never uses "born of water" to refer to physical birth. It uses terms like "born of a woman" (Job 14:1), "born of women" (Mt 11:11), or just "born" (Gen 4:18) to refer to this birth. Scripture does use the word "water" of H_2O, but this word was also used to picture God's word.

The LORD is called "the fountain of living waters" (Jer 2:13), and the word of the LORD is pictured as something people thirst for:

"Behold, the days come, saith the Lord GOD, that I will send a famine in the land, not a famine of bread, nor a thirst for water, but of hearing the words of the LORD" (Amos 8:11-13).

Job said, "I have esteemed the words of his [God's] mouth more than my necessary *food*" (Job 23:12). The consumption of the words of the LORD was also described this way, "thy words were found, and I did eat them" (Jer 15:16). So, is God's word as critical to life as food and water? ["If any would not work, neither should he eat" (2Th 3:10) is usually taken to be about physical food. But might this also apply to the eating of the word of God (i.e., "our daily bread" (Mt 6:11)) as we see pictured in scripture? (cf. Eze 2:8 & 3:1-3, Rev 10:9-10)]

Questions to Consider

"The washing of **water by the word**" is used by Jesus to "sanctify and cleanse" the church (Eph 5:26). The brethren are "born again, not of corruptible seed, but of incorruptible, **by the word of God**" (1Pt 1:23). So, the word of God produces regeneration and "water" was used to portray God's word. Since the birth that is produced by God's word is non-physical, the phrase "born of water" is likely portraying being begotten (i.e., regenerated) by the word of God. In light of this, consider the implications of the following passage:

"Then will I sprinkle clean water upon you, and ye shall be clean: from all your filthiness, and from all your idols, will I cleanse you. A new heart also will I give you, and a new spirit will I put within you: and I will take away the stony heart out of your flesh, and I will give you a heart of flesh. And I will put my spirit within you, and cause you to walk in my statutes, and ye shall keep my judgments, and do *them*" (Eze 36:25-27).

Was the term "born of water" describing this sort of change? It is left to the reader to weigh the rest of what was said between Jesus and Nicodemus. [Verses like Galatians 4:28-31, where the terms "born after the flesh" and "after the Spirit" were used to describe Old Testament events, can shed more light on this topic.]

As you study this topic further, here are some other questions that emerge when we consider how the words of scripture fit together:

- The picture of birth is presented in "born again" and "born of water and *of* the Spirit" (Fourth gospel 3:3 & 5-8). So, would a birthright be included in this, since the birthright is a key concept in scripture? If so, then the warning to not be like "Esau, who for one morsel of meat sold his birthright" (Heb 12:16) that was directed to the brethren also needs to be weighed when we are evaluating these word pictures.
- What can we learn about the difference between seeing and entering the kingdom of God from other passages?
- Why did Nicodemus speak flattering words to Jesus on behalf of the Pharisees, even though they did not submit to John the Baptist and they did not receive the witness of Jesus? Jesus threw the merchants out of the temple and was working miracles. Surely, this made the Jewish religious leaders look bad. So, did Nicodemus visit Jesus to see if he could cozy up to him and get him to play ball with the Pharisees?
- Scripture presents us with the following identifying mark, "everyone that doeth righteousness is born of him [God]" (1Jo 2:29). Still, some say, *'if you feel bad when you sin, this proves you are born again/are a child of God.'* If someone presents an idea like this we can either judge their words by the written word of God or we can let their words shape our view of scripture.
- If we want to get more insight into the topic of "born again" and/or "born of water and *of* the Spirit," what do we do? Since these phrases do not occur in the Old Testament, we need to look for the subject matter, not just the words.

Jesus said, "not everyone that saith unto me, Lord, Lord, shall enter into the kingdom of heaven; but he that doeth the will of my Father which is in heaven" (Mt 7:21). Nicodemus and his fellow religious leaders did not receive the witness of Jesus, so they were not doing God's will. Thus, if they did not change, they were not going to enter this kingdom and unless Jesus' words applied only in that era, his words are still a standard for us today.

Chapter 4 – Learning from God's Word

If someone asks about a man in the jungle who has not heard about God, what should we say? Does God accept people before they believe in the name of Jesus? How is repentance a blessing? This chapter will address questions like these.

The Reliability of the Scriptures

Scripture is the only source that gives us an authoritative record of the things Jesus said and did. It was inspired by God (cf. 2Ti 3:16), and Jesus affirmed the reliability of the scriptures in his day when he said, "till heaven and earth pass, one jot or one tittle shall in no wise pass from the law, till all be fulfilled" (Mt 5:18). He believed God is able to preserve his word and had done so over the centuries, in spite of all the copies that had to be made and even though the scriptures in Jesus' day had come down through the hands of "backsliding Israel" and "treacherous Judah" (Jer 3:2). Even their episodes of rebellion could not handicap God's ability to preserve his word until Jesus' day. The point is, despite what man may do, we can trust God is still able to preserve his inspired word.

As has been noted, the scriptures written before Jesus' birth have the same authority as the scriptures written after his resurrection. We cannot pick and choose when it comes to scripture, since all of scripture has equal authority, as James 2:10-11 will show later. The Old Testament is ignored by some, yet Jesus said, "had ye believed Moses, ye would have believed me: for he wrote of me" (Fourth gospel 5:46). The words of Jesus and the apostles teach us to value the Old Testament, for they consistently cited scripture and they taught people to have consistent respect for its authority.

The Foundation of Peter's Message

Scripture was stressed on the day of Pentecost when Peter cited:

- the prophet Joel (Acts 2:16-21, cf. Joel 2:28-32),
- Psalm 16 (Acts 2:25-28, cf. Ps 16:8-11),
- Psalm 16 again (Acts 2:31, cf. Ps 16:10), and
- Psalm 110 (Acts 2:34-35, cf. Ps 110:1).

He proved that scripture foretold Jesus' resurrection and he said God raised Jesus from the dead "because it was not possible that he should be holden of it" (Acts 2:24). [Why could death not hold him? Because "scripture cannot be broken" (Fourth gospel 10:35).] Peter then went on to cite another passage of scripture and said:

"David speaketh concerning him, I foresaw the Lord always before my face, for he is on my right hand, that I should not be moved: Therefore did my heart rejoice, and my tongue was glad; moreover also my flesh shall rest in hope: Because thou wilt not leave my soul in hell, neither wilt thou suffer thine Holy One to see corruption. Thou hast made known to me the ways of life; thou shalt make me full of joy with thy countenance" (Acts 2:25-28).

Peter proved these words *of* David were not *about* David when he said, David "is both dead and buried, and his sepulcher is with us unto this day" (Acts 2:29).

Paul also tied the words, "thou shalt not suffer thine Holy One to see corruption" (Acts 13:35) to Jesus' resurrection. Paul showed this could not be speaking about David when he said, "David, after he had served his own generation by the will of God, fell on sleep, and was laid unto his fathers, and saw corruption" (Acts 13:36).

Since David was still dead, Psalm 16:8-11 had to be talking about someone else. This was confirmed by Peter when he pointed out David's words were a prophecy about Christ:

"Therefore being a prophet, and knowing that God had sworn with an oath to him, that of the fruit of his loins, according to the flesh, he would raise up Christ to sit on his throne; He seeing this before **spake of the resurrection of Christ**, that **his** soul was not left in hell, neither **his** flesh did see corruption" (Acts 2:30-31).

So, when David said, "thou wilt not leave my soul in hell, neither wilt thou suffer thine Holy One to see corruption," he was not speaking about himself. He was speaking about "the resurrection of Christ."

In Acts 2:32-33, Peter told the people Jesus was raised by God, the disciples were witnesses of this, and Jesus caused the events of that day (the events in Acts 2:1-12). Peter proved Psalm 110:1 was about Christ, not David because David was not in heaven:

"David is not ascended into the heavens: but he saith himself, The Lord said unto my Lord, Sit thou on my right hand, Until I make thy foes thy footstool. Therefore let all the house of Israel know assuredly, that God hath made that same Jesus, whom ye have crucified, both Lord and Christ" (Acts 2:34-36).

Peter's resurrection message relied on the authority of scripture, i.e., the Old Testament, and not merely his personal testimony. While he did cite the apostles' witness to show the promise of a risen Christ was fulfilled in their day, the words of scripture were his primary evidence for Jesus' resurrection. He pointed people to what was written in God's word, then he built upon this foundation. The record of that day ends with this report:

"they were pricked in their heart, and said unto Peter and to the rest of the apostles, Men *and* brethren, what shall we do? Then Peter said unto them, Repent, and be baptized every one of you in the name of Jesus Christ for the remission of sins, and ye shall receive the gift of the Holy Ghost. For the promise is unto you, and to your children, and to all that are afar off, *even* as many as the Lord our God shall call. And with many other words did he testify and exhort, saying, Save yourselves from this untoward generation. Then they that gladly received his word were baptized: and the same day there were added *unto them* about three thousand souls" (Acts 2:37-41).

The Blessing of Repentance

When they asked, "what shall we do," Peter did not say, *'there is nothing you can do, all you have to do is believe.'* He told them what to do, and step number one was to "repent." Today, what is typically called a gospel presentation does not feature this word. Yet, it was the first thing out of Peter's mouth.

Not using the word repent may seem to make God's word more user-friendly. But repentance is part of the gospel and omitting it deprives people of a blessing. While some view repentance as a hard saying, notice what Peter told the men of Israel in Acts 3:26, "unto you first God, having raised up his Son Jesus, sent him to bless you, in turning away every one of you from his iniquities." The blessing God wanted them to get from his risen Son involved them turning away from their iniquities. Thus, if we fail to mention the need to repent or if we downplay this idea to make people feel more comfortable, then we keep people from this blessing.

Those who think they help God if they make scripture sound more winsome to people may actually be stealing the LORD's word from their neighbor (cf. Jer 23:30). The LORD said, "he that hath my word, let him speak my word faithfully" (Jer 23:28) and turning people from their iniquities is a blessing God intended for people to receive from Jesus. So, we must faithfully present the call to repentance as part of the gospel. When Jesus met with his disciples after his resurrection, he told them, "repentance and remission of sins should be preached in his name" (Lk 24:47). They did this and we should also. Peter told a crowd in the temple, "repent ye therefore, and be converted, that your sins may be blotted out, when the times of refreshing shall come from the presence of the Lord" (Acts 3:19). If both repenting and being converted must take place before one's sins can be blotted out, then the need to repent is not merely a portion of the gospel message, it is step one!

A Belief that Went Nowhere?

Belief without repentance seems to be what led to a situation we find in Acts 8. [Note: belief is not faith, as will be shown later.] Philip went to the city of Samaria and "preached Christ unto them" (Acts 8:5). They "gave heed unto those things which Philip spake, hearing and seeing the miracles which he did" (Acts 8:6).

It also mentions "a certain man, called Simon, which beforetime in the same city used sorcery, and bewitched the people of Samaria" (Acts 8:9). "To him they had regard, because that of long time he had bewitched them with sorceries" (Acts 8:11). However, even with this background, he believed and was baptized:

"But when they believed Philip preaching the things concerning the kingdom of God, and the name of Jesus Christ, they were baptized, both men and women. Then Simon himself <u>believed</u> also: and when he <u>was baptized</u>, he <u>continued with Philip</u>, and wondered, beholding the miracles and signs which were done" (Acts 8:12-13).

We are not told how long this situation lasted. But news of this made its way back to Jerusalem and subsequent verses tell us:

"when the apostles which were at Jerusalem heard that Samaria had received the word of God, they sent unto them Peter and John: Who, when they were come down, prayed for them, that they might receive the Holy Ghost: (for as yet he was fallen upon none of them: only they were baptized in the name of the Lord Jesus.) Then laid they *their* hands on them, and they received the Holy Ghost. And when Simon saw that through laying on of the apostles' hands the Holy Ghost was given, he offered them money, Saying, Give me also this power, that on whomsoever I lay hands, he may receive the Holy Ghost" (Acts 8:14-19).

Simon's offer showed he had not repented, and this is why Peter indicated Simon's thoughts were still the root of Simon's problem:

"But Peter said unto him, Thy money perish with thee, because thou hast thought that the gift of God may be purchased with money. Thou hast neither part nor lot in this matter: for thy heart is not right in the sight of God. Repent therefore of this thy wickedness, and pray God, if perhaps the thought of thine heart may be forgiven thee. For I perceive that thou art in the gall of bitterness, and *in* the bond of iniquity" (Acts 8:20-23).

He was in the bond of iniquity. Until he repented and turned from his iniquities, he could not receive the blessing of repentance.

Acts 8:13 says Simon believed, was baptized, and had continued with Philip. Thus, these things are not sufficient to prove a person is converted – because Simon did those things without repenting.

Peter warned him, "repent therefore of this thy wickedness, and pray God, if perhaps the thought of thine heart may be forgiven thee." The words "if perhaps" and "may" show us Peter was not saying God was obliged to accept whatever qualified as repenting in Simon's eyes.

Is God obliged to act in accord with our judgment of what is right? Not according to this, "let God be true, but every man a liar; as it is written, That thou [God] mightest be justified in thy sayings, and mightest overcome **when thou art judged**" (Rom 3:4). If men judge an act of God to be unjust or unloving, does it mean they are right? No. Yet, if God does not meet their standard of what qualifies as loving or right, then in their mind, he is unjust and is not their God.

Simon's actions meant he was not using a godly measure of right and wrong. His heart was the problem and unless he repented, he would remain in bondage and continue to judge wrongly.

Simon's Decision Versus God's Draw?

When Simon chose to believe, he did not become a child of God at that point. What about others who believe without repenting? Jesus once talked about people who "receive the word with joy" and **"for a while believe**," but who later "in time of temptation fall away" (Lk 8:13). This proves people can stop believing after a time. This would seem to describe Simon's situation and, later, we will see what scripture says about the need to continue in belief.

The Bible says, "whosoever shall call on the name of the Lord shall be saved" (Acts 2:21) and "believe on the Lord Jesus Christ, and thou shalt be saved, and thy house" (Acts 16:31). Yet, if Simon "believed" when he was not "saved," how are we to resolve this?

Jesus said, "no man can come to me, except the Father which hath sent me draw him" (Fourth gospel 6:44). What should we make of this statement if we view it according to the measure of scripture?

Did Jesus mean the choice to come to him was up to men? No. "Can" refers to ability. Thus, in order for a man to "come to" Jesus, the Father must "draw" that man to Jesus.

The word "draw" translates a Greek word (^{G1670}) that describes people being moved against their will (cf. Acts 16:19, Jas 2:6) or an object moved by force, such as draw a sword or draw in a net of fish (cf. Fourth gospel 18:10 & 21:6). Each time, the power of the "draw" forced a person or thing to move. It did not prompt a voluntary response. [In James 4:8, "draw nigh to God" refers to a voluntary choice, but here the word "draw" translates a different Greek word (^{G1448}) and that word does involve a volitional decision.]

How Does the Father Draw People to Jesus?

When Jesus said men could come to him only if the Father draws them, he also taught *how* God draws people. He said:

> "No man can come to me, except the Father which hath sent me draw him: and I will raise him up at the last day. It is written in the prophets, And they shall be all taught of God. Every man therefore that hath heard, and hath learned of the Father, cometh unto me" (Fourth gospel 6:44-45).

"No man" can come to Jesus unless he is drawn by the Father, but "every man" who has heard and learned of the Father comes. One verse excludes all except those who the Father draws, the other includes all who meet the condition ("hath heard, and hath learned of the Father"). But in the middle of this contrast, he said, "it is written in the prophets, And they shall be all taught of God" (v. 45). Thus, the Father draws people to Jesus by teaching them. Jesus proved this by citing "they shall be all taught of God" and adding this explanation, "every man therefore that hath heard, and hath learned of the Father, cometh unto me." So, the phrase "taught of God" did not mean being taught about God but being taught by God! Further proof of this will be cited later when we return to this topic to discuss how this happens. For now, though, consider what occurs when God's word teaches us. It is "powerful" (Heb 4:12). It also gives life, as Peter showed when he talked about **"being born again**, not of corruptible seed, but of incorruptible, **by the word of God**, which liveth and abideth forever" (1Pt 1:23). This parallels an idea Jesus expressed when he told his disciples, "the words that I speak unto you, *they* are spirit, and *they* are life" (Fourth gospel 6:63).

Jesus linked the idea of the Father teaching people to the result of people coming to him. If this is how people come to Jesus, then resisting the teaching of God is a dangerous thing. [This may be why the writer of Hebrews quoted "today if ye will hear his voice, harden not your hearts" three times (Heb 3:7-8 &15, 4:7). This warning to the brethren shows the word of God is not winsome. Rather, it indicates God says things that people may not want to hear.]

When Jesus went on to explicitly say no man can come to him unless God gives him this gift, "many of his disciples went back, and walked no more with him" (Fourth gospel 6:66). Think about this. They were his disciples but what he said made them forsake him! Let us consider what caused those followers to leave Jesus.

<u>Disciples Who Permanently Abandoned Jesus</u>

Fourth gospel, Chapter 6, reports the following sayings of Jesus led up to the moment many disciples forsook him on that day:

- "the bread of God is he which cometh down from heaven, and giveth life unto the world" (v. 33),
- "I am the bread of life: he that cometh to me shall never hunger; and he that believeth on me shall never thirst" (v. 35),
- "I am that bread of life" (v. 48),
- "I am the living bread which came down from heaven: if any man eat of this bread, he shall live for ever: and the bread that I will give is my flesh, which I will give for the life of the world" (v. 51),
- "except ye eat the flesh of the Son of man, and drink his blood, ye have no life in you. Whoso eateth my flesh, and drinketh my blood, hath eternal life; and I will raise him up at the last day. For my flesh is meat indeed, and my blood is drink indeed. He that eateth my flesh, and drinketh my blood, dwelleth in me, and I in him. As the living Father hath sent me, and I live by the Father: so, he that eateth me, even he shall live by me. This is that bread which came down from heaven: not as your fathers did eat manna, and are dead: he that eateth of this bread shall live forever" (v. 53-58).

Many did not like what he said on that day. Verse 41 says, "the Jews then murmured at him, because he said, I am the bread which came down from heaven." Also, after verses 53-58 it says, "many therefore of his disciples, when they had heard *this*, said, This is a hard saying; who can hear it?" (Fourth gospel 6:60) They were not happy, but they were still there. Then Jesus said something they would not submit to:

"When Jesus knew in himself that his disciples murmured at it, he said unto them, Doth this offend you? *What* and if ye shall see the Son of man ascend up where he was before? It is the spirit that quickeneth; the flesh profiteth nothing: the words that I speak unto you, *they* are spirit, and *they* are life. But there are some of you that believe not. For Jesus knew from the beginning who they were that believed not, and who should betray him. And he said, Therefore said I unto you, that no man can come unto me, except it were given unto him of my Father. From that *time* many of his disciples went back, and walked no more with him" (Fourth gospel 6:61-66).

Jesus referred to eating his flesh and drinking his blood earlier in the passage. When "his disciples murmured at it," he did not offer words of comfort. Instead, what he said caused them to leave. Earlier he had said, "no man can come to me, except the Father which hath sent me draw him." But when Jesus said, "no man can come unto me, except it were given unto him of my Father," it was the straw that broke the camel's back! "From that *time* many of his disciples went back, and walked no more with him."

No doubt, their distress over what he said earlier contributed to their decision to leave. Still, it was the issue of God being in control – the inability to come to Jesus unless God gives us this ability – that ultimately led those disciples to walk away. Saying, "no man can come unto me, except it were **given** unto him of my Father" showed men lack the ability to come to Jesus by their own will. The Father must act first. If the ability to come to Jesus is a gift, then the Father can give this gift as he chooses. This is contrary to the view that assumes having a free will and being able to make choices means anyone can come to Jesus whenever they want, *whether or not* the Father gives them the ability to come to Jesus.

Jesus' words do not suggest the Father gives this gift to all men and draws everyone. If the Father did this, then it seems all men will come to Jesus, for he said every man who "hath heard, and hath learned of the Father, cometh unto me" (Fourth gospel 6:45). It is fair to ask, how does this reconcile with these often cited words from 2 Peter 3:9, "the Lord is... not willing that any should perish," or similar passages? We will tackle this question later in this book.

The words of Jesus "are spirit" and "life" (Fourth gospel 6:63). In taking offense at his words, his disciples gave up the benefits that come to those who hear his words, and this also applies to the words of his apostles, as will be shown. If people are exposed to the truth and turn away from it, then a love of the truth is obviously lacking.

Continue in the Truth

The following was written to the brethren about another time when people walked away from the truth: "they went out from us, but they were not of us; for if they had been of us, they would *no doubt* have continued with us: but *they went out,* that they might be made manifest that they were not all of us" (1Jo 2:19). It sounds sad, but the writer says their departure, "made manifest that they were not all of us." Moreover, he called them "antichrists."

The prior verse says, "ye have heard that antichrist shall come, even now are there many antichrists; whereby we know that it is the last time" (1Jo 2:18). "They went out from us" are the words that immediately follow, so this tells us where "antichrists" come from – they come from inside the church. The word "antichrist" appears in only four verses (1Jo 2:18 & 22, 2:22, 2Jo 1:7), and here we see it was used of those who seemed to be for Christ until they walked away and, thereby, showed they were against him.

Similarly, this was written to the church in Corinth, "there must be also heresies among you, that they which are approved may be made manifest among you" (1Cor 11:19). So, the divisions caused by "heresies" help "they which are approved" among the brethren to be made manifest. We can see how this would happen because truth unites the brethren and divides them from those who are not, while error turns people away from the standard of God.

Jesus once told a group of Jews who demanded he declare if he was the Christ, "ye believe not, because ye are not of my sheep" (Fourth gospel 10:26). Then he said, "my sheep hear my voice, and I know them, and they follow me" (v. 27). These verses contrasted two groups that arose from his earlier teaching on the shepherd:

"the sheep hear his voice: and he calleth his own sheep by name, and leadeth them out. And when he putteth forth his own sheep, he goeth before them, and the sheep follow him: for they know his voice. And a stranger will they not follow" (Fourth gospel 10:3-5).

Those who follow heresy follow a wrong voice and those who are "approved" are made manifest by heresies because they will not.

1 John 4:1-5 says the "beloved" are "of God" and it contrasts them with those who are "of the world" and "not of God." Verse 6 then states, "we are of God: he that knoweth God heareth us; he that is not of God heareth not us. Hereby know we the spirit of truth, and the spirit of error" (1Jo 4:6). The difference is that those who are "of God" hear the truth, while those who are "not of God" will not. This seems to express the same dividing line that was highlighted by Jesus when he appointed the seventy. He told them, "he that heareth you heareth me; and he that despiseth you despiseth me; and he that despiseth me despiseth him that sent me" (Lk 10:16). Likewise, Jesus tied the authority of the disciples to his own when he said, "if they have kept my saying, they will keep yours also" (Fourth gospel 15:20). So, we honor Jesus when we continue to hear the word of the apostles in scripture and we keep their sayings.

What If Someone Dies Before Being Told About Jesus?

What happens to a man in the jungle or any others who die without hearing about Jesus? Various forms of this question are raised and sometimes people in the church struggle to respond, but they need not do so. Scripture gives us the answer and it also shows the question is based on a false assumption. The answer is found in the context of Peter learning a critical lesson about people who have not yet heard about Jesus. He learned a new perspective on this issue and God's word can open our eyes on this issue also.

Peter's insight on this subject is found in Acts 10, and verses 1-8 provide the backstory for this episode:

"a certain man in Caesarea called Cornelius, a centurion of the band called the Italian band, A devout *man*, and one that feared God with all his house, which gave much alms to the people, and prayed to God always. He saw in a vision evidently about the ninth hour of the day an angel of God coming in to him, and saying unto him, Cornelius. And when he looked on him, he was afraid, and said, What is it, Lord? And he said unto him, Thy prayers and thine alms are come up for a memorial before God. And now send men to Joppa, and call for *one* Simon, whose surname is Peter: He lodgeth with one Simon a tanner, whose house is by the seaside: he shall tell thee what thou oughtest to do. And when the angel which spake unto Cornelius was departed, he called two of his household servants, and a devout soldier of them that waited on him continually; And when he had declared all *these* things unto them, he sent them to Joppa."

Cornelius was "a devout *man*" and "feared God with all his house." As head of the household, he ensured the fear of God was taught to those who were in his house. He gave much alms to the people and prayed to God always and his good deeds made a difference. Notice, the angel said, "thy prayers and thine alms are come up for a memorial before God." Cornelius' deeds were noted by God, and this should encourage all who do similar things.

More striking, however, may be the fact that the angel spoke to him but did not tell him how to be saved. Instead of preaching the gospel to Cornelius, the angel told him to send men to Joppa and get Peter. When the angel left, three men were sent to fetch Peter.

Acts 10 tells us as the men neared the city, Peter "became very hungry, and would have eaten: but while they made ready, he fell into a trance" (v. 10). Then he saw a "vessel descending unto him" (v. 11) that contained "four-footed beasts of the earth, and wild beasts, and creeping things, and fowls of the air" (v. 12). A voice told him, "rise, Peter; kill, and eat" (v. 13) but he said, "not so, Lord; for I have never eaten anything that is common or unclean" (v. 14).

Then Peter heard, "what God hath cleansed, that call not thou common" (v. 15). After this happened three times, "the vessel was received up again into heaven" (v. 16). This vision was showing him he needed to judge according to God's standard and not his own.

The Jews in that day did not go into the houses of uncircumcised men or eat with them. We know this because when Peter returned to Jerusalem after he met Cornelius, he was confronted on this:

"when Peter was come up to Jerusalem, they that were of the circumcision contended with him, Saying, Thou wentest in to men uncircumcised, and didst eat with them" (Acts 11:2-3).

The beasts in the vision came from heaven, yet Peter judged them to be unclean. If the LORD can make "crooked things straight" (Isa 42:16), then he can cleanse something that was unclean and make it clean. (Peter had to learn to judge according to God's judgment on all matters, including what to eat and who he could eat with.)

Acts 10:17 tells us Peter wondered what the vision meant, then the passage goes on to say:

"While Peter thought on the vision, the Spirit said unto him, Behold, three men seek thee. Arise therefore, and get thee down, and go with them, doubting nothing: for I have sent them" (Acts 10:19-20).

In reality, the three men who had come to visit him were not sent merely by Cornelius. They were sent by the Spirit, who told Peter, "I have sent them."

When Peter went out to the men and asked them why they had come, they said, "Cornelius the centurion, a just man, and one that feareth God, and of good report among all the nation of the Jews, was warned from God by a holy angel to send for thee into his house, and to hear words of thee" (Acts 10:22).

Peter had the men stay with him that night. Then, the next day, Peter and six of the brethren (cf. Acts 11:12) accompanied the men back to the house of Cornelius.

In the meantime, Cornelius "called together his kinsmen and near friends" (Acts 10:24), since the angel had told him Peter would speak "words, whereby thou and all thy house shall be saved" (Acts 11:14). His actions show he sought to take full advantage of this promise.

Acts 10:25-33 tells of Peter's arrival and Cornelius's report to him about being visited by the angel. Then he told him, "now therefore are we all here present before God, to hear all things that are commanded thee of God." At this point, Peter realized something and he said:

"Of a truth I perceive that God is no respecter of persons: But **in every nation he that feareth him**, **and worketh righteousness, is accepted with him**" (Acts 10:34-35).

Take a minute to ponder this. This was an eye-opening moment for Peter and it can be for us as well. In that instant, he realized people did not have to be part of the Jewish nation to fear God.

Amazingly, in Peter's declaration, Bible readers have always had the answer to the man in the jungle question! How so? Because "in every nation" people are "accepted" with God so long as they:

A. fear God, and
B. work righteousness.

Peter's words teach us that all over the earth there are people like Cornelius, who fear God and work righteousness. All such people are accepted with God, as was Cornelius, and we should note this was Cornelius' status before Peter even arrived on the scene.

Accepted

How would he respond when he heard Peter's words? Jesus said, "he that is faithful in that which is least is faithful also in much" (Lk 16:10). Cornelius most likely was not raised to have a regard for God's word. As a gentile, he was not part of the nation that had a history rooted in the God of Abraham, Isaac, and Jacob. Yet, he still ended up being faithful to God. Does this suggest he would fit the definition of one who was faithful in that which is least?

If Cornelius was faithful in that which is least, how would he react when he learned about Jesus and the resurrection? The principle taught by Jesus (in Luke 16:10) indicates Cornelius would *stay* faithful. He had established a habit of doing works that pleased God. Thus, learning more truth would not cause him to become less faithful. Peter learned Cornelius was accepted with God after he arrived at Cornelius' home, but God knew this before he sent the angel. Cornelius's fear of God also lets us know he would rightly receive the news about Jesus' resurrection when he heard it from Peter.

2 Thessalonians 2:10 speaks about, "them that perish; because they received not the love of the truth, that they might be saved." If someone fears God and works righteousness, can we conclude that person is exhibiting a love of the truth? Also, if someone who loves the truth, learns about Jesus being raised from the dead, will that person hear this message or will they stop their ears and reject it? The answer to both questions is self-evident.

Why did Peter not tell Cornelius to repent? Do those who fear God and work righteousness need to repent, or did they already do so and they should now keep doing as they are? This answer is also self-evident. If they continue to honor God, then their status as "accepted" with God would certainly continue as well.

Continue does not mean no change. In fact, change is necessary, and Peter's note of warning to the beloved in 2 Peter 3:17-18 helps to show this. Verse 17 shows even the beloved risk "being led away with the error of the wicked" and, if this happens, then they will "fall from" their "own steadfastness." Then verse 18 says: "but grow in grace, and *in* the knowledge of our Lord and Savior Jesus Christ." The word "but" introduces a contrast that shows the way to avoid falling prey to error is to grow!

Behavior that Honors God

Knowledge is important for growth, but a knowledge of the written law is not required for people to behave in a God-honoring way. Before the written law, Enoch and Abraham honored God (Heb 11:5, Jas 2:23). After the written law, even those who did not know the law could honor God and scripture explicitly tells of people who did so.

Romans 2:14 speaks about Gentiles who do not have the law but "do by nature the things contained in the law" (Rom 2:14). It does not say how they came to have a "nature" that caused them to do this. Still, given what the Bible tells us about Cornelius, it seems he was the kind of Gentile this verse was talking about. [We need to weigh the popular idea of *'a sin nature'* (that causes people to sin) against this verse which says their "nature" caused those Gentiles to do the things contained in the law (i.e., not to sin, but to obey).]

In 1 Timothy 2:2, Paul talked of living "a quiet and peaceable life in all godliness and honesty" and he went on to say such behavior is "good and acceptable in the sight of God our Savior" (v. 3). Is this an unattainable goal or can people live this way and please God by doing so? We will return to this question later.

Micah 6:8 asks this, "what doth the LORD require of thee, but to do justly, and to love mercy, and to walk humbly with thy God?" Did the LORD require this only of a subset of men in that day or should men act this way even if they do not have the written law? Consider the two key commandments that were cited by Jesus:

"Thou shalt love the Lord thy God with all thy heart, and with all thy soul, and with all thy mind. This is the first and great commandment. And the second *is* like unto it, Thou shalt love thy neighbor as thyself" (Mt 22:37-39).

Can people act in accord with these commandments even if they have not read scripture? If so, this would explain why God-fearers like Cornelius are accepted with God, and how men do the things contained in the law even if they do not have the written law.

Keep in mind, however, Peter was told, "what God hath cleansed, *that* call not thou common" (Acts 10:15). It is evident this did not refer to a self-cleansing. Rather, this cleansing was done by God.

"The washing of water by the word" (Eph 5:26) cleanses those who are in the church. But could this also apply to Cornelius or others who do not have the written law? How one answers this depends on the authority of the "voice" and the "words" that have gone out to every human over all time as described in the verses below:

"The heavens **declare** the glory of God; and the firmament **showeth** his handiwork. Day unto day **uttereth speech**, and night unto night **showeth knowledge**. *There is* no speech nor language, *where* **their voice** is not heard. **Their line** is gone out through all the earth, and **their words** to the end of the world" (Ps 19:1-4).

Since God is the source, this handiwork, knowledge, and voice carry the same authority as scripture (and Romans 10:18 affirms the worldwide reach of God's word). So, if people hear the words described in Psalm 19, the effect will be similar to the washing that occurs when we submit to the authority of God's written word.

If God teaches people via the words noted in Psalm 19, then this will also draw them to Jesus because being taught by God is what draws people to Jesus (cf. Fourth gospel 6:45).

We are not told what led Cornelius to fear God, but the things in Psalm 19 surely had an effect. He was honoring God even before he was told about Jesus. If he had a love of the truth, then he was going to hear it when Peter brought him more of it. Also, since he had already been "accepted" with God, it makes no sense to think Cornelius would have been tormented for eternity if he had died before he got to hear Peter's message. [Lord willing, the next book in this series will weigh scripture's testimony on the resurrection and will further consider what it means to be "accepted" with God.]

Focus on the Reward

Hebrews 6:10 says, "God *is* not unrighteous to forget your work and labor of love, which ye have showed toward his name," and while this was written to the brethren, it expresses a principle that would also apply to the works of Cornelius. It is also in harmony with the principle of rewards emphasized in other passages like, "he that cometh to God must believe *that* he is, and that he is a rewarder of them that diligently seek him" (Heb 11:6). It is easy to see why no one comes to God unless they believe he is God. But we also have to believe "he is a rewarder of them that diligently seek him." Therefore, this principle is of the utmost importance, and this lets us know diligence in seeking God will be rewarded!

Scripture tells us Moses rightly valued these rewards, "esteeming the reproach of Christ greater riches than the treasures in Egypt: for he [Moses] had respect unto the recompense of the reward" (Heb 11:26). The treasures in Egypt were not the only game in town and Moses recognized "greater riches" come from honoring God.

In this passage, Jesus told how our treasure is tied to our thinking:

"Lay not up for yourselves treasures upon earth, where moth and rust doth corrupt, and where thieves break through and steal: But lay up for yourselves treasures in heaven, where neither moth nor rust doth corrupt, and where thieves do not break through nor steal: For where your treasure is, there will your heart be also" (Mt 6:19-21).

Moses "had respect unto the recompense of the reward." This is where his treasure was. Jesus also looked forward to a reward.

"Jesus the author and finisher of our faith; who for the joy that was set before him endured the cross" (Heb 12:2). This gives us a look into the mind of Jesus and his regard for the reward. He "endured the cross" because he esteemed "the joy that was set before him."

In any case, these words apply, "the Lord shall judge his people" (Heb 10:30). If we do not trust the Lord to judge rightly, then we will resist his authority. So, a little bit later, we will look at the evidence that shows the Lord can be trusted to judge rightly.

Case Study: The Case of the Eleven

A Math Problem?

If we find something in scripture that raises a difficulty or looks like an error, what should we do? If we believe there are mistakes in scripture, our confidence in God's word will be shaken. But as this case study will show, what looks like an irreconcilable problem could easily be the result of us having a blind spot.

The night of Jesus' resurrection, "he appeared unto the eleven as they sat at meat, and upbraided them with their unbelief and hardness of heart, because they believed not them which had seen him after he was risen" (Mk 16:14). Since Judas was dead by that point (Mt 27:5), many assume the eleven means the twelve minus Judas. However, scripture also says: "but Thomas, one of the twelve, called Didymus, was not with them when Jesus came" (Fourth gospel 20:24). Thus, the question is, who was at this event?

As will be shown, neither Thomas nor Judas were there when Jesus met "the eleven" and twelve minus two is ten. So, how could Jesus have met with "the eleven" on that night?

When this dilemma is pointed out, some say this shows there are errors in scripture, but they are wrong.

Now is your opportunity to check your Bible on this. Write down your thoughts about the answer. Then go on to the case study and learn why questions raised by scripture are best answered by God's word itself.

The Case of the Eleven

The Twelve Apostles

Revelation 21 describes "the holy city, new Jerusalem" and says, "the wall of the city had twelve foundations, and in them the names of the twelve apostles of the Lamb" (v. 14). Some say Paul's name will be one of those names because he was used mightily by God. They defend this idea by saying Paul replaced Judas and became one of the twelve. But scripture does not say this, and this view will also keep a person from being able to answer the question that we are considering in this case study.

After Jesus ascended into heaven, Peter talked to the disciples and in Acts 1:20-22 he said this about Judas:

"it is written in the book of Psalms, Let his habitation be desolate, and let no man dwell therein: and his bishopric [office] let another take. Wherefore of these men which have companied with us all the time that the Lord Jesus went in and out among us, Beginning from the baptism of John, unto that same day that he was taken up from us, must one be ordained to be a witness with us of his resurrection".

The passage goes on to tell us:

"And they appointed two, Joseph called Barsabas, who was surnamed Justus, and Matthias. And they prayed, and said, Thou, Lord, which knowest the hearts of all *men*, show whether of these two thou hast chosen, That he may take part of this ministry and apostleship, from which Judas by transgression fell, that he might go to his own place. And they gave forth their lots; and the lot fell upon Matthias; and he was numbered with the eleven apostles" (Acts 1:23-26).

They prayed and asked for the Lord's guidance. Is there a reason to conclude the Lord did not hear their prayer and answer it? No. Why did they cast lots? Perhaps they believed the words, "the lot is cast into the lap; but the whole disposing thereof *is* of the LORD" (Prv 16:13) and other verses like:

- "by lot was their inheritance, as the LORD commanded by the hand of Moses" (Jos 14:2), and
- "the children of Israel gave by lot unto the Levites these cities with their suburbs, as the LORD commanded by the hand of Moses" (Jos 21:8).

At times, the LORD wanted the lot to be used, and there is nothing that suggests the disciples were wrong to cast lots to find out who God had chosen to take Judas' place among the twelve. Paul was chosen to be an apostle. But Paul never became one of the twelve and scripture proves he could not have taken the place of Judas.

What was Jesus' purpose in choosing Paul? Jesus told Paul:

"I have appeared unto thee for this purpose, to make thee a minister and a witness both of these things which thou hast seen, and of those things in which I will appear unto thee" (Acts 26:16).

Jesus said nothing about Paul replacing Judas or being counted as one of the twelve. Paul was called to be a witness of the things he had seen and would see. Did this make him the replacement for Judas? No. When Paul was called Saul of Tarsus, he did not meet Jesus until their first conversation on the road to Damascus (cf. 1Tm 1:13). He could witness to his encounters with Jesus from then on, but he could not be a witness to things he never saw.

Paul called Jesus' appearance to him on the Damascus Road a vision. This vision and others enabled Paul to testify Jesus was alive. Still, he did not see what the twelve saw. They saw the risen Jesus in a flesh and bone body, they saw him multiple times over forty days, and they watched as Jesus was taken up into heaven. In one of those appearances, he showed himself to his disciples and said, "behold my hands and my feet that it is I myself: handle me, and see; for a spirit hath not flesh and bones, as ye see me have" (Lk 24:39). Then after Jesus ascended into heaven, Peter told the disciples one of them had to **"be ordained to be a witness with us of his** [Jesus'] **resurrection"** (Acts 1:22). Paul could not be this witness because he did not see what they saw. In order to be a witness "with" the disciples, a person had to see what they saw.

Disciples, Apostles, and the Twelve

We use different terms to make distinctions and God's word also does this. The terms disciples, apostles, and the twelve denoted distinct groups. There is some overlap because the twelve were all apostles and every apostle was a disciple. Yet, all the disciples were not apostles and not every apostle was one of the twelve. There were many disciples and far fewer apostles. But the twelve were a unique group and Paul is never called one of the twelve.

Jesus had more than twelve disciples during his earthly ministry for Peter said Judas' replacement had to be one of the men "which have companied with us all the time that the Lord Jesus went in and out among us, Beginning from the baptism of John, unto that same day that he was taken up from us" (Acts 1:21-22). At one point, Jesus chose twelve of the disciples and named them "apostles" (Mt 10:1-2, Mk 3:13-14, Lk 6:13). Yet, he still had other disciples. The terms "the twelve" and "apostles" denoted the same group of men until the events of the Book of Acts, when the term "apostle" was used of others, such as Barnabas, Paul, and James (cf. Acts 14:14, Gal 1:19).

There are more than twelve apostles in scripture, but the number in the twelve was always twelve. Judas forfeited his position in this group. Thereafter, "the twelve" referred to this same group, only with Matthias having taken the place (the bishopric) of Judas. Scripture says, "the lot fell upon Matthias; and he was numbered with the eleven apostles" (Acts 1:26). Then after this, we see "Peter, standing up with the eleven" (Acts 2:14) on the day of Pentecost, not with the ten. This confirms Matthias had to be one of the twelve. Otherwise, Peter could not have stood up *with* "the eleven." Also, Acts 6:2 says, "the twelve called the multitude of the disciples." The term "twelve" in this verse makes no sense without Matthias.

The Apostle Matthias

After the author of the Book of Acts told of "Peter, standing up with the eleven," he referred to these men as, Peter and "the rest of the apostles" (Acts 2:37). He also used the term "apostles" at least a dozen times in Acts before he even mentioned Saul of Tarsus. Also remember, Peter stated the purpose of Judas' replacement:

"of these men which have companied with us all the time that the Lord Jesus went in and out among us, Beginning from the baptism of John, unto that same day that he was taken up from us, must one be ordained to be a witness with us of his [Jesus'] resurrection" (Acts 1:20-22).

The replacement for Judas did not merely fill an open slot among the twelve. This person was to be ordained as a witness of Jesus' resurrection and had to be with Jesus throughout his ministry. Matthias was with the disciples "all the time that the Lord Jesus went in and out among" them (Acts 1:21). He was also with them on the day Jesus ascended into heaven and this must affect our view of what Acts 1:2-4 says about that day:

"the day in which he [Jesus] was taken up, after that he through the Holy Ghost had given commandments unto the apostles whom he had chosen: To whom also he showed himself alive after his passion by many infallible proofs, being seen of them forty days, and speaking of the things pertaining to the kingdom of God: And, being assembled together with *them*, commanded them that they should not depart from Jerusalem, but wait for the promise of the Father, which, *saith he*, ye have heard of me."

The writer of Acts included Matthias with the apostles in reporting on the day of Pentecost (cf. Acts 2:14 & 37) and also when he said, Jesus was "taken up, after that he through the Holy Ghost had given commandments unto the apostles whom he had chosen."

The events in Acts took place long before they were written down, so the writer was looking back when he used the word "apostles" in verses where it had to include Matthias. Also, when Jesus told his disciples what would happen after he sent the Spirit, he said, "ye also shall bear witness, because ye have been with me from the beginning" (Fourth gospel 15:27). So, Jesus himself connected their witness to them being with him from the beginning.

Learning What God Already Knew

After Jesus was taken up into heaven, Peter and the disciples:

"prayed, and said, Thou, Lord, which knowest the hearts of all *men*, show whether of these two thou hast chosen, That he may take part of this ministry and apostleship, from which Judas by transgression fell" (Acts 1:24-25).

The past tense in their request lets us know they were not asking the Lord to make a choice. They wanted him to show them who had already been chosen! "Jesus knew from the beginning... who should betray him" (Fourth gospel 6:64), but the disciples did not know Judas was the betrayer until after the fact.

Something similar occurred in Acts 1:15-26. The Lord knew who would replace Judas, but the disciples did not know who this was until the lot revealed the Lord's choice to them.

The gospels were written after the events of Acts 1 had occurred. So, the gospel writers knew Matthias had been given the "ministry and apostleship, from which Judas by transgression fell" (Acts 1:25), and this knowledge is reflected in their words. When Mark 16:14 and Luke 24:33-36 tell us Jesus met "the eleven" on the day of his resurrection, the term "the eleven" included Matthias (just as in Acts 2:14). It excluded Thomas because he was not present.

By the time Jesus rose from the dead, Judas was no longer one of the twelve, because his part in the "ministry and apostleship" had been forsaken in his act of "transgression" (cf. Acts 1:25).

Judas was one of the twelve until he betrayed Jesus with a kiss (Mt 26:47, Mk 14:43, Lk 22:47). After that, he was never again referred to as one of the twelve. Every time the twelve is mentioned from that point on, Matthias was included in this number, just as we see on the night of Jesus' resurrection.

The Conclusion to the Case of the Eleven

The gospels could refer to "the eleven" when Thomas was absent because Matthias replaced Judas by the time they were written. Yet, some say since Matthias is not mentioned again after Acts 1, this means he was not a legitimate apostle. So, what happens if we subject this inference to biblical scrutiny?

In Acts 1:12, Andrew, Thomas, and Bartholomew are mentioned, but they were not named again in scripture. Does this mean those three apostles became insignificant or irrelevant? No. That view is based on a false assumption, so it would not apply to Andrew, Thomas, Bartholomew, or Matthias. While it is true to say Matthias is not mentioned by name after the events of Acts 1, this also offers us an example of how men can draw false inferences from true statements. This is why it is good to validate our beliefs.

Is there sufficient evidence to prove the identification of Matthias by lot was valid? Yes, because scripture requires it, since terms like "the eleven" make no sense without him, as has been shown.

Also, we are told the risen Jesus met with "the twelve" (1Cor 15:5). Paul was not known to the disciples at that point, so this meeting could only have happened if this number included Matthias.

Lastly, notice what Paul said when he discussed the witnesses of Jesus' resurrection. He did not claim to be one of them, but rather in Acts 13:30-31, he said:

> "God raised him [Jesus] from the dead: And he was seen many days of them which came up with him from Galilee to Jerusalem, who are his witnesses unto the people."

Paul indicated Jesus' witnesses were the ones who came up with him from Galilee to Jerusalem and saw him many days. If Paul did not count himself in that group, then neither should we.

On the morning of Jesus' resurrection, women who learned about this miracle, "returned from the sepulcher, and told all these things unto the eleven, and to all the rest" (Lk 24:9). Judas was not there. Matthew 27:5 tells us, Judas "went and hanged himself" and then six verses later it says, "Jesus stood before the governor" (Mt 27:11). So, Judas died before Jesus did.

While scripture does not explicitly mention if Thomas was absent on that morning, it does tell us he was not with the eleven later that evening. Thus, this would indicate he was also the one who was absent when those women brought their report to the eleven.

Peter said God raised Jesus and "showed him openly" (Acts 10:40). Then he added, "**not to all the people**, but unto witnesses chosen before of God, *even* to us, who did eat and drink with him after he rose from the dead" (Acts 10:41). This gives us another fact that must be considered. He specified that the witnesses who had been chosen before by God were those who ate and drank with Jesus after he rose from the dead. However, since Paul never did this, he could not have been one of these witnesses.

Matthias, on the other hand, was with Jesus, "beginning from the baptism of John, unto that same day that he was taken up" (Acts 1:22). So, Matthias was one of those who ate and drank with him in the days between the time he rose from the dead and was taken into heaven.

The end of the Case of the Eleven

Chapter 5 – Build on a Firm Foundation

This chapter will discuss some principles that directly relate to our ability to distinguish truth from error. As will be shown, the critical first step is to avoid the trap of acting as if it is okay to give non-Bible sources and scripture equal consideration.

The Authority of Scripture

Jesus said, "he that is faithful in that which is least is faithful also in much: and he that is unjust in the least is also unjust in much" (Lk 16:10). Thus, the way we handle little things is also the way we handle bigger matters. Holding to the truth on big issues depends on allegiance to the truth on little matters.

A consistent regard for God's word is also taught in this passage:

"whosoever shall keep the whole law, and yet offend in one *point,* he is guilty of all. For he [God] that said, Do not commit adultery, said also, Do not kill. Now if thou commit no adultery, yet if thou kill, thou art become a transgressor of the law" (Jas 2:10-11).

"He" refers to God (cf. Ex 20:13). We are "guilty of all" if we disrespect God's law in one area because we are disrespecting his authority and he gave <u>all</u> of the law. Some will say, *'sin is sin'* and suggest this passage teaches all sins are equally bad, but this is not what the passage is teaching. Rather, it shows God stands behind all of God's word. James cites the law, but the same logic applies to any portion of scripture since they come from the same source.

The Source of the Message

"God, who at sundry times and in divers manners spake in time past unto the fathers by the prophets" (Heb 1:1) and "all scripture *is* given by inspiration of God" (2Ti 3:16) are just two of the verses that tell us God is the source of scripture. So, it carries God's authority. But the things men say about scripture do not have this authority. This is why we must hold scripture above the opinions of men and be diligent to speak God's word faithfully.

Jesus told the men of his day, "had ye believed Moses, ye would have believed me" (Fourth gospel 5:46). They convinced themselves they believed Moses, but they were wrong. Likewise, we can be mistaken about things we believe. He went on to say, "if ye believe not his writings, how shall ye believe my words?" (Fourth gospel 5:47) In refusing to believe Moses' writings, they set their minds against the truth, which meant they could not believe Jesus' words either. This also applied to God's other prophets, for Jesus said: "if they hear not Moses and the prophets, neither will they be persuaded, though one rose from the dead" (Lk 16:31). If people will not respond to God's written word, then a miracle as great as someone rising from the dead will not change them, for God is the source of both.

While a formal education can teach people the words of scripture, it does not guarantee a person will hear God's voice or do his will. "The Pharisees and lawyers rejected the counsel of God against themselves" (Lk 7:30) and "the chief priests and the scribes and the chief of the people sought to destroy" Jesus (Lk 19:47). Moreover, Jesus told his disciples to beware of "the doctrine of the Pharisees and of the Sadducees" (Mt 16:12). He did not urge his disciples to adopt the views of the educated elite, he cautioned them against doing so. Why? Perhaps it is because when people learn to value the teachings of men, then they do not seek the honor that comes "from God only" (Fourth gospel 5:44-47), as will be shown later.

The words "study to show thyself approved unto God, a workman that needeth not to be ashamed, rightly dividing the word of truth" (2Ti 2:15) set a high bar. The word translated as "study" in this verse is more often translated as either "be diligent," "give diligence," or "do thy diligence" (2Ti 4:9 & 21, Titus 3:12, 2Pt 1:10 & 3:14). "Rightly dividing the word of truth" takes time and effort but it is worth it, for God "is a rewarder of them that diligently seek him" (Heb 11:6).

Saul of Tarsus

Jesus once told his disciples, "the time cometh, that whosoever killeth you will think that he doeth God service" (Fourth gospel 16:2). This describes Saul of Tarsus. He was "a Hebrew of the Hebrews; as touching the law, a Pharisee" (Phl 3:5). This highly educated man believed it was a good thing to persecute the followers of Jesus.

Before Jesus confronted Saul on the road to Damascus, surely Saul thought he understood scripture. But his beliefs were based on what men told him about scripture and not on God's word itself! No doubt, Saul felt assured because he believed like his teachers. Later, he learned he was wrong and called himself "a blasphemer, and a persecutor, and injurious," but he also said God had mercy on him because he "did *it* ignorantly in unbelief" (1Ti 1:13).

Although Saul knew the words of scripture, he had misconstrued their meaning. Putting confidence in men had left him unable to rightly divide God's word, therefore, his method of assessing truth had to change if he was going to honor God and stand corrected.

Errors in the Church?

The brethren were told to "be not deceived" (Lk 21:8, et al.), and Paul asked the churches in Galatia, "who hath bewitched you, that ye should not obey the truth?" (Gal 3:1) So, we know the brethren can be deceived. The Corinthian church even tolerated contrary ideas on the resurrection and it earned them a reprimand: "if Christ be preached that he rose from the dead, how say some among you that there is no resurrection of the dead?" (1Cor 15:12)

Jesus sent a warning to the angel of the church of the Laodiceans that included a rebuke: "thou sayest, I am rich, and increased with goods, and have need of nothing; and knowest not that thou art wretched, and miserable, and poor, and blind, and naked" (Rv 3:17). How can a church think they are "rich" and have "need of nothing" when they *are* "poor, and blind, and naked?" How did they get into such a state? This lets us know one cannot assume ideas that are accepted in a church are necessarily correct. So, let us consider some of the reasons the brethren fall prey to mistaken beliefs.

God's Word Offers Good Counsel

The idea that there is 'safety in numbers' leads many to assume it is safe to adopt the beliefs of the majority. Is this wise?

If scripture says, "in the multitude of counselors there is safety" (Prv 11:14), what should we conclude?

Popularity is not a measure of truth. Thus, Proverbs 11:14 is not suggesting if a large number of people hold the same view on an issue, then one should assume that view is right or true.

In response to Jesus "some said, He is a good man: others said, Nay; but he deceiveth the people" (Fourth gospel 7:12). Acts 14:4 says, "the multitude of the city was divided: and part held with the Jews, and part with the apostles." When groups hold opposing views is the one that is in the majority necessarily correct? Of course not. Once during Paul's ministry, "the multitude of the people followed after, crying, away with him." Neither their number nor their unity meant their words were wise. "In the multitude of counselors there is safety" cannot mean the opinions of the majority are right, for scripture also tells us, "thou shalt not follow a multitude to *do* evil" (Ex 23:2). We need to get good counsel and the more of it we get, the better off we will be.

If Jesus, Moses, Jeremiah, etc., were our counselors, we would be better off. A multitude of their counsel would help to keep us safe from false ideas and to correct us when we have missed the truth. Psalm 33:11 says, "the counsel of the LORD standeth forever" and in Psalm 119:24 it says, "thy testimonies also *are* my delight *and* **my counselors**." So, scripture is the place to go for wise counsel. Looking to the opinions of men is not the same thing. In scripture, we see that when the people listened to all of the religious experts in Jesus' day, it did not lead them to the truth. This does not mean we should never seek the counsel of others, but we should always remember to seek God's counsel and to value it above all else.

Put Traditions to the Test

If an idea is called a tradition, does that make it true? No. Jesus said the religious experts of his day were making God's word void through their "tradition" (Mk 7:13) and the word tradition is still used to give an air of authority to the opinions of men. Colossians 2:8 offered the brethren this caution, "beware lest any man spoil you through philosophy and vain deceit, after the tradition of men, after the rudiments of the world, and not after Christ." How can a person tell a God-honoring tradition from a tradition which makes the word of God of no effect? Test it.

The source of a tradition is what makes the difference! This is seen in verses like: "now we command you, brethren, in the name of our Lord Jesus Christ, that ye withdraw yourselves from every brother that walketh disorderly, and not after the tradition which he received of us" (2Th 3:6). So, consider the source. The teachings of the apostles have God's authority. A tradition of men does not. When the traditions of men are promoted, it leads people to trust the authority of men. When this happens, then the authority of the word of God has taken a backseat.

Do the credentials issued by men ensure accuracy when it comes to God's word? No. People who are ordained or who have PhDs often hold opposite views on what the Bible tells us. This same problem shows up in scripture when people were taught to rely on the teachings of men.

The Sadducees and the Pharisees were the two leading religious groups in Jesus' day. Those two groups held contrary views, "the Sadducees say that there is no resurrection, neither angel, nor spirit: but the Pharisees confess both" (Acts 23:8). Since both groups could not be right, this proves large groups and trained experts can espouse beliefs that are not true. Also, notice that although the Pharisees believed in a resurrection, getting this issue right did not mean their teachings honored God.

Trust in the Teachings of Men Makes God's Word Powerless

Both the Sadducees and the Pharisees undermined the authority of the word of God. Jesus warned his disciples about this when he said, "take heed and beware of the leaven of the Pharisees and of the Sadducees" (Mt 16:6). After he explained these words to the disciples, "then understood they how that he bade them not beware of the leaven of bread, but of the doctrine of the Pharisees and of the Sadducees" (Mt 16:12).

He spoke of "the doctrine" of the Pharisees and Sadducees, so this shows they had this in common. Therefore, his warning was not regarding their views on certain issues, since they disagreed on many points. However, both groups used the teachings of men to convince people to adopt their group's views on God's word.

Why did he use leaven to portray their doctrine? Scripture says, "a little leaven leaveneth the whole lump" (Gal 5:9). When leaven is added to a lump of dough it will spread throughout the dough until all of it becomes leavened. This pictures how the teachings of men take over. The minute a person trusts those teachings to define what is true, they take over for God's word as the measure of truth. According to Jesus, the Pharisees and scribes were "making the word of God of none effect through" their "tradition" (Mk 7:13). How does this take place? Scripture has authority because it is of God. But this authority is usurped when the traditions of men are taught as if they have authority, i.e., should be trusted or deserve respect.

Honor? From What Source?

A group of men was once asked by Jesus, "how can ye believe, which receive honor one of another and seek not the honor that *cometh* from God only?" (Fourth gospel 5:44) When these words were cited earlier, it was noted that in this question Jesus linked belief to honor and he contrasted the two sources of honor. The words "how can ye believe" imply an inability. So, valuing the honor we get from others, keeps us from seeking the honor that comes from God only and doing so apparently hinders being able to believe.

Jesus indicated seeking the honor that comes "from God only" is a good thing to do. Scripture also says, "before honor *is* humility" (Prv 15:33, 18:12). Moreover, this goes along with what was said in James 4:10, "humble yourselves in the sight of the Lord, and he shall lift you up." This counsel perfectly parallels something else James said in a passage where he contrasted the different results yielded by pride and humility:

"God resisteth the proud, but giveth grace unto the humble. Submit yourselves therefore to God" (Jas 4:6-7).

Peter made the same point when he wrote this to the elect:

"be subject one to another, and be clothed with humility: for God resisteth the proud, and giveth grace to the humble. Humble yourselves therefore under the mighty hand of God" (1Pt 5:5-6).

Humbly submitting to God's word is what makes the difference (cf. 1Th 2:13). James also told the brethren, "draw nigh to God, and he will draw nigh to you" (Jas 4:8). So, if we want to be closer to God, we need to move in that direction. How can we do this? One way is to "let this mind be in you, which was also in Christ Jesus" (Phl 2:5). Jesus revealed his mind in this verse, "my judgment is just; because I seek not mine own will, but the will of the Father which hath sent me" (Fourth gospel 5:30). Instead of seeking his own will, Jesus sought the will of the Father – and this caused his judgment to be just. If we want our judgment to be just, then we should do the same.

Now, notice what Jesus said after he contrasted the two sources of honor that were discussed a moment ago:

"How can ye believe, which receive honor one of another, and seek not the honor that *cometh* from God only? Do not think that I will accuse you to the Father: there is one that accuseth you, *even* Moses, in whom ye trust. For had ye believed Moses, ye would have believed me: for he wrote of me. But if ye believe not his writings, how shall ye believe my words?" (Fourth gospel 5:44-47)

Moses was their accuser! God preserved the writings of Moses, and they were dishonoring Moses and God by not believing him. Instead, they believed men who told them they were followers of Moses, even though Moses' own words proved otherwise.

Jesus said Moses wrote of him. So, we can learn about Jesus by reading what Moses wrote. Moreover, he said, "but if ye believe not his writings, how shall ye believe my words?" (Fourth gospel 5:47) He could say this because the authority of God was the foundation for both the words of Moses and the words of Jesus.

According to the Scriptures

Many will say, *'the gospel is the most important thing.'* Yet, if the gospel is not taught according to the scriptures, then the gospel of scripture is not being taught! Paul referred to "the gospel" (1Cor 15:1) and said this:

"Christ died for our sins **according to the scriptures**; And that he was buried, and that he rose again the third day **according to the scriptures**" (1Cor 15:3-4).

This means "the gospel" is tied to the authority of the scriptures that we call the Old Testament. Jesus and the apostles repeatedly used the term "it is written" and cited God's word on matters they were dealing with. If they linked their teaching to scripture, then the Old Testament surely deserves our attention.

Paul certainly preached the gospel and in Acts 26:22-23 when he spoke to Agrippa he indicated the things he taught about Jesus had already been prophesied in the Old Testament:

"I continue unto this day, witnessing both to small and great, saying none other things than those which the prophets and Moses did say should come: That Christ should suffer, and that he should be the first that should rise from the dead, and should show light unto the people, and to the Gentiles."

This shows why those who will not believe Moses' writings will not believe in Jesus. The Hebrew people should have known better since God's word warned them against trusting in "lying words." Jeremiah told those in Judah who sought to worship the LORD, "trust ye not in lying words" (Jer 7:4) and "ye trust in lying words, that cannot profit" (Jer 7:8). He wrote those words to people who had been deceived by the teachings of men. The remedy?

"Thus saith the LORD of hosts, the God of Israel, Amend your ways and your doings" (Jer 7:3).

Learning from Other People's Mistakes

The LORD used Jeremiah to rebuke religious leaders who did not know the LORD and yet spoke their own words while attributing them to the LORD. For example, the LORD said, "they that handle the law knew me not: the pastors also transgressed against me, and the prophets prophesied by Baal, and walked after *things that do not profit*" (Jer 2:8). In other verses, the LORD had Jeremiah write very similar descriptions:

- "from the prophet even unto the priest everyone dealeth falsely" (Jer 8:10),
- "many pastors have destroyed my vineyard" (Jer 12:10),
- "the LORD said unto me, the prophets prophesy lies in my name: I sent them not, neither have I commanded them, neither spake unto them: they prophesy unto you a false vision and divination, and a thing of naught, and the deceit of their heart" (Jer 14:14),
- "woe be unto the pastors that destroy and scatter the sheep of my pasture! saith the LORD" (Jer 23:1),
- "thus saith the LORD of hosts, Hearken not unto the words of the prophets that prophesy unto you: they make you vain: they speak a vision of their own heart, and not out of the mouth of the LORD" (Jer 23:16).

If the words of men are assumed to be true, it keeps people from the word of God that can turn them around, as in this passage:

"I have not sent these prophets, yet they ran: I have not spoken to them, yet they prophesied. But if they had stood in my counsel, and had caused my people to hear my words, then they should have turned them from their evil way, and from the evil of their doings" (Jer 23:21-22).

Instead of standing in the LORD's counsel and causing people to hear his words, they shared their own opinions. But the LORD gave them counsel that would avoid this; **"he that hath my word, let him speak my word faithfully"** (Jer 23:28). The Jewish leaders did not do this. Instead, they attributed the ideas of men to the LORD. They became thieves when they did this, for they were stealing the word of the LORD:

"I *am* against the prophets, saith the LORD, that steal my words everyone from his neighbor. Behold, I *am* against the prophets, saith the LORD, that use their tongues, and say, He saith" (Jer 23:30-31).

Still, those leaders were not the only ones at fault. The LORD said, "the prophets prophesy falsely, and the priests bear rule by their means; and my people love to have it so" (Jer 5:31).

Holding Contrary Beliefs is Unreasonable

What makes the difference when God's word offers to correct us is how we respond. If scripture shows we were mistaken, will we be thankful for it or embarrassed by it? We must avoid letting the fear of others influence us, for "the fear of man bringeth a snare: but whoso putteth his trust in the LORD shall be safe" (Prv 29:25).

Jesus said, "I am the way, the truth, and the life" (Fourth gospel 14:6). Since he identified himself with the truth, the way we treat the truth is an indication of how we would treat Jesus.

When the truth is contrary to their beliefs, some people act as if it is fine to believe mutually exclusive ideas. This is what the people of Israel were doing when Elijah the prophet challenged them on their practice of honoring contrary views. "Elijah came unto all the people, and said, how long halt ye between two opinions? if the LORD be God, follow him: but if Baal, then follow him" (1Kgs 18:21). When he told them to follow Baal if Baal is God, he showed their divided loyalty meant they were not really following either belief.

Yet, his most critical barb was not against Baal worship. Rather, it was against their double-mindedness and their willingness to live in the space "between two opinions."

The premise is clear. The LORD and Baal cannot both be God, so it is foolish to follow them both. The claims are mutually exclusive. If one is true, the other must be false. By behaving as if both could be true, they were tolerating falsehood. In worshipping other gods and the LORD, they showed they were believing contrary ideas. But in order to hold contradictory beliefs, a person must set aside a commitment to honest reasoning.

Unity, According to the Scriptures

For many churches, a spirit of unity is a top priority. A spirit of unity may sound good, but it is not a biblical idea. It is wrong because it makes unity the goal. However, scripture tells us we should be "endeavoring to keep the unity of the Spirit" (Eph 4:3), and the fact that people switch those words around should raise a big red flag!

The "unity of the Spirit" and a spirit *of unity* are not the same. A spirit of unity might exist at a ball game or a Baal worship meeting. However, the "unity of the Spirit" has a built-in condition, for this refers to the Spirit of truth. Thus, we need to look at the basis of the unity that is being promoted or sought.

Scripture talks about "salvation through sanctification of the Spirit and belief of the truth" (2Th 2:13) and Jesus talked about "the Spirit of truth" (Fourth gospel 14:17). If the Spirit and truth go hand in hand, a unity established apart from truth is not the "unity of the Spirit."

Furthermore, the truth causes division. Jesus identified himself with the truth and also said, "suppose ye that I am come to give peace on earth? I tell you, Nay; but rather division" (Lk 12:51). So, if the truth causes division, how is the unity of the Spirit achieved? It comes about because <u>the truth divides</u> people who do not want the truth from those who do, <u>while it also unites</u> people who have a love of the truth by drawing them and opening their eyes.

Psalm 86:11 says, "teach me thy way, O LORD; I will walk in thy truth: unite my heart to fear thy name." It appears, therefore, that a heart committed to a respect for God's authority is linked to:

A. being taught by God, and
B. a willingness to heed his word and conform our life to it.

When the believers were said to be of one accord in Acts 2:46, this was not achieved by avoiding the truth. It resulted from being led by the Spirit of truth, for unity among the brethren is fostered by a willingness to submit to the authority of God.

<u>One or the Other</u>

Jesus stated this principle, "no man can serve two masters: for either he will hate the one, and love the other; or else he will hold to the one, and despise the other" (Mt 6:24).

So, what about the men of Elijah's day who worshiped the LORD and Baal. Were they serving two masters? Not at all. They were showing contempt for the LORD by worshipping Baal.

No doubt, they convinced themselves they were serving the LORD and Baal. But their belief did not make it so, for "no man can serve two masters."

When people hold a belief that is not justified by scripture, some will act as if that issue is a matter of personal preference because on such issues, we are the judge. Scripture tells us certain issues *are* matters of conscience, but this does not mean we get to play pick and choose with God's word. Scripture is inspired by God, so its content is not a matter of personal preference. If the Bible says an issue is a conscience issue, then one's conscience before God is what rules on that issue. But there are two things to note here. The first is, scripture gets to make the call as to what qualifies as a matter of conscience. We cannot put behaviors in this category simply to give ourselves an excuse to continue doing them.

Second, personal preference and conscience before God are not the same. These are vastly different and must not be confused, because one of these two standards does not include God as a fixed point of reference, while the other one does.

Chapter 6 – A Change for the Better

What does it mean to be taught by God? How can we grow in spiritual discernment? This chapter will consider these and other points that can help us to build on a firm foundation.

How Repentance Relates to Truth

The idea of repentance may bring to mind the idea of giving up particular sins, and such a change is good. But repentance is also required to receive the truth since we must stop resisting the truth if we are going to receive it. Scripture speaks in these terms when it talks about "repentance to the acknowledging of the truth" (2Ti 2:25), and Paul told Timothy how proper instruction might bring this change about in people who "oppose themselves." We learn this from an admonition found in 2 Timothy 2:24-25:

"the servant of the Lord must not strive; but be gentle unto all *men*, apt to teach, patient, in meekness instructing those that oppose themselves; if God peradventure will give them repentance to the acknowledging of the truth."

What does it mean for people to "oppose themselves?" The term makes perfect sense and it identifies the problem. No one says they want to believe a lie. People always claim they want the truth. So, when people resist the truth, they are opposing the very thing they claim they want. People also "oppose themselves" when they hold contradictory beliefs, for to believe mutually exclusive ideas requires one to engage in thinking that opposes itself. The people whom Elijah rebuked for worshipping the LORD and Baal engaged in this kind of thinking, and followers of Jesus can also fall prey to self-contradictory thinking, as we see in this rebuke for doing so:

"If Christ be preached that he rose from the dead, how say some among you that there is no resurrection of the dead? But if there be no resurrection of the dead, then is Christ not risen" (1Cor 15:12-13).

Belief in one who "rose from the dead" is not compatible with the idea of "no resurrection of the dead." Both ideas cannot be true.

In tolerating falsehood, the Corinthians were acting as if light and darkness can coexist. But verses like "what communion hath light with darkness" (2Cor 6:14) show these two things are not compatible. The Corinthians were rebuked because one cannot respect Jesus who rose from the dead and also respect those who say there is no resurrection. They claimed to believe in Jesus but sacrificed honesty in their reasoning for the sake of inclusiveness.

Respect for the truth is not shown when contrary ideas are treated as equals. Jesus said, "to this end was I born, and for this cause came I into the world, that I should bear witness unto the truth. Every one that is of the truth heareth my voice" (Fourth gospel 18:37). The link between Jesus and the truth is unbreakable. So, when contradictory views (i.e., truth and falsehood) are both considered to be valid, Jesus is not being honored.

Divided Loyalties

How can people justify God? In Luke 7:29-30 we see how:

> "the people that heard *him* [John the Baptist], and the publicans, **justified God**, being baptized with the baptism of John. But the Pharisees and lawyers **rejected the counsel of God against themselves**, being not baptized of him."

When they were confronted with the truth, some of those people repented and submitted to God's authority. They "justified God" because to receive correction, they had to admit they were wrong and conform to God's standard of what is right. Being educated did not lead the Pharisees and lawyers to invite correction, for this would call into question their training and the authority of the men whom they followed. This is why training and/or group affiliations can lead people to resist correction. If we have loyalty to a man or group that holds beliefs that are contrary to God's word, this will pit us against the truth. We tend to associate with those who think like us. But if we take our cues on what to believe from those who we associate with, we are not relying on God's word. (Relying on the views of those who agree with us is a self-validating fallacy.) If people resist the truth, they are rejecting the counsel of God, instead of justifying God.

Who Decides What is Important?

When scripture tells us what issues are more important, we need to heed that counsel. For example, Jesus discussed "the first and great commandment" (Mt 22:38) and went on to say, "the second *is* like unto it" (Mt 22:39). Therefore, one of them is ahead of the other. But God's word gets to make this call, not us. Jesus once said, "woe unto you, scribes and Pharisees, hypocrites! for ye pay tithe of mint and anise and cumin, and have omitted the weightier *matters* of the law, judgment, mercy, and faith: these ought ye to have done, and not to leave the other undone" (Mt 23:23). Here we see Jesus and the scholars did not weigh things the same way.

Those leaders claimed they valued the law, yet in their opinion, the "tithe" was more important than "judgment, mercy, and faith." If they had said, *'those are minor issues, the tithe is the main thing'* would this have made it so? No, because the opinions of men are not the measure of what issues are weightier. Judgment, mercy, and faith were the "weightier *matters* of the law" long before he rebuked those scholars on this issue. We will take a closer look at this passage a little later. The point for now though is God's word establishes what things are more important, not men.

If we rightly identify the weightier issues, it does not mean we can ignore lesser issues, for Jesus also told them, "these ought ye to have done." We do not get to discount what the Bible teaches on the things we decide are secondary and only respect it on issues we say are essential.

Of God or of Men?

A verse written to the church of the Thessalonians reveals our real moment of decision. When the word of God is presented to us, how will we receive it? When God's word was presented to them, they made the right choice, as we see in this verse – "when ye received the word of God which ye heard of us, ye received *it* not *as* the word of men, but as it is in truth, the word of God, which effectually worketh also in you that believe" (1Th 2:13). They rightly distinguished between what was "of God" and what was "of men" and, as a result, God's word effected the way they lived their lives.

If we rightly receive God's word, we can get the same blessing of having it effectually work in our life. But this blessing only happens if we properly distinguish between words that have God's authority and those that do not. Furthermore, as we seek to subject ideas to biblical scrutiny, we may not always do so accurately. Even so, in seeking to do this we uphold scripture as the standard of truth and this keeps us grounded in "the fear of the LORD" (Prv 1:7).

A scale measures weight, not length. Likewise, the method used to assess truth on biblical issues must be appropriate to the task. If we rely on the opinions of others to tell us what is true, then we are using a wrong approach.

As to the Lord

- "Whatsoever ye do in word or deed, do all in the name of the Lord Jesus" (Col 3:17).
- "Whatsoever ye do, do it heartily, as to the Lord, and not unto men" (Col 3:23).

What would happen if we applied these admonitions to our study of the Bible? It would remind us our approach to scripture should please the Lord. The traditions of men lure people by seeming to offer a shortcut to the truth. Some say tradition ought to be given the benefit of the doubt. But Jesus never encouraged this, nor did his apostles. They pointed people to scripture and we should also do this when we are discussing biblical issues.

If everything in God's word has already been discovered by men, why read the Bible? If the scholars have it all figured out, why not just read their writings?

If we read scripture we might misunderstand it, but if we follow experts then this will guarantee we know the truth, right? No.

The religious groups in Jesus' day advocated this sort of thinking and he rebuked them for it, calling them "blind leaders of the blind" (Mt 15:14). In that verse, he went on to say, "if the blind lead the blind, both shall fall into the ditch." So, the question this raises is, how can people determine if they are following a blind leader?

The followers of blind leaders end up in the ditch, but they do this to themselves, since they pick who they will follow. Is there hope for them? Yes. It happens when scripture or anything else reveals something is amiss. This is their "fall into the ditch" moment, and they should thank God for this wake-up call.

1 Corinthians 13:6 says love rejoices "in the truth," so if we love the truth, we will change and strive to do better when evidence or some experience proves we have been misled. If a man says, *'Jesus will return on April 1st,'* what happens if we believed this (because we put confidence in that man)? If April 2nd passes and Jesus has not come, it is our "fall into the ditch" moment. We were wrong. The question is, what will we do next?

When the data proves people have been misled, only some will admit they were wrong. Others will assume the error was about one issue, like date-setting in the example above. But the fact is, their standard of judgment led them to choose to follow someone who was blind, and *this* is why they ended up falling into the ditch.

Judgment, Based on What?

A challenge was put to Jesus when "the Pharisees and scribes asked him, Why walk not thy disciples according to the tradition of the elders?" (Mk 7:5) What authority did they cite? What they used to judge the disciples of Jesus was the tradition of the elders. They did not cite God's word! The opinions of men had supplanted scripture as their measure of right and wrong. Mark 7:6-7 tells us how Jesus responded when they pointed to those traditions:

"He answered and said unto them, Well hath Esaias prophesied of you hypocrites, as it is written, This people honoreth me with *their* lips, but their heart is far from me. Howbeit in vain do they worship me, teaching *for* doctrines the commandments of men."

This shows the bait and switch that was involved. Here we see religious leaders who claimed they were honoring God, but they were "teaching *for* doctrines the commandments of men" (Mk 7:7). In their eyes, their views about scripture could not be wrong.

They promoted a substitute authority, and their desire to hold on to their traditions is what led them to do so. We know this because Jesus identified their self-interested motive when he told them:

A. "laying aside the commandment of God, ye hold the tradition of men" (Mk 7:8), and
B. "ye reject the commandment of God, that ye may keep your own tradition" (Mk 7:9).

Their belief in what they had been taught came before God's word. Jesus said they were "making the word of God of none effect" through their "tradition" (Mk 7:13). They could not have it both ways, since "no man can serve two masters" (Mt 6:24). So, either scripture or our beliefs will dictate how we view things, but it cannot be both.

If we view God's word through the lens of our beliefs, then we have made our opinion the measure of truth. "Forever, O LORD, thy word is settled in heaven" (Ps 119:89) and "O LORD: give me understanding according to thy word" (Ps 119:169) are just two of many passages that teach us God's word is the right measure.

The Antidote for Error

Paul gave Timothy this warning regarding deception, "evil men and seducers shall wax worse and worse, deceiving, and being deceived" (2Ti 3:13). Then he added this:

"But continue thou in the things which thou hast learned and hast been assured of, knowing of whom thou hast learned them; And that from a child thou hast known the holy scriptures, which are able to make thee wise unto salvation through faith which is in Christ Jesus" (2Ti 3:14-15).

Would Timothy have thought the words "knowing of whom thou hast learned them" referred to some human teacher? No.

Lois, Eunice, and Paul all taught Timothy. However, if Timothy received this teaching "not as the word of men, but as it is in truth, the word of God" like the Thessalonians had done (cf. 1Th 2:13), then he was taught those things by God.

Paul also told Timothy, "the holy scriptures" could make him "wise unto salvation" (2Ti 3:15). Those who delivered God's word to him played a role, but the holy scriptures are what made Timothy wise unto salvation.

Truth is the antidote for error. So, Paul urged Timothy to "preach the word" consistently, even though it would cause some people to turn away just as he forewarned Timothy in this passage:

"Preach the word; be instant in season, out of season; reprove, rebuke, exhort with all longsuffering and doctrine. For the time will come when they will not endure sound doctrine; but after their own lusts shall they heap to themselves teachers, having itching ears; and they shall turn away *their* ears from the truth, and shall be turned unto fables" (2Ti 4:2-4).

"A fool despiseth his father's instruction: but he that regardeth reproof is prudent" (Prv 15:5). Even so, the words, "today if ye will hear his voice, harden not your hearts" (Heb 3:7-8) were directed to the holy brethren. So, the brethren may be tempted to resist when the voice of God calls on them to change. Furthermore, there is no reason to think the followers of Jesus today are immune from this temptation. In fact, this temptation may be even greater in our internet age when people can "turn away *their* ears from the truth" and "be turned unto fables" in a few clicks.

People joke, *'it must be true because it was on the Internet.'* However, we make the same mistake if we think something is true because a famous person said it or because it was said in a book or because it appears in notes that have been added alongside the words of scripture in our Bible.

<u>Taught by God?</u>

Jesus said, "I thank thee, O Father, Lord of heaven and earth, because thou hast hid these things from the wise and prudent, and hast revealed them unto babes" (Mt 11:25, Lk 10:21). Unless God no longer does this, being wise and prudent would not ensure that a man or any group of men would be more likely to have the truth.

While others may understand scripture better than us, scripture urges against letting others tell us what to think simply because they are more educated. Why not let God teach us?

The idea of being taught by God may sound strange to us, and it may have sounded strange to the brethren in Ephesus when they first read the words, "if so be that ye have **heard him** [God], and have been **taught by him**" (Eph 4:21). Thus, their teacher was God. They "heard him" and were "taught by him." The question is, since this was written to "the faithful in Christ Jesus" (Eph 1:1), would it also apply to those who follow Jesus today?

Who teaches us? "All scripture *is* given by inspiration of God" (2Ti 3:16). Therefore, when we are taught by scripture, God teaches us!

Jesus told his disciples, "the Holy Ghost, whom the Father will send in my name, he shall teach you all things" (Fourth gospel 14:26). One way this happens is via God's word.

Jesus also cited this prophecy: "it is written in the prophets, And they shall be all taught of God" (Fourth gospel 6:45). Then he went on to show this did not mean being taught about God, it meant being taught by God, as we saw when we looked at this verse earlier.

God's Word Can Change People

After noting that the Ephesians had been taught by God, the letter to the Ephesians went on to say, Christ "loved the church, and gave himself for it; that he might <u>sanctify and cleanse it with the washing of water by the word</u>" (Eph 5:26). We find a similar idea when Jesus told his disciples, "ye are <u>clean through the word</u> which I have spoken unto you" (Fourth gospel 15:3). So, the word works to cleanse the brethren. But the cleansing effect of God's word is undermined when the opinions of men are treated as an authority.

James cited another work of the word when he told the brethren the Father had begotten them "with the word of truth" (Jas 1:18). This same idea was also taught in this verse: "being born again, not of corruptible seed, but of incorruptible, by the word of God, which liveth and abideth for ever" (1Pt 1:23).

God's word brings about birth, growth, cleansing, correction, etc., and faith comes by hearing the word (cf. Rom 10:17); so let us dive in.

Not everyone has a Bible or the ability to read, let alone access to the Internet which lets people utilize a wide array of free Bible study tools. Those of us who have those things need to thank God for them. We can show our gratitude by making a diligent effort to let scripture be a lamp to our feet and a light to our path.

Scripture says, "unto whomsoever much is given, of him shall be much required" (Lk 12:48) and, for us, this verse must be weighed considering the resources we can easily access in this age.

Once when Jesus prayed for his disciples, he asked the Father to "sanctify them through thy truth: thy word is truth" (Fourth gospel 17:17). We must uphold this standard because God's word was, and still is, what changes and sanctifies those who believe in Jesus.

Wise? By What Standard?

Men sometimes will raise other measures of truth, such as when the chief priests and Pharisees asked this about Jesus, "have any of the rulers or of the Pharisees believed on him?" (Fourth gospel 7:48) Notice, their question implied the beliefs of the religious leaders determine what is true and it suggested only a fool would disagree with highly educated men. Because nobody wants to be the target of ridicule, such questions work to bully people into going along with the views of those who are seen as scholars.

2 Timothy 2:23 says, "foolish and unlearned questions avoid" and Titus 3:9 says, "avoid foolish questions" for "they are unprofitable and vain." So, we must distinguish such questions from questions that further the cause of truth. The prior paragraph showed how a foolish question can be used to turn people away from God's word and how the opinions of experts can be used to bully people into putting confidence in men. Jesus did not let the teachings of men dictate his view of God's word, but the rulers and Pharisees did. Since they had no evidence against Jesus, those scholars cited their own beliefs and implied he was not worthy of anyone's belief simply because the scholars had chosen not to believe on him.

The people who trusted the scholars in Jesus' day were led astray. Can this still happen today? Yes, it can. This happens whenever the opinions of men shape our view of God's word. We can avoid making this mistake if we get into the habit of putting everything to the test of scripture.

When men cite their own beliefs or other sources instead of citing the word of God, let this be a red flag. Does it make sense to cite a lesser source if a greater authority is available? No. So, when people cite a source other than scripture, we should wonder why they would not just cite scripture if it actually supported their view.

Some think 'objectivity' means looking at a lot of ideas that men have proposed and picking the one that seems best. Such people will be led astray more often than not because they are not using a God-honoring method, just as the counsel of God's word shows.

Jesus once said, "whosoever heareth these sayings of mine, and doeth them, I will liken him unto a wise man, which built his house upon a rock" (Mt 7:24). He defined godly wisdom as hearing and doing his sayings. 1 Corinthians 3:20 says, "the Lord knoweth the thoughts of the wise, that they are vain." Obviously, this is not referring to people like the "wise man, which built his house upon a rock." So, by what standard do we define the word "wise?"

"The wisdom of this world is foolishness with God" (1Cor 3:19), so what some consider to be wisdom is the opposite in God's eyes. If we want to employ godly wisdom, we need the right measure when we are making judgments.

After Jesus said the "wise man" built "upon a rock," he talked of those who are foolish. He said, "everyone that heareth these sayings of mine, and doeth them not, shall be likened unto a foolish man, which built his house upon the sand" (Mt 7:26).

The "foolish man" thinks what he is doing is fine because he is using a wrong measure. "The way of a fool *is* right in his own eyes" (Prv 12:15). Thus, foolish thinking is self-justifying and Isaiah 5:21 says, "woe unto *them that are* wise in their own eyes, and prudent in their own sight!"

Becoming Skillful by Exercising Discernment

In Luke 16:17 Jesus said, "it is easier for heaven and earth to pass, than one tittle of the law to fail." A few verses later, his teaching on Lazarus and the rich man ended with the following words, "if they hear not Moses and the prophets, neither will they be persuaded, though one rose from the dead" (Lk 16:31). As was noted earlier, those who reject the word of God that comes via scripture will not be persuaded by a miracle (since both manifest God's authority). A consistent regard for the authority of God is needed for proper judgment. When this is lacking, one's ability to make right judgments will be impaired.

Drunkenness impairs both a man's ability to drive and his capacity to judge his fitness to drive. Similarly, false assumptions will impair our ability to discern the truth and our capacity to judge whether our judgment is good or not. When we put confidence in a man or group, we assume that this is a wise thing to do when it is not.

Being persuaded by the conclusions of others is not the same as being persuaded by the evidence. If someone says, *'here is what I think...,'* what should we do? If people tell us what they believe, we know what they think, but not why.

The cause of truth is better served if we ask people to tell us about the biblical evidence that led them to hold their view. Weighing this data for ourselves will help to keep us from falling into the trap of basing our beliefs on the conclusions of someone else.

When a person says, *'the Bible says...,'* then it is up to us to check to see if they are speaking the word of God faithfully or not.

If you were on a jury and a witness testified, *'that man was driving that car and he ran over that woman,'* you would weigh it one way. Yet, if the witness said, *'I believe that man was driving that car and I think he ran over that woman,'* you would have a reason to be skeptical. On biblical issues, when someone says, *'I think...'* or *'I believe...,'* they are telegraphing their punch and letting us know they are giving us their opinion. At that point, we should ask them why they did not quote scripture if it teaches what they say it does?

When people cite their beliefs, one way to get the focus back on what scripture says, is to ask questions like, Where can I find that in the Bible? or What statements in scripture teach that view?

Jesus said, "thou shalt love the Lord thy God with all thy heart, and with all thy soul, and with all thy mind" (Mt 22:37). Those of us who have access to the Bible have been given a great gift. So, we should heed the admonitions of scripture that urge us to think on God's word throughout our day (cf. Jos 1:8, Ps 1:2 & 119:97, et al.).

The Book of Hebrews contrasted the brethren who were "dull of hearing" and "unskillful in the word of righteousness" (Heb 5:11 & 13), with those "who **by reason of use** have their senses exercised to discern both good and evil" (Heb 5:14). The growth that comes from exercising discernment will not happen when we let other people do our discerning for us. To avoid becoming "dull of hearing," we need to have our "senses exercised to discern both good and evil" and this comes about "by reason of use." So, we must keep it up.

We All Have Blind Spots

If we are not aware of something, we have a blind spot. This was the case with Apollos, who we meet in Acts 18:24-25. It says he was "mighty in the scriptures," "instructed in the way of the Lord," and "spake and taught diligently the things of the Lord," but he only knew about "the baptism of John." When Aquila and Priscilla "expounded unto him the way of God more perfectly" (Acts 18:26), he received the correction, updated his teaching, and immediately started sharing what he had learned (cf. Acts 18:27-28). His willingness to change after he was corrected is a good example for anyone who wants to honor God. As we saw earlier, Jesus linked himself to truth when he said, "to this end was I born, and for this cause came I into the world, that I should bear witness unto the truth" (Fourth gospel 18:37). We are urged to be vigilant and loyal to God's standard in verses such as, "prove all things; hold fast that which is good" (1Th 5:21), "let God be true, but every man a liar" (Rom 3:4), and "blessed is that man that maketh the LORD his trust, and respecteth not the proud, nor such as turn aside to lies" (Ps 40:4). A bible study process that puts no trust in the opinions of men and relies only on the data in God's word conforms to these verses.

As has been noted, scripture says, "*it is* better to trust in the LORD than to put confidence in man" (Ps 118:8). Still, many seek to learn what the Bible says by turning to non-Bible sources and weighing the opinions of men. But the practice of relying on the teachings of men was rejected by Jesus and it should also be rejected today. Moreover, if opinions from non-Bible sources are held in esteem, people tend to drop their guard.

For example, if someone says world-class Bible scholars believe a certain idea, many people will assume the idea is true and think there is no reason to subject it to biblical scrutiny. Yet verses like, "let God be true, but every man a liar" make no exception for world-class scholars or other elites.

The LORD said, "them that honor me I will honor" (1Sa 2:30). If we want the LORD to honor us, we must first honor him. We honor him when we exercise a high regard for his word. This takes more than just knowing what it says. James wrote to the beloved brethren who had been begotten "with the word of truth" (Jas 1:18) and in his letter he told them "be ye doers of the word, and not hearers only, deceiving your own selves" (Jas 1:22). People who hear God's word and do not act in accord with what it says, cause themselves to be deceived.

The Pillar and Ground of the Truth

Paul talked of "the house of God, which is the church of the living God, the pillar and ground of the truth" (1Tm 3:15), yet some restate his words and say, '*the church is the pillar and ground of the truth.*' What happens when scripture is edited in this way? In the verse, "the house of God" is "the church of the living God" and "the living God" is "the pillar and ground of the truth." In the restated version, "the church" is said to be "the pillar and ground of the truth," i.e., the church replaces the living God as the fixed point of reference. But, Paul would not say this because he knew those in the church, including church leaders, could be in error. He made this clear in verses like, "O foolish Galatians, who hath bewitched you" (Gal 3:1), and in his criticism of Peter and others who "walked not uprightly according to the truth of the gospel" (Gal 2:14), and in his rebuke of the church in Corinth (cf. 1Cor 15:12).

Whenever the church strays from the standard of the word of God, it runs into trouble. Jesus provided a critical lesson on this in the Book of Revelation. Read the letters to the seven churches and consider what caused these churches to become the targets of a whole series of stern rebukes from Jesus (cf. Rv 1:4, 11, & 20, 2:1-3:22).

When people let the church be their measure of truth, they are failing to obey a directive that was repeated by Jesus seven times. He said, "he that hath an ear, let him **hear what the Spirit saith unto the churches"** (Rv 2:7, et al.).

Jesus did not say his followers should hear what the church says. He directed those who have an ear, to hear what the Spirit says *to* the churches. So, what is said by those who are in the church must not come before the word of God.

Case Study: The Case of Jesus Wept

The Shortest Verse

In Chapter 11 of the fourth gospel, verse 35 is comprised of just two words, "Jesus wept." This is the shortest verse in the Bible. These words occur in the context of Jesus' visit to the tomb of his friend Lazarus, which leads many to read various emotions into the passage and causes people to say things like:

A. *Jesus cried because he missed his friend Lazarus and he shared Mary and Martha's burden of grief,* or
B. *Jesus' tears show he identified with all of us who have ever lost someone they loved.*

Get a Bible and consider the words "Jesus wept" in their context. Make some notes on what you think the context of this passage teaches us. Then return to this case study and see if the evidence in scripture supports either of the common views noted above or if scripture intended to teach something else.

The Case of Jesus Wept

A Time to Mourn?

Visiting a tomb where mourners are weeping could easily move one to tears, and the grief of Mary and Martha surely tugged at the heart of Jesus. Does scripture suggest this is why he wept? The verses below present Jesus' tears in context:

"a certain *man* was sick, *named* Lazarus, of Bethany... When Jesus heard *that,* he said, This sickness is not unto death, but for the glory of God, that the Son of God might be glorified thereby. Now Jesus loved Martha, and her sister, and Lazarus. When he had heard therefore that he was sick, he abode two days still in the same place where he was. Then after that saith he to *his* disciples, Let us go into Judea... Our friend Lazarus sleepeth; but I go, that I may awake him out of sleep. Then said his disciples, Lord, if he sleep, he shall do well. Howbeit Jesus spake of his death: but they thought that he had spoken of taking of rest in sleep. Then said Jesus unto them plainly, Lazarus is dead. And I am glad for your sakes that I was not there, to the intent ye may believe; nevertheless let us go unto him... Then Martha, as soon as she heard that Jesus was coming, went and met him: but Mary sat *still* in the house. Then said Martha unto Jesus, Lord, if thou hadst been here, my brother had not died... she went her way, and called Mary her sister... Then when Mary was come where Jesus was, and saw him, she fell down at his feet, saying unto him, Lord, if thou hadst been here, my brother would not have died. When Jesus therefore saw her weeping, and the Jews also weeping which came with her, he groaned in the spirit, and was troubled, and said, Where have ye laid him? They said unto him, Lord, come and see. Jesus wept. Then said the Jews, Behold how he loved him! And some of them said, Could not this man, which opened the eyes of the blind, have caused that even this man should not have died?" (Fourth gospel 11:1-37)

This shows the words "Jesus wept" are not to be compared to the tears we shed when we go to the funeral of a friend or loved one.

Unlike us when we go to a memorial service and unlike the people who were mourning the death of Lazarus, Jesus was not there for a funeral. He was there to raise Lazarus from the dead! Jesus told the disciples, "our friend Lazarus sleepeth; but I go, that I may awake him out of sleep." Then it says, "Jesus spake of his death." Jesus knew Lazarus would rise from the dead and his knowledge of this needs to inform our view of this passage.

Taking account of his purpose will keep us from making the same false assumption about his tears as the Jews who saw him weep. They said, "behold how he loved him." They assumed Jesus wept because he loved Lazarus, but they did not know what Jesus was going to do, so this inference was based on ignorance. However, when he told his disciples, "Lazarus is dead" he added, "I am glad for your sakes that I was not there, to the intent ye may believe." Jesus' use of the word "glad" in talking about the death of Lazarus should grab our attention. He looked forward to what would occur because Lazarus' death and his being raised would work together for the disciples' benefit.

When Did Jesus Weep?

Jesus loved Lazarus (cf. Fourth gospel 11:5). Yet, he did not weep when:

- he heard Lazarus was sick (Fourth gospel 11:3),
- he knew Lazarus was dead (Fourth gospel 11:14),
- he met with grieving Martha (Fourth gospel 11:20),
- he met with grieving Mary and "saw her weeping, and the Jews also weeping which came with her" (Fourth gospel 11:33).

Still, many think identification with the mourners prompted Jesus to weep, even though the evidence does not fit this assumption.

He did not cry when he saw Martha or when Mary and the Jews came to him weeping. So, what brought on his tears when he eventually did cry?

The scriptures only tell us about one other time when Jesus wept in public. Luke 19:41-44 gives us the report on the time Jesus rode into Jerusalem on a colt:

"when he was come near, he beheld the city, and wept over it, Saying, If thou hadst known, even thou, at least in this thy day, the things which belong unto thy peace! but now they are hid from thine eyes. For the days shall come upon thee, that thine enemies shall cast a trench about thee, and compass thee round, and keep thee in on every side, And shall lay thee even with the ground, and thy children within thee; and they shall not leave in thee one stone upon another; because thou knewest not the time of thy visitation."

They should have known the time of their visitation but they had missed it. Their ignorance prompted his tears on that day.

What caused him to weep when he wept at the tomb of Lazarus? It was the response of the Jews to his question!

He asked them, "where have ye laid him? They responded, Lord, come and see" (Fourth gospel 11:34). At that point, Jesus wept.

Their answer to his question is what moved him to tears. But why? Here is what scripture says next:

"Then said the Jews, Behold how he loved him! And some of them said, Could not this man, which opened the eyes of the blind, have caused that even this man should not have died?" (Fourth gospel 11:36-37)

Later, we will see how their words contributed to Jesus' weeping. At this point, however, let us consider a time when Jesus heard someone say words that triggered a completely different reaction.

A Necessary Detour

Jesus once said, "I have not found so great faith, no, not in Israel" (Mt 8:10, Lk 7:9). What led him to say this? It was hearing the words of a centurion with a sick servant who he wanted Jesus to heal.

While Jesus was making his way to the centurion's house to heal the servant, the centurion sent word to Jesus. Luke 7:6-9 tells us what that message was and what happened when Jesus heard it:

"Lord, trouble not thyself: for I am not worthy that thou shouldest enter under my roof: Wherefore neither thought I myself worthy to come unto thee: but say in a word, and my servant shall be healed. For I also am a man set under authority, having under me soldiers, and I say unto one, Go, and he goeth; and to another, Come, and he cometh; and to my servant, Do this, and he doeth *it*. When Jesus heard these things, he marveled at him, and turned him about, and said unto the people that followed him, I say unto you, I have not found so great faith, no, not in Israel."

The centurion realized he and Jesus had something in common, for he said, "I also am a man set under authority." Being a man under authority, his word had power and his orders were carried out because of the one who he represented, and in his case that was Caesar. He recognized Jesus was also a man under authority and concluded Jesus could say the word and his servant would be healed. People who help the sick physically interact with them to give aid, comfort, etc. However, miracles overcome the things of this world, so physical interaction or nearness is not required. The authority to do miracles is not of this world. Thus, anyone who is under authority and doing miracles is not bound by the rules of this world. Follow this reasoning through to its logical conclusion. This tells us Jesus did not have to be physically present to bless someone with a miracle. He only needed to give the order. Still, the centurion's logic is not what impressed Jesus; it was his faith. He acted on that reasoning and sent word for Jesus not to come, and showed he truly respected the power and authority of God.

Why Did Jesus Go to the Tomb?

Jesus did not go to the tomb to be close enough for Lazarus to hear him say, "Lazarus, come forth" (Fourth gospel 11:43). Since he was dead, getting closer to Lazarus' corpse would not increase the chance of Jesus' voice being heard.

Jesus had to go and raise Lazarus in the presence of his disciples for this miracle to impact *their* belief. Remember, Jesus told them, "Lazarus is dead" (Fourth gospel 11:14) and said, "I am glad for your sakes that I was not there, to the intent ye may believe" (v. 15).

He raised Lazarus so his disciples would believe. Still, they were not the only ones who would witness this miracle. Jesus had not reached the town when Mary and the Jews who were weeping with her went out to meet him:

"Jesus therefore saw her weeping, and the Jews also weeping which came with her, he groaned in the spirit, and was troubled, And said, Where have ye laid him? They said unto him, Lord, come and see. Jesus wept. Then said the Jews, Behold how he loved him! And some of them said, Could not this man, which opened the eyes of the blind, have caused that even this man should not have died? Jesus therefore again groaning in himself cometh to the grave" (Fourth gospel 11:33-38).

How should the Jews have responded when Jesus asked, "where have ye laid him?" If they knew he had the power to stop death, this should have led them to say, *'you do not need to go there, just say the word and he shall be raised.'*

Their words prove they knew Jesus represented a power and authority that was not of this world. Yet, they did not follow this to its logical conclusion and act in faith as the centurion had done.

No, Not in Israel

The centurion said Jesus did not need to come, but the Jews said, "Lord, come and see." The centurion had less evidence to go on than they did. They had a heritage built on the word of God, he did not. Also, they knew Jesus had opened the eyes of the blind and it is likely they knew of other miracles as well. He did so many that people made note of it. "Many of the people believed on him, and said, When Christ cometh, will he do more miracles than these which this man hath done?" (Fourth gospel 7:31) Beyond this, they had other reasons to know Jesus had been sent by God.

In his teaching and his confrontations with the religious leaders, Jesus honored the authority of God. Moreover, every person who obeyed God knew Jesus was honoring God. This principle was taught by Jesus when he said:

"My doctrine is not mine, but his that sent me. **If any man will do his will, he shall know of the doctrine, whether it be of God, or** whether **I speak of myself**" (Fourth gospel 7:16-17).

Despite knowing what Jesus had done and taught, when he asked them where they had laid Lazarus, the Jews offered to show him the tomb. Only then did Jesus weep. It was a sad moment, but it may be wrong to assume he wept simply because of sadness over their lack of faith. Men shed tears for lots of reasons. Some weep for joy at weddings. Indignation moves others to tears at injustices like human trafficking. So, let us look again to see if scripture has more to say on this.

Overcoming the Language Barrier

Scripture was written mostly in Hebrew and Greek. We who use an English Bible can often benefit by looking at the words used by the writers of scripture. In the "Jesus wept" passage, the words "groaned," and "groaning" were used before Jesus asked where Lazarus was laid. After the Jews acknowledged he had the power to stop death it says, "Jesus <u>therefore</u> again groaning in himself cometh to the grave" (Fourth gospel 11:38). If we relate these uses of groan to other verses with the English word groan we might get a wrong impression if we do not check the source text.

The Greek word that is translated as "groaned" and "groaning" in the passage in question was used in only three other places. Twice it was translated as "straightly charged" and once as "murmured against" (Mt 9:30, Mk 1:43 & 14:5). It means to be moved with indignation, to be angry, and to sternly charge.

The verses where the word was translated as "straightly charged" tell of Jesus giving a command to men who then went out and directly disobeyed him (Mt 9:30-31 & Mk 1:43-45). This Greek word was only used one other time. It was when "some that had indignation within themselves" had "murmured against" a woman who gave Jesus an expensive gift (Mk 14:4-5). Since we intend to let the word of God lead us, then we ought to take account of the fact that a response of "indignation" is linked to this Greek word elsewhere in scripture.

Thus, in the Jesus wept passage the Greek word translated as "groaned" and "groaning" may indicate Jesus was moved with indignation at the Jews. Why? Because they knew he did miracles but, in spite of this, they did not act in faith.

[Researching the words used by the God-inspired writers of scripture may sound difficult. However, the internet offers access to various tools that make this a relatively easy task. Links to free Bible tools can be found at www.ABetterBibleStudyMethod.com.]

The Conclusion of the Case of Jesus Wept

Arguably, the greatest public miracle of Jesus' earthly ministry is the raising of Lazarus. Jesus knew it was going to happen before he went to Lazarus' tomb. Beyond this, we are told the moment Jesus wept, and it was when he heard the response of the Jews to his question, "where have ye laid him?" (Fourth gospel 11:34) This, combined with the other data reported in scripture, indicates it was their ignorance and/or their lack of faith that moved him to tears, and not grief or identification with the sadness of the mourners. Therefore, those who say things like, 'Jesus wept over the death of his friend,' are not speaking the word of God faithfully.

Jeremiah 23:28 is where the LORD said, "he that hath my word, let him speak my word faithfully." So, how can we show respect for the counsel of God that is in this verse?

When we speak and think on biblical issues, we should seek to conform our words and our thinking to the words and the thoughts that come from God's inspired writers and teachers in scripture. Developing a habit of seeking to do this as much as possible will help us to become better at speaking the word of God faithfully.

The end of the Case of Jesus Wept

Chapter 7 – According to the Scriptures

What did Able do to offend Cain? How did Jesus offend men in his day? How can we know what matters in scripture are the more important ones? These questions, and the danger posed by double standards, will be addressed in this chapter.

Milk Versus Meat

The consumption of information is sometimes pictured as eating and information is sometimes portrayed as food. We see this in verses where milk and meat were used to picture the difference between concepts that are easily digested and those that take time and thought to comprehend. Here is one such passage:

"I, brethren, could not speak unto you as unto spiritual, but as unto carnal, *even* as unto babes in Christ. I have fed you with milk, and not with meat: for hitherto ye were not able to *bear it,* neither yet now are ye able. For ye are yet carnal: for whereas *there is* among you envying, and strife, and divisions, are ye not carnal, and walk as men? For while one saith, I am of Paul; and another, I *am* of Apollos; are ye not carnal" (1Cor 3:1-4).

They were not able to handle teaching that qualified as meat, yet they were still brethren. So, if people cannot handle what scripture teaches on an issue, it does not mean they are not true followers of Jesus. Scripture indicates their inability to handle meat resulted from a willingness to identify with only part of the truth.

At that point, the whole truth was not their authority. They elevated their judgment over God's will when they decided to identify with one of God's messengers, but not another. The passage below shows why this was an unreasonable thing to do.

"Who then is Paul, and who is Apollos, but ministers by whom ye believed, even as the Lord gave to every man? I have planted, Apollos watered; but God gave the increase. So then neither is he that planteth anything, neither he that watereth; but God that giveth the increase" (1Cor 3:5-7).

The authority of God was the unifying factor. Both men were teaching God's word. Therefore, there was no reason for anyone to assume either one of them had greater authority than the other. "God gave the increase." To go by what is right in the sight of God would require people to honor the teaching of both men equally, because the combination of their efforts is what God used to give the increase. Planting and watering are different functions that occur at different times, but they are unified in the result, for they work together to produce fruit, and both are needed.

If we judge according to God's goal of producing increase, then the work of Paul and Apollos will be seen to be equally necessary, and we will realize how God works these things together for good. Of course, the planting and watering of 1 Corinthians 3:6-7 is not about physical seeds or H_2O. In scripture, the word of God was portrayed both by seeds (Mt 13:19-23) and by water (Eph 5:26). So, if Paul was planting the word of God and Apollos was watering with the word of God, then it is easy to see why Paul said, "God gave the increase" (1Cor 3:6).

Acting as if God's message can be divided against itself was shown to be a foolish idea earlier in the same letter:

"Now this I say, that every one of you saith, I am of Paul; and I of Apollos; and I of Cephas; and I of Christ. Is Christ divided?" (1Cor 1:12-13)

Jesus said, "I am the way, the truth, and the life." The truth is not divided against itself. So, claiming to be of Christ based on a *part* of the truth from his messengers will not work because Jesus said, "he that receiveth whomsoever I send receiveth me; and he that receiveth me receiveth him that sent me" (Fourth gospel 13:20).

In Corinth, they had pit one messenger of God against another, and this type of reasoning still produces divisions among those in the church. Self-willed people grant themselves the authority to make judgments based on their opinion and, as a result, they take a pick and choose approach to scripture. In any case, the two most important things a person can learn are the authority of God (1Chr 29:11-12, et al.) and the authority of God's word (1Pt 1:25, et al.).

Milk and Meat Portray Levels of Knowledge

Milk and meat also appear as word pictures in Hebrews 5:12-14 when the holy brethren were rebuked with these words:

"the time ye ought to be teachers, ye have need that one teach you again which *be* the first principles of the oracles of God; and are become such as have need of milk, and not of strong meat. For everyone that useth milk *is* unskillful in the word of righteousness: for he is a babe. But strong meat belongeth to them that are of full age, even those who by reason of use have their senses exercised to discern both good and evil."

This was said to people who had been in the church long enough that the writer said they should have been teachers by this point. So, we should realize that the length of time someone has been a follower of Jesus does not equate to a deeper understanding of God's word. [See Hebrews 5:12 & 6:1-3 for further proof of this.]

Rather than "grow in grace, and in the knowledge of our Lord and Savior Jesus Christ" (2Pt 3:18), they did the opposite and regressed to the point where they became "such as have need of milk." The picture was they became intellectual babies who could not digest "strong meat." Being told this would not have made those brethren feel good about themselves. But being made aware of their state might provoke them to change.

While hearing this might hurt the feelings of those brethren, God led the writer of Hebrews to highlight this problem. Undoubtedly, this challenge was meant to wake them up and encourage them to change and start growing.

The Word of God Versus the Teachings of Men

The men in groups such as the Pharisees, Sadducees, scribes, chief priests, etc., were formally trained and they knew the words of scripture. But they did not get the message that was conveyed by the words. What caused this? It was because they let tradition, i.e., the teachings of men, shape their view of scripture.

Jesus publicly berated the scribes and Pharisees and told them "ye reject the commandment of God, **that ye may keep your own tradition**" (Mk 7:9). Their beliefs came before God's word [much like the statements of beliefs and creeds of many groups]. This is why Jesus also said they made the word of God void by their tradition (cf. Mk 7:23). The misrepresentation of God's word that resulted from people being taught to trust the traditions of men was something Jesus challenged repeatedly. A prime example of this can be seen in the stark contrast of Jesus' words that show up in Matthew 5 as the opening words of the following six pairs of verses:

- "ye have heard that it was said by them of old time... "
- "but I say unto you... " (Mt 5:21 & 22),

- "ye have heard that it was said by them of old time... "
- "but I say unto you... " (Mt 5:27 & 28),

- "it hath been said... "
- "but I say unto you... " (Mt 5:31 & 32),

- "ye have heard that it hath been said by them of old time... "
- "but I say unto you... " (Mt 5:33 & 34),

- "ye have heard that it hath been said... "
- "but I say unto you... " (Mt 5:38 & 39),

- "ye have heard that it hath been said... "
- "but I say unto you... " (Mt 5:43 & 44).

Take a moment to read all of these verses and you will see Jesus contrasting error and truth on a wide range of issues. The words quoted above show he was putting the spotlight on the thing that caused the errors. It was the practice of quoting the words of men and getting people to put confidence in them. Jesus showed it is wrong to rely on beliefs that may be commonly accepted or that were believed by people who lived long ago. Listening to men is not the problem. Giving authority to their teachings is the problem. When the words of men are cited to sell people on an idea today, it is fair for us to wonder why are people being encouraged to trust in non-Bible sources?

Jesus stated, "I have not spoken of myself; but the Father which sent me, he gave me a commandment, what I should say, and what I should speak" (Fourth gospel 12:49). Jesus honored the authority of God. He did not honor the teachings of men.

Honoring the Words of Men Results in a Double Standard

As the bullet list above shows, judging by what others say leads people to be misled on a whole range of issues, for "a little leaven leaveneth the whole lump" (Gal 5:9). This principle lets us know that if people allow the teachings of men to be their measure of truth on *any* issue, they have already agreed to accept a substitute for the authority of God's word. If they do it in one instance, they can do it anytime they please, so God's word is not their standard.

In Jesus' day, the opinions of men had been presented as if they were true, but they did not accurately reflect what scripture taught. Since men can misunderstand God's word, believing something just because it has been said by others, now or in the past, is not a wise thing to do. Conversely, we can rely on what scripture says because the writers were inspired by God. It all comes down to the issue of source. Consider the source!

If God is the source of a message, then anyone who is accurately conveying that message is speaking the truth. When Jesus said, "but I say unto you... " in the passages above, he presented a different way to understand those issues. Those who heard him had a choice to make: keep following the "it hath been said" crowd or stop doing so, switch, and get in the habit of letting God's word be their only standard.

An Exercise in Discernment

If scripture says, "divers weights, *and* divers measures, both of them *are* alike abomination to the LORD" (Prv 20:10), how should we take these words? People who think this condemns stealing say, *'dishonest merchants used altered weights to deceive customers into paying for more than they received.'* Charging for more than is delivered is a form of stealing. But is this really what the verse is talking about?

The word "divers" is not simply an old spelling of the word diverse. "Divers" expresses a difference in quantity. It means an indefinite number, not a great number but more than one, i.e., several. Diverse is all about a difference in quality. It means differing from one another, i.e., dissimilar, distinct, separate, unlike.

Does the verse require us to conclude it is talking about stealing? No. The words steal, cheat, or theft do not appear in the verse. So, why assume this is the topic of the verse? Does the context suggest this verse is about merchants who cheat their customers? Not at all. The verse before says, "who can say, I have made my heart clean, I am pure from my sin?" (Prv 20:9) The verse after says, "even a child is known by his doings, whether his work *be* pure, and whether *it be* right" (Prv 20:11).

Scripture says, "thou shalt not steal" (Ex 20:15), "ye shall not steal" (Lev 19:11), "let him that stole steal no more" (Eph 4:28), etc. The word "abomination" was not used in any verse where the words steal, stole, thief, theft, or rob appear. So, why are "divers weights, *and* divers measures" an abomination to the LORD? If we think this is all about merchants using shaved weights to cheat people, where would that leave us? Not many things are called an abomination in scripture. Since stealing itself is not called an abomination but "divers weights, *and* divers measures" are, is the verse telling us using shaved weights is uniquely despicable? This cannot be. So, the verse must refer to something else, and the word abomination lets us know this involves a heavyweight issue.

What Do the Words Mean?

"Divers weights, *and* divers measures" is about having more than one weight or measure, for "divers" means more than one. At a basic level, therefore, <u>this is talking about inconsistent standards</u>. A godly perspective is not founded on the cares of this world, so Proverbs 20:10 is likely talking about something more important than petty theft. How do inconsistent standards impact the things of God? If "all scripture *is* given by inspiration of God" (2Ti 3:16), a regard for God's authority will require a consistent standard when we deal with scripture. Still, far too often, an inconsistent regard is shown for the words that were inspired by God.

We employ a double standard if we say the Bible is God's word, but we dismiss verses that conflict with our views. If we assume we can decide when scripture must be respected and when it can be ignored, we are disregarding God's authority. This practice is dangerous because scripture indicates an inconsistent approach keeps people from a proper understanding of God's word. Let us take a look at several instances of this.

Weight and Measure

Consider the term "divers weights." If this is not speaking about physical weights, what does it mean? Jesus said something when he was rebuking the scribes and Pharisees that can help on this:

"Woe unto you, *ye* blind guides, which say, Whosoever shall swear by the temple, it is nothing; but whosoever shall swear by the gold of the temple, he is a debtor! *Ye* fools and blind: for whether is **greater**, the gold, or the temple that sanctifieth the gold? And, Whosoever shall swear by the altar, it is nothing; but whosoever sweareth by the gift that is upon it, he is guilty. *Ye* fools and blind: for whether *is* **greater**, the gift, or the altar that sanctifieth the gift? Whoso therefore shall swear by the altar, sweareth by it, and by all things thereon. And whoso shall swear by the temple, sweareth by it, and by him that dwelleth therein. And he that shall swear by heaven, sweareth by the throne of God, and by him that sitteth thereon. Woe unto you, scribes and Pharisees, hypocrites! for ye pay tithe of mint and anise and cumin, and have omitted the **weightier** *matters* of the law, judgment, mercy, and faith: these ought ye to have done, and not to leave the other undone. *Ye* blind guides, which strain at a gnat, and swallow a camel" (Mt 23:16-24).

They did not give proper weight to the issues. As we saw when we previously looked at verse 23, rather than stick to God's word, they did what was right in their own eyes and they taught others to do as they did. They were not always wrong, for right after Jesus said, "ye pay tithe of mint and anise and cumin" he said, "these ought ye to have done." However, they were inconsistent in their regard for scripture.

Those experts said, "the gold," "the gift," and a "tithe of mint and anise and cumin" were what mattered. This put "the temple that sanctifieth the gold," "the altar that sanctifieth the gift," and "the weightier *matters* of the law" in an inferior position. Trust in their own opinion led them to "strain at a gnat, and swallow a camel," for in making their own opinion the measure of truth, they made God's word void.

A reversal of priorities resulted from switching the standard by which truth is judged. Their unwillingness to let scripture be the sole measure of what was important, i.e., weightier, meant they did not have a consistent standard of truth and this caused them to take a pick and choose approach to what scripture said.

[Notice, "strain at a gnat, and swallow a camel" was not a critique of people who seek to pay attention to the details in God's word. It was about men who ignore or fail to obey what scripture says.]

How about the word "measure?" If we looked for verses with this word, we might notice when Jesus said, "take heed what ye hear: with what measure ye mete, it shall be measured to you" (Mk 4:24). Here the word had nothing to do with a physical measure. When we refer to the measure of a man's character, others know this is a non-physical measure because the context clues them in, as it does in phrases like "the measure of faith" (Rom 12:3).

While the idea of physical weights and measures may seem to fit Proverbs 20:10 at first glance, upon closer inspection that idea is ruled out by both the immediate context and the rest of scripture.

Balance

Proverbs 20:23 says, "divers weights *are* an abomination unto the LORD; and a false balance *is* not good." So, how was "balance" used in scripture?

In interpreting the handwriting on the wall, Daniel told the king, "thou art weighed in the balances, and art found wanting" (Dan 5:27), and it is clear those "balances" were not physical. Moreover, in the Bible, we find these other uses of the word "balance:"

- "Oh that my grief were thoroughly weighed, and my calamity laid in the balances together" (Job 6:2),
- "Let me be weighed in an even balance, that God may know mine integrity" (Job 31:6),
- "Who hath measured the waters in the hollow of his hand, and meted out heaven with the span, and comprehended the dust of the earth in a measure, and weighed the mountains in scales, and the hills in a balance?" (Isa 40:12)

The word "balance" was used in a physical sense when Jeremiah bought a field. He said, "I subscribed the evidence, and sealed *it,* and took witnesses, and weighed *him* the money in the balances" (Jer 32:10). But the meaning of words is not always obvious, so it is good to get in the habit of taking the time to check the context.

Weightier Matters

God's word should carry more weight than the words of men, yet too often, people are swayed by the views of others. This is why the scholars of Jesus' day had an erroneous view of scripture. Here again is a portion of Matthew 23:15-24 for you to consider:

"Woe unto you, *ye* blind guides, which say, Whosoever shall swear by the temple, it is nothing; but whosoever shall swear by the gold of the temple... whether is greater, the gold, or the temple that sanctifieth the gold?... ye pay tithe of mint and anise and cumin, and have omitted the weightier *matters* of the law, judgment, mercy, and faith: these ought ye to have done, and not to leave the other undone."

When it comes to weighing various matters, something cannot be greater than the thing that sanctifies it. Also, notice what this is telling us about the Old Testament. Since "the weightier *matters* of the law" are "judgment, mercy, and faith," these three ideas are taught by God's law. Some see the law as being harsh or out of date, but this is not how Jesus saw it. Judgment, mercy, and faith are neither harsh nor out of date. To see the law that way is to miss "the weightier *matters* of the law." Regardless, even if one does not think of faith as being a matter of the law, Jesus' words prove it is!

If men give more weight to their own opinion than to God's word, their judgment acts as a false balance, since it is tilted in favor of their own view.

The Problem with Double Standards

If weights and measures are not a problem by themselves, why would more than one ["divers"] of them be an abomination?

Consider physical weights. One pound is a standard of weight and anything that is not one pound differs from the standard.

So, even physical weights show truth demands there be only one standard. Having a double standard will mean our weights and measures are not consistent.

Proverbs 11:1 says, "a false balance *is* abomination to the LORD: but a just weight *is* his delight." Here we see two methods, one is "false" and one is "just" and they have vastly different outcomes. The principle in this verse does apply to physical things, but it also applies to how a jury ought to weigh the evidence in a trial.

Earlier we saw where Jeremiah 23:30 pictures a more dangerous type of theft – "I *am* against the prophets, saith the LORD, that steal my words everyone from his neighbor." How were they stolen?

Throughout Jeremiah 23, we find the LORD rebuking the pastors, priests, and prophets who were promoting the ideas of men while they claimed to be conveying what the LORD had said. It starts in verses 1-2:

> "Woe be unto the pastors that destroy and scatter the sheep of my pasture! saith the LORD. Therefore, thus saith the LORD God of Israel against the pastors that feed my people; Ye have scattered my flock, and driven them away"

The LORD continued his rebuke of those religious leaders in the verses that led up to his accusation of stealing (in verse 30):

- "both prophet and priest are profane; yea, in my house have I found their wickedness, saith the LORD" (Jer 23:11),

- "thus saith the LORD of hosts, Hearken not unto the words of the prophets that prophesy unto you: they make you vain: they speak a vision of their own heart, *and* not out of the mouth of the LORD. They say still unto them that despise me, The LORD hath said, Ye shall have peace; and they say unto everyone that walketh after the imagination of his own heart, No evil shall come upon you" (Jer 23:16-17),
- "I have not sent these prophets, yet they ran: I have not spoken to them, yet they prophesied. But if they had stood in my counsel, and had caused my people to hear my words, then they should have turned them from their evil way, and from the evil of their doings" (Jer 23:21-22).

The people were deceived because they were listening to men who gave their own words authority – "they speak a vision of their own heart, *and* not out of the mouth of the LORD." Notice also, "they say unto everyone that walketh after the imagination of his own heart, No evil shall come upon you" (Jer 23:17). Here, men who claimed to speak for God offered unconditional promises to those who did not walk after the LORD. But they had no right to do so.

They ascribed to the words of men an honor due only to the words of God. Scripture tells us how things would have been different if those leaders had respected the authority of the word of the LORD: "but if they had stood in my counsel, and had caused my people to hear my words, then they should have turned them from their evil way, and from the evil of their doings" (Jer 23:22). By substituting their own words for the words of the LORD, they robbed people of the opportunity of being changed by his living and active word.

No one should think Jeremiah's warnings only applied in his day, for Romans 15:4 says, "whatsoever things were written aforetime were written for our learning." Thus, it is worth our time to think on the admonitions that are found in Jeremiah 23.

Abomination, According to Who?

Finding other verses that use the term "abomination to the LORD" is also helpful. Here are just two of many such verses:

- "the sacrifice of the wicked *is* an abomination to the LORD: but the prayer of the upright *is* his delight" (Prv 15:8),
- "the way of the wicked *is* an abomination unto the LORD: but he loveth him that followeth after righteousness" (Prv 15:9).

Knowing the LORD's view on these things helps us to understand other passages. For example, scripture states:

"the LORD had respect unto Abel and to his offering: But unto Cain and to his offering he had not respect" (Gen 4:4-5).

Because "Cain brought of the fruit of the ground an offering unto the LORD" (Gen 4:3), many assume he offered the wrong kind of gift. Yet, rather than make inferences, why not consult scripture? If we took the time to do a search on offerings, we would find this verse, "hath the LORD *as great* delight in burnt offerings and sacrifices, as in obeying the voice of the LORD? Behold, to obey *is* better than sacrifice" (1Sa 15:22). The problem was not what Cain offered. It was the one who made the offering. Consider this description, "Cain, *who* was of that wicked one, and slew his brother. And wherefore slew he him? **Because his own works were evil, and his brother's righteous**" (1Jo 3:12). Cain killed Abel because of Abel's righteous works. Cain's works were evil, so by doing right, Abel was making Cain look bad and this offense cost him his life! [Note: the Jewish leaders took offense at Jesus and killed him for the same reason, i.e., his righteousness hardened their heart.]

The LORD had no respect "unto Cain and to his offering" because he was wicked. To assume a different type of offering would make a difference is to ignore the fact that an offering does not change a person. To change, an evildoer must repent. Cain did not, and "the sacrifice of the wicked *is* an abomination to the LORD" (Prv 15:8). So, the LORD could not respect Cain nor *any* gift from him. The LORD said, "if thou doest well, shalt thou not be accepted?" (Gen 4:7) Yet, Cain decided to kill Abel instead. His "works were evil, and his brother's righteous." This explains the difference between the offerings of these two men that was noted here: "by faith Abel offered unto God a more excellent sacrifice than Cain" (Heb 11:4). Thus, Abel's offering was "more excellent," not due to the type of gift he offered, but because he offered his gift "by faith."

What Hurts People More?

As has been noted, the term "abomination to the LORD" is not tied to stealing or theft in commerce. So, Proverbs 20:10 must be describing a problem that is deeper than this.

Proverbs 6:16-19 tells us, "a false witness *that* speaketh lies, and he that soweth discord among brethren" are "an abomination" to the LORD. Who qualifies as a false witness? How about the men who spoke "a vision of their own heart, *and* not out of the mouth of the LORD?" (Jer 23:16)

What about those who do the other things noted in Jeremiah 23, like those who the LORD said, "cause my people to err by their lies, and by their lightness?" (Jer 23:32) Ponder what we are told about the extreme action Jesus took when he:

"went into the temple, and began to cast out them that sold therein, and them that bought; Saying unto them, It is written, My house is the house of prayer: but ye have made it a den of thieves" (Lk 19:45-46).

Why did he do this? It does not say people were overcharged, and Jesus also cast out "them that bought." So, perhaps it is wrong to assume he took this action simply to protest price gouging.

However, if those thieves had been stealing the word of the LORD, then he cast them out because they were doing something much worse than making obscene profits.

Written Law Versus Oral Tradition?

Earlier we saw where Jesus debunked beliefs that were promoted based on phrases like "it was said," etc. (Mt 5:21-44) The teachings of men that were cited as having authority are sometimes called *'the oral law,'* yet the very idea of an *'oral law'* is a problem.

Scripture gave the law. If the traditions of men are presented as another source of law, then people are given a double standard. The way to avoid this trap is to stick to the standard of God's word.

Jesus taught the written word of God is the right measure of truth. For starters, consider his words in this statement:

"Think not that I am come to destroy the law, or the prophets: I am not come to destroy, but to fulfill. For verily I say unto you, Till heaven and earth pass, one jot or one tittle shall in no wise pass from the law, till all be fulfilled" (Mt 5:17-18).

This taught regard for scripture's details since the jot and tittle are the smallest characters in the Hebrew language that was used to write the scriptures. This did not apply to any oral hand-me-down teachings because characters are not used in spoken language.

We use words to speak. We use characters to write. Thus, Jesus' statement applied to the written scriptures.

Jesus and his apostles did teach orally, but all their references to scripture showed the authority for their teaching was the written word of God. Men will often promote trust in the teachings of men. Jesus and the apostles never did. At times, they cited things that had been said by men, yet they never cited them as an authority. In Matthew 5:21-44, Jesus noted what men had said, yet it did not mean those men were correct. This was obvious in that instance. Scripture is a true record. However, not all the statements of men in scripture are true. Consider this statement, "one of themselves, *even* a prophet of their own, said, The Cretians *are* always liars, evil beasts, slow bellies" (Titus 1:12). This was said by a prophet from another group, not by a follower of Jesus. Did Paul quote this to ascribe authority to a non-scriptural source? No. Yet, after saying "the Cretians *are* always liars," Paul wrote "this witness is true" (Titus 1:13). Did Paul think everyone from Crete was a non-stop liar?

The only other time the "Cretians" are mentioned in scripture is in Acts 2:11, where they were identified as "Cretes" and were among the "devout men, out of every nation under heaven." They heard the apostles on the day of Pentecost and said, "we do hear them speak in our tongues the wonderful works of God" (cf. Acts 2:5 & 11). They did not lie when they said this. Thus, the claim, "the Cretians *are* always liars" is not a true statement. So, why would the words, "this witness is true" follow that quote?

Paul wrote this to Titus, "for this cause left I thee in Crete, that thou shouldest set in order the things that are wanting, and ordain elders in every city" (Titus 1:5). If he thought all Cretians were liars, he would not have told Titus to ordain some of them, because he said candidates for ordination should be "blameless" (Titus 1:6, et al.).

Paul expected that the ones who were ordained would "be able by sound doctrine both to exhort and to convince the gainsayers" (Titus 1:9). He also went on to note the problems those "gainsayers" were causing, and he said their teaching had to be overcome with sound doctrine:

"there are many unruly and vain talkers and deceivers, specially they of the circumcision: Whose mouths must be stopped, who subvert whole houses, teaching things which they ought not, for filthy lucre's sake. One of themselves, *even* a prophet of their own, said, The Cretians *are* always liars, evil beasts, slow bellies. This witness is true. Wherefore rebuke them sharply, that they may be sound in the faith; Not giving heed to Jewish fables, and commandments of men, that turn from the truth" (Titus 1:10-14).

Paul told Titus, "vain talkers and deceivers" were teaching things "for filthy lucre's sake" – and one of them even said, "the Cretians *are* always liars." Paul then told Titus to "rebuke them sharply, that they may be sound in the faith; Not giving heed to Jewish fables." What Jewish fables?

In this passage, Paul gave an example of the teaching he wanted Titus to rebuke. Paul stated, "one of themselves, *even* a prophet of their own" had said, "the Cretians *are* always liars, evil beasts, slow bellies." So, this was a "Jewish fable" that was being taught by "vain talkers and deceivers" who were "of the circumcision." Like a man saying all people of a certain race are lazy, this was a slur against the Cretians that was outrageous and obviously false.

Also, consider how plain old common sense shows the idea must be untrue. If people move into Crete, do they become liars? If they move out, do they stop being liars? No, because residency is not what dictates a person's behavior, character does that.

In court, highlighting the fact that a person made a false statement impeaches his or her testimony. This lets people know to be wary of believing other things that have been said by the one who made the false statement. This also goes on outside the courtroom.

If a man makes a prejudiced statement that is patently false, it can be cited to show others they cannot trust what that man has said. If a co-worker states, *'The boss said, ____, I'm telling you it's true,'* how would you take those words? Do they mean the boss spoke the truth? Or was the boss' statement so outrageous that people might doubt the report, so the one reporting this news felt led to testify the quote is accurate? Both scripture and common sense show this second option is what Paul was doing in Titus 1:12 &13.

When Paul said, "this witness is true" he was not affirming what this prophet said. Rather, he was testifying that such ideas were being taught, and giving Titus an example of the kind of teachers he was referring to when he told Titus to rebuke them sharply.

Who was the Good Samaritan?

Another passage that is often misunderstood is Luke 10:25-29, where a "lawyer stood up and tempted" Jesus saying:

"what shall I do to inherit eternal life? He [Jesus] said unto him, What is written in the law? how readest thou? And he answering said, Thou shalt love the Lord thy God with all thy heart, and with all thy soul, and with all thy strength, and with all thy mind; and thy neighbor as thyself. And he [Jesus] said unto him, Thou hast answered right: this do, and thou shalt live. But he, willing to justify himself, said unto Jesus, And who is my neighbor?"

Unlike men who talk down about God's law, Jesus pointed people *to* God's law, not away from it. The lawyer asked, "what shall I do to inherit eternal life?" Jesus then pointed him to God's word when he said, "what is written in the law?"

When the man then cited the law properly, Jesus said, "thou hast answered right: this do, and thou shalt live."

But the man did not like that answer and sought to justify himself, so he asked Jesus, "who is my neighbor?" Below is the exchange found in Luke 10:30-37 that followed after he asked his question:

"Jesus answering said, A certain *man* went down from Jerusalem to Jericho, and fell among thieves, which stripped him of his raiment, and wounded *him*, and departed, leaving *him* half dead. And by chance there came down a certain priest that way: and when he saw him, he passed by on the other side. And likewise a Levite, when he was at the place, came and looked *on him*, and passed by on the other side. But a certain Samaritan, as he journeyed, came where he was: and when he saw him, he had compassion *on him*, And went to *him*, and bound up his wounds, pouring in oil and wine, and set him on his own beast, and brought him to an inn, and took care of him. And on the morrow when he departed, he took out two pence, and gave *them* to the host, and said unto him, Take care of him; and whatsoever thou spendest more, when I come again, I will repay thee. Which now of these three, thinkest thou, was neighbor unto him that fell among the thieves? And he said, He that showed mercy on him. Then said Jesus unto him, Go, and do thou likewise."

How to Identify the Neighbor

Jesus gave a long answer to a short question. Why? Why not say, *'everyone is your neighbor'* if this was that simple? In his reply, Jesus did not refer to everyone or all men. Instead, he contrasted the response of a priest, a Levite, and a Samaritan to the plight of an assault victim who was half dead.

When the priest and the Levite saw the man, they "passed by on the other side." Jesus went on to show how the response of those who had religious training differed from the response of someone who did not. The Samaritans lacked such training since the Jews had no dealings with them (cf. Fourth gospel 4:9). Worse yet, as we saw with the Samaritan woman who talked with Jesus at Jacob's well, the Samaritans had a muddled history regarding religious ideas. Even so, in Jesus' teaching, the men with religious training did not exhibit compassion, while the one without it did.

Jesus indicated the deeds of the Samaritan offered the answer to the "neighbor" question, as we see in this exchange:

"Which now of these three, thinkest thou, was neighbor unto him that fell among the thieves? And he said, He that showed mercy on him. Then said Jesus unto him, Go, and do thou likewise" (Lk 10:36-37).

The "neighbor" was not the person who "fell among the thieves." In his teaching, Jesus defined the neighbor as the one who was willing to exhibit outrageous compassion for someone who was in a half-dead condition, who was not their family member or friend.

Jesus answered the question, "who is my neighbor?" by indicating how a true neighbor behaves. But who fits this description? In the parable, the Samaritan did not just stop to help the victim. He also took time to bind his wounds "and he brought him to an inn, and took care of him." Then Jesus raised the bar even further.

He also said, "on the morrow when he departed, he took out two pence, and gave *them* to the host, and said unto him, Take care of him; and whatsoever thou spendest more, when I come again, I will repay thee" (Lk 10:35). He obligated himself to pay a debt of an unlimited amount for a man who did not even know him. Wow!

Who does such a thing?

Who does such a thing is one who obeys the law of God – "love the Lord thy God with all thy heart, and with all thy soul, and with all thy strength, and with all thy mind; and thy neighbor as thyself." In order "to justify himself," the lawyer asked Jesus, "who is my neighbor?" (Lk 10:29) Jesus' response was a rebuke to this lawyer, for it showed men can obey the law even if they were not raised with the scriptures, as was the case with the Samaritans.

The lawyer did not need Jesus to tell him how to act, scripture already did this. He knew what the law said, but he was not willing to obey it. Yet, he *was* willing to "justify himself" and this exposed a double standard. He acted as if he respected God's word and he also believed he was justified in not doing what it said.

Instead of obedience, he chose self-justification, and in order to make himself look good, he portrayed the law as unreasonable. He asked, "who is **my** neighbor?" in order "to justify himself," so he was not asking who he should act this way toward. Rather, he was asking who was acting this way toward him. Why? Because he would be justified in not obeying this commandment if scripture raised an impossible standard, and his question was supposed to show this, since he assumed there was no way to answer it.

Who was the Lawyer's Neighbor?

Jesus asked which of the three was "neighbor unto him that fell among the thieves?" The lawyer replied, "he that showed mercy on him." If men can do this, then God's law is not unreasonable. When Jesus said, "go, and do thou likewise," he indicated men, including this lawyer, could do what God's word said.

However, Jesus also indicated someone *was* acting as a neighbor to the lawyer. Who recognized he needed help, had compassion on him, took time to tend to his half-dead condition, and got him to where he might recover from his fall among the thieves?

This parable of Jesus raised the idea of someone who agreed to take on an unknown, uncapped amount of debt to help a man who did not know him. This pictured what Jesus did when he took on an unspecified degree of debt for people who did not know him. Jesus acts this way toward people! So, he answered the question, "who is my neighbor?" by portraying what he was willing to do for the lawyer.

Was the image of the man who had fallen among the thieves picturing the lawyer? Is this what happens when men steal the LORD's word and cause people to have minds that are prejudiced to believe that God's law requires people to do the impossible?

The lawyer asked about eternal life but did not care about truth, for he tempted Jesus when he asked, "what shall I do to inherit eternal life?" (Lk 10:25) He wanted to justify himself, i.e., be justified without changing. But with his unrepentant heart, he fit the picture of a man who was half dead.

Some people might assume Jesus would never portray himself as a Samaritan. But the Jews did exactly this. Consider one of the many insults that were raised against Jesus in his lifetime. "Then answered the Jews, and said unto him [Jesus], Say we not well that thou art a Samaritan, and hast a devil?" (Fourth gospel 8:48)

The phrase "say we not well" suggests this slur about Jesus had existed for some time.

Might this be why he used a Samaritan to portray the neighbor, i.e., the person who showed mercy, in his example?

All of us would want someone to do for us as the Samaritan did. But not everyone would do as the Samaritan did!

Chapter 8 – The Love of the Truth

In this chapter, we will consider what it means to have a love of the truth. We will also address these questions: Is there a limited time to respond to truth? Can the brethren do good and be holy? When God corrects us, what does this prove?

When the Truth is Unwanted

Paul asked the Galatians, "am I therefore become your enemy, because I tell you the truth?" (Gal 4:16), so he knew the truth could cause division among the brethren. Those who resisted the truth would naturally see Paul as an adversary because they would not want to be proven wrong.

Resisting the truth did not mean they were not counted among the brethren, for three verses later Paul wrote: "my little children, of whom I travail in birth again until Christ be formed in you" (Gal 4:19). He considered them his spiritual children, yet they had only been conceived spiritually. Their birth had not occurred for he said he was still in "travail" regarding them and would be until Christ was formed in them. But what happens if this growth process is cut-off before Christ is formed in a person?

Jesus once said, "because I tell you the truth, ye believe me not" (Fourth gospel 8:45). Think about that. The truth is what caused them not to believe. Worse yet, he said this to men who believed on him moments earlier:

> "Then said Jesus to those Jews which believed on him, If ye continue in my word, *then* are ye my disciples indeed; And ye shall know the truth, and the truth shall make you free" (Fourth gospel 8:31-32).

They believed on him, but the truth did not set them free, since a little later he said, "because I tell you the truth, ye believe me not." Thus, they did not continue in his word. He presented the truth and they did not want to hear it. Although the phrase, "the truth shall make you free" may sound good to us, they took offense at it!

"They answered him, We be Abraham's seed, and were never in bondage to any man: how sayest thou, Ye shall be made free? Jesus answered them, Verily, verily, I say unto you, Whosoever committeth sin is the servant of sin" (Fourth gospel 8:33-34).

Physical bondage was not the issue, as he showed when he said, "whosoever committeth sin is the servant of sin." They thought they had a free will and could do as they pleased, but they had sold themselves into bondage by serving sin. So, they were not free to obey God, for "no man can serve two masters" (Mt 6:24).

When the Truth is Divisive

In Matthew 10:34-36, Jesus indicated he would cause division:

"Think not that I am come to send peace on earth: I came not to send peace, but a sword. For I am come to set a man at variance against his father, and the daughter against her mother, and the daughter in law against her mother in law. And a man's foes shall *be they* of his own household."

Does the reference to a man's foes being of his own household picture instances like those above, where the truth caused those who believed on Jesus to turn on him? While it is good to believe on Jesus, this has to be done on God's terms, including the need for people to "continue" in his word.

Scripture speaks of "them that perish; because they received not the love of the truth, that they might be saved" (2Th 2:10). This shows that receiving the love of the truth is critical to being saved.

Let us always welcome the truth, even if it means we will have to change our views because the alternative is deadly:

"they received not the love of the truth, that they might be saved. And **for this cause God shall send them strong delusion, that they should believe a lie**: That they all might be damned who believed not the truth, but had pleasure in unrighteousness" (2Th 2:10-12).

This parallels what the LORD said to those who chose "their own ways" (Isa 66:3). He said, "I also will choose their delusions, and will bring their fears upon them; because when I called, none did answer; when I spake, they did not hear: but they did evil before mine eyes, and chose *that* in which I delighted not" (Isa 66:4).

Scripture reports on a time when the people who respected the LORD's word were cast out by those who gave it mere lip service. "Hear the word of the LORD, **ye that tremble at his word**; <u>Your brethren that hated you, that cast you out for my name's sake, said, Let the LORD be glorified</u>: but he shall appear to your joy, and they shall be ashamed" (Isa 66:5). Notice, the ones who *said*, "let the LORD be glorified," hated and cast out those who truly feared "his word." This shows deeds do not always follow words and this verse warns us to practice discernment. Do not assume people love God just because they say they do.

We are told, "let us not love in word, neither in tongue; but in deed and in truth" (1Jo 3:18). A deed is something that is done, so mere words will not suffice. The love of the truth must be in deed and in truth, just as our love of God and our neighbor must be.

God's view on resisting the truth should be clear. As we just saw, for those who did not receive the love of the truth, indifference to the truth led God to send them strong delusion. Playing games with the truth is no small matter, for this puts people at odds with the "God of truth" (Dt 32:4). When Jude wrote to people who were "sanctified by God the Father, and preserved in Jesus Christ" (Jude 1:1), he warned them that "the Lord, having saved the people out of the land of Egypt, afterward destroyed them that believed not" (Jude 1:5). Verses like this show the need to continue in belief (and in the love of the truth) does not stop when people join the church.

Respond While Light is Available?

Five days before Jesus' last Passover, he told a group of people, "while ye have light, believe in the light, that ye may be the children of light" (Fourth gospel 12:36). Unless this was only for them or only for that time, we need to heed his counsel about responding to light while we can. Here is what scripture said next:

"though he had done so many miracles before them, yet they believed not on him: That the saying of Esaias the prophet might be fulfilled, which he spake, Lord, who hath believed our report? and to whom hath the arm of the Lord been revealed? Therefore they could not believe, because that Esaias said again, He hath blinded their eyes, and hardened their heart; that they should not see with *their* eyes, nor understand with *their* heart, and be converted, and I should heal them. These things said Esaias [Isaiah], when he saw his glory, and spake of him" (Fourth gospel 12:37-41).

Although Jesus did many miracles, they still did not believe on him. After reporting this, the author cited a prophecy that showed this response did not come as a surprise to God. At first, it indicates they would not believe. Then it says, "therefore they could not believe... " and it cites another Isaiah prophecy that said the Lord, "blinded their eyes, and hardened their heart." So, those who would not believe became those who could not believe, and it says this was the Lord's doing. This may sound familiar because it aligns with verses that were discussed just a few moments ago:

"they received not the love of the truth, that they might be saved. And for this cause God shall send them strong delusion, that they should believe a lie" (2Th 2:10-11).

God caused some to not be able to see in this passage also:

"Israel hath not obtained that which he seeketh for; but the election hath obtained it, and the rest were blinded (According as it is written, **God hath given them the spirit of slumber**, **eyes that they should not see**, **and ears that they should not hear**;) unto this day. And David saith, Let their table be made a snare, and a trap, and a stumbling block, and a recompence unto them: Let their eyes be darkened..." (Rom 11:7-10).

Thus, God is not always seeking to make things understandable. If people say things like, *'God is infinitely patient,' God's grace is inexhaustible,'* etc., they may think it makes God look good to men when they talk this way. But scripture presents a different picture.

Paul and Barnabas said the following to the Jews who resisted their message. "It was necessary that the word of God should first have been spoken to you: but seeing ye put it from you, and judge yourselves unworthy of everlasting life, lo, we turn to the Gentiles" (Acts 13:46). Does this teach infinite patience? No. It teaches when people resist God's word, their actions are evidence of a judgment against themselves.

Jesus indicated "the light" that is in a person can "be darkness" (Mt 6:23). It seems this would apply when what people think is true, leads them to reject truth. Conversely, "in thy [God's] light shall we see light" (Ps 36:9) shows God's light is what enables us to see light, and this standard is how we can tell what is light and what is not.

The Lord's Chastisement is Reserved for the Children

How can we tell who is a child of God? One way is chastisement. The writer of Hebrews told the brethren:

> "whom the Lord loveth he chasteneth, and scourgeth every son whom he receiveth. If ye endure chastening, God dealeth with you as with sons; for what son is he whom the father chasteneth not? But if ye be without chastisement, whereof all are partakers, then are ye bastards, and not sons" (Heb 12:6-8).

The words, "whom the Lord loveth" would make no sense if God loves everybody. Who does God chasten? It says, "whereof all are partakers" but clearly "all" refers only to all of those who God deals with as sons, because it cannot possibly include all of those who are "without chastisement."

Also, notice who gets chastened in Jesus' message to the church of the Laodiceans. "As many as I love, I rebuke and chasten" (Rv 3:19). So, only those who he loves benefit from his correction.

"Blessed is the man whom thou chastenest, O LORD" (Ps 94:12) shows the chastening of the LORD results in a blessing. Moreover, in Proverbs 3:11 it says, "my son, despise not the chastening of the LORD; neither be weary of his correction."

"Whom the LORD loveth he correcteth" (Prv 3:12) is another verse that shows correction is reserved for those who God loves. Who is left out? All who are not corrected (like those who do not receive the love of the truth, for God will "send them strong delusion, that they should believe a lie" (2Th 2:11)).

When people say, *'God loves everybody,'* ask them if everybody is corrected by God? This is how to wield "the sword of the Spirit, which is the word of God" (Eph 6:17).

Flesh Ties Versus Faith Ties

In the passage where Jesus told "those Jews which believed on him, If ye continue in my word, *then* are ye my disciples indeed" (Fourth gospel 8:31), he went on to talk about the difference between Abraham's seed and Abraham's children.

Notice Jesus' basis for making this distinction, and how he proved those who he spoke to were not God's children. He told them:

> "ye are Abraham's seed; but ye seek to kill me, because my word hath no place in you. I speak that which I have seen with my Father: and ye do that which ye have seen with your father. They answered and said unto him, Abraham is our father. Jesus saith unto them, If ye were Abraham's children, ye would do the works of Abraham. But now ye seek to kill me, a man that hath told you the truth, which I have heard of God: this did not Abraham. Ye do the deeds of your father. Then said they to him, We be not born of fornication; we have one Father, *even* God. Jesus said unto them, If God were your Father, ye would love me: for I proceeded forth and came from God; neither came I of myself, but he sent me. Why do ye not understand my speech? *even* because ye cannot hear my word. Ye are of *your* father the devil" (Fourth gospel 8:37-44).

Here we see dueling claims. While those men claimed their father was Abraham, Jesus said they were not Abraham's children. Because they were using different standards to define the terms, they came to different conclusions.

Their assumption that a physical connection to Abraham is what made a person a child of Abraham was wrong. They did not honor Abraham by doing as he had done. Thus, they were not acting as children of Abraham; they were merely his physical offspring.

What was it that distinguished Abraham's seed from his children? It was works. Jesus said, "if ye were Abraham's children, ye would do the works of Abraham."

Furthermore, a fleshly link to Abraham will not make a person do as Abraham did. Below we see those who are of faith believe God and this is what Abraham did, so they are counted as his children:

"as Abraham believed God, and it was accounted to him for righteousness. Know ye therefore that **they which are of faith, the same are the children of Abraham**. And the scripture, foreseeing that God would justify the heathen through faith, preached before the gospel unto Abraham, *saying*, In thee shall all nations be blessed. So, then they which be of faith are blessed with faithful Abraham" (Gal 3:6-9).

"The gospel" was preached to Abraham in this promise, "in thee shall all nations be blessed." All nations do not physically descend from him, so how can they be blessed? By faith – "in every nation he that feareth him [God], and worketh righteousness, is accepted with him" (Acts 10:35). The brethren were told, "ye are all the children of God by faith in Christ Jesus" and "if ye *be* Christ's, then are ye Abraham's seed, and heirs according to the promise" (Gal 3:26 & 29). So, faith in Christ Jesus made them both Abraham's seed and the children of God, and we will look at this further in the next chapter.

The Children of God

Since "God that made the world and all things therein" (Acts 17:24) "giveth to all life, and breath, and all things" (Acts 17:25), people are called "the offspring of God" (Acts 17:29). This does not make them his children, however, because the children of God are known by their deeds. Scripture makes this point in verses like, "as many as are led by the Spirit of God, they are the sons of God" (Rom 8:14) and "he that doeth good is of God" (3Jo 1:11).

Jesus also knew fleshly ties are not the basis for God's family ties. Once as Jesus was speaking, he was told his mother and brothers were standing outside and wanted to speak with him (cf. Mk 3:32). He would not speak with them, and Mark 3:33-35 tells us he said:

"Who is my mother, or my brethren? And he looked round about on them which sat about him, and said, Behold my mother and my brethren! For whosoever shall do the will of God, the same is my brother, and my sister, and mother."

So, how can we join Jesus in God's family? "Do the will of God."

What is his will? God "commandeth all men everywhere to repent" (Acts 17:30). If men can obey this command, then it is wrong to say, '*I was born this way, so I cannot stop sinning.*'

Scripture says, "let him that stole steal no more" (Eph 4:28). This is a radical change and it shows it is possible for people who steal to stop doing so. If men can permanently stop stealing, can they also stop their other sins?

The Foundation of Repentance

John the Baptist told men to produce "fruits meet for repentance" (Mt 3:8). Jesus said, "I came not to call the righteous but sinners to repentance" (Mk 2:17). When he sent out the twelve, "they went out, and preached that men should repent" (Mk 6:12).

In Acts 2:38 & 3:19, Peter told the assembled crowd to repent. This was also key to Paul's teaching.

Paul told the elders in Ephesus that everywhere he had been he testified "both to the Jews, and also to the Greeks, repentance toward God, and faith toward our Lord Jesus Christ" (Acts 20:21). In Acts 26:20, Paul said his message to people was "that they should repent and turn to God, and do works meet for repentance."

Repentance is not sorrow but they are linked, for sorrow precedes it. Also, there are two kinds of sorrow. One yields a good result, the other does not. In 2 Corinthians 7:9-10 Paul wrote this:

"I rejoice, not that ye were made sorry, but that ye sorrowed to repentance... For godly sorrow worketh repentance to salvation not to be repented of: but the sorrow of the world worketh death" (2Cor 7:9-10).

Godly sorrow results in a permanent change, a salvation that will not be repented of. This is far different than the sorrow of the world that leads to death. A temporary pang of conscience will produce no permanent change.

The Book of Hebrews speaks of "the foundation of repentance from dead works" (Heb 6:1). So, repentance is foundational. It is a necessary first step. This lets us know the brethren can repent from dead works. All men will not obey the command for "all men everywhere to repent." Yet, the following verse seems to tell us all the true brethren will do so – "the Lord is not slack concerning his promise, as some men count slackness; but is longsuffering to us-ward, not willing that any should perish, but that all should come to repentance" (2Pt 3:9).

It is not uncommon for people to quote, "the Lord is... not willing that any should perish" and they think this accurately represents this verse. Does it?

Any and All?

An ellipsis is used to let people know some of the words of a quote were omitted for brevity. When this is done in oral communication, those who hear the quote will not know part of the verse is left out unless they know the verse. Either way, the question of accuracy is what we must address.

When an ellipsis is used correctly, the quote will still accurately represent the source material. But if the omitted words will cause a quote to misrepresent the source material, then the ellipsis has been misapplied and must be corrected.

An ellipsis can be useful in highlighting key points. However, if it is used carelessly it will lead people into error and 2 Peter 3:9 is a prime example of this. Compare the following two quotes:

A. "The Lord is... not willing that any should perish."
B. "The Lord is... longsuffering to us-ward, not willing that any should perish."

Item A distorts scripture by deleting the context of the word "any." This implies the Lord is not willing to allow any person to perish. But what 2 Peter 3:9 says is, "the Lord is not slack concerning his promise, as some men count slackness; but is longsuffering to **us-ward**, not willing that any should perish, but that all should come to repentance." Therefore, the words "any" and "all" refer to the brethren ["us"]. We also see that repentance is what keeps a person from perishing and, because of his promise, the Lord is patient toward all of the brethren while this process takes place.

The term "us-ward" was merely a shortened way to say toward us or regarding us. It translates a word that was also translated as "us," "we," and "our." "Us-ward" also shows up in a verse where Paul talked about "the exceeding greatness of his [God's] power to us-ward who believe" (Eph 1:19).

The word "us-ward" defines a group and Peter wrote his letter "to them that have obtained like precious faith with us through the righteousness of God and our Savior Jesus Christ" (2Pt 1:1). [Notice, it says they obtained this faith through the righteousness of God and Jesus.] While the word "us" can be used to refer to all humans, it is not often used this way. Moreover, the words "us," "we," and "our" that show up elsewhere in Peter's letter were never used to refer to the whole human race.

Since "us-ward" refers to the brethren, the words "any" and "all" must refer to the same subset in this context. Therefore, the verse is indicating the Lord is patient with the brethren and he will not let any of *them* perish, for they all will repent. However, repenting is just a first step, for the process of salvation then follows.

What does the Bible say about this process?

Salvation Through Sanctification

Consider this passage:

"we beseech you, brethren, and exhort *you* by the Lord Jesus, that as ye have received of us how ye ought to walk and to please God, *so* ye would abound more and more. For ye know what commandments we gave you by the Lord Jesus. For this is the will of God, *even* your sanctification, that ye should abstain from fornication: That every one of you should know how to possess his vessel in sanctification and honor" (1Th 4:1-4).

"This is the will of God, *even* your sanctification" did not apply only to the brethren in Thessalonica. God expects righteous behavior, and the commandments of the apostles show Jesus also wanted his followers to behave in a godly way. "God hath not called us unto uncleanness, but unto holiness" (1Th 4:7). Was this exhortation only for the Thessalonians? No. Peter had a similar admonition for those who love Jesus:

"as he which hath called you is holy, so be ye holy in all manner of conversation; Because it is written, Be ye holy; for I am holy" (1Pt 1:15-16).

[Note: the word "conversation" does not mean mere talk. When the KJV was written the word meant behavior, conduct, i.e., one's walk. The word we use today to express this idea is 'lifestyle.']

Paul said Jesus Christ "gave himself for us, that he might redeem us from all iniquity, and purify unto himself a peculiar people, zealous of good works" (Titus 2:14). He also hoped "that they which have believed in God might be careful to maintain good works" (Titus 3:8). Similarly, Timothy was told to urge those who are rich in this world "that they do good, that they be rich in good works" (1Ti 6:18). If Jesus gave himself for us with the intent of purifying to himself a people zealous of good works, then let us acknowledge this is what Jesus wanted to achieve.

Nobody Does Good?

Scripture indicates it is possible to "lead a quiet and peaceable life in all godliness and honesty" (1Ti 2:2). Despite this, some think the following passage teaches us no one can do good:

"As it is written, There is none righteous, no, not one: There is none that understandeth, there is none that seeketh after God. They are all gone out of the way, they are together become unprofitable; there is none that doeth good, no, not one" (Rom 3:10-12).

If someone tells us, *'this teaches no one does good'* what should we do? "As it is written" is citing a source. So, first off, we could take a look at the context of the quote.

Surely, the above passage does not describe the apostles and or Cornelius, a man who "feared God." It also cannot apply to those who live "in all godliness and honesty" or to:

- Abraham, "the Friend of God" (Jas 2:23),
- Noah, "a preacher of righteousness" (2Pt 2:5),
- Job, who "was perfect and upright, and one that feared God, and eschewed evil" (Job 1:1), or
- John the Baptist's parents, who "were both righteous before God, walking in all the commandments and ordinances of the Lord blameless" (Lk 1:6).

The idea that no person ever does good is contrary to scripture. We know men can do good, since James 4:17 says, "to him that knoweth to do good, and doeth it not, to him it is sin." People were also taught to do good in passages such as these:

- "depart from evil, and do good" (Ps 34:13),
- "if ye do good to them which do good to you, what thank have ye? for sinners also do even the same" (Lk 6:33),
- "love ye your enemies, and do good" (Lk 6:35),
- "eschew evil, and do good" (1Pt 3:11),
- "beloved, follow not that which is evil, but that which is good. He that doeth good is of God" (3Jo 1:11).

Jesus said, "a good man out of the good treasure of his heart bringeth forth that which is good" (Lk 6:45). Therefore, such people must exist. Tabitha "was full of good works" and Barnabas "was a good man" (Acts 9:36 & 11:24). Paul thought people could do good, for he often said things like:

- "abound to every good work" (2Cor 9:8),
- "walk worthy of the Lord unto all pleasing, being fruitful in every good work" (Col 1:10),
- "be a vessel unto honor, sanctified, and meet for the master's use, *and* prepared unto every good work" (2Ti 2:21).

Titus taught the brethren "to be ready to every good work" (Titus 3:1).

Paul told the saints in Ephesus "we are his [God's] workmanship, created in Christ Jesus unto good works" (Eph 2:10). He also said, "whatsoever good thing any man doeth, the same shall he receive of the Lord" (Eph 6:8). This parallels something Jesus said:

> "all that are in the graves shall hear his [the Son of man's] voice, And shall come forth; they that have done good, unto the resurrection of life; and they that have done evil, unto the resurrection of damnation" (Fourth gospel 5:28-29).

Even the resurrection is tied to doing good. God's word tells us, "overcome evil with good" and "do that which is good" (Rom 12:21 & 13:3). So, why would some suggest the phrase "there is none that doeth good" in Romans 3:12 applies to all mankind in all times?

Check the Reference

"They are all gone aside, they are *all* together become filthy: *there is* none that doeth good, no, not one" (Ps 14:3). "Every one of them is gone back: they are altogether become filthy; *there is* none that doeth good, no, not one" (Ps 53:3). Romans 3:10-12 appears to be citing one of these verses, so let us consider Psalm 14 in context:

> "**The fool** hath said in **his** heart, *There is* no God. **They** are corrupt, **they** have done abominable works, *there is* none that doeth good. The LORD looked down from heaven upon **the children of men**, to see if there were **any** that did understand, *and* seek God. **They** are *all* gone aside, **they** are all together become filthy: *there is* none that doeth good, no, not one. Have **all the workers of iniquity** no knowledge? who eat up my people *as* they eat bread, and call not upon the LORD" (Ps 14:1-4).

Here we have two groups, those who the Lord calls "my people" and those who eat them up.

Also, the Psalm opens with "the fool," i.e., someone who "said in his heart, *There is* no God." This is who is meant when it says, "**they** are corrupt, **they** have done abominable works." They are also called "the children of men" and "the workers of iniquity."

Psalm 53:1-4 is almost identical to Psalm 14:1-4, and since one of them was being cited in Romans 3:10-12, we must consider them if we want to exercise due diligence. With this in mind, let us now look at Romans 3:10-18 to get a look at the broader context:

"As it is written, There is none righteous, no, not one: There is none that understandeth, there is none that seeketh after God. They are all gone out of the way, they are together become unprofitable; there is none that doeth good, no, not one. Their throat *is* an open sepulcher; with their tongues they have used deceit; the poison of asps *is* under their lips: Whose mouth *is* full of cursing and bitterness: Their feet *are* swift to shed blood: Destruction and misery *are* in their ways: And the way of peace have they not known: There is no fear of God before their eyes."

In Psalms 14 and 53, the word "they" refers to people who are acting as "the fool." This must inform our view of Romans 3:10-18.

Yet even if we miss this, it should be evident Romans 3:12 cannot be teaching no human does good. Why? Because the statement, "there is no fear of God before their eyes" cannot apply to people who did fear God according to scripture or who do fear God today.

All Have Sinned

We do find a statement on the human condition in Romans 3, but it is not in the passage discussed above. Rather, it is this verse, "all have sinned, and come short of the glory of God" (Rom 3:23).

If "all have sinned" describes the condition of every human being, what can human beings do about this?

Both Jews and Gentiles need to "repent and turn to God, and do works meet [fit] for repentance" (Acts 26:20). But no one repents if they do not think they need to do so. This seems to be the issue Paul had to face when it came to many of his fellow Jews. Notice what was said before and after Romans 3:10-18:

- "are we better *than they*? No, in no wise: for we have before proved both Jews and Gentiles, that they are all under sin" (Rom 3:9).
- "now we know that what things soever the law saith, it saith to them who are under the law: that every mouth may be stopped, and all the world may become guilty before God" (Rom 3:19).

"Them who are under the law" referred to the Jews and converts who joined them in seeking to follow the law. Thus, the context on either side of Romans 3:10-18 helps us to see this passage was teaching that having God's law did not make the Jews better. Owning a Bible does not make someone a better person or mean that person is closer to God than people who do not have one. Likewise, having the law did not keep the Jews from sinning and it did not mean they were automatically better than non-Jews.

Some Jews thought they *were* better, and this issue is what was being addressed in Romans 3:9 & 19. They failed to remember "there is no respect of persons with God" (Rom 2:11), and the earlier part of Romans already laid the groundwork on this issue.

Romans 2 set forth "the righteous judgment of God" (v. 5), starting with this affirmation, God "will render to every man according to his deeds" (v. 6).

The next two verses then stated the conditions and the rewards. **"To them who by patient continuance in well doing** seek for glory and honor and immortality, eternal life" (v. 7). "But **unto them that are contentious, and do not obey the truth**, but obey unrighteousness, indignation and wrath" (v. 8).

Romans 2:9-11 then put these ideas in terms of the sequence of their presentation to Jews and Gentiles:

"Tribulation and anguish, upon every soul of man that doeth evil, of the Jew first, and also of the Gentile; But glory, honor, and peace, to every man that worketh good, to the Jew first, and also to the Gentile: For there is no respect of persons with God."

God gave the law to the Hebrews, but they promoted a view of the law that allowed men to think they were righteous if they kept the letter of the law. Yet, "the letter killeth, but the spirit giveth life" (2Cor 3:6) because the spirit leads people to see the law differently.

Jesus contrasted two views of "thou shalt not kill," one concluded "whosoever shall kill shall be in danger of the judgment" (Mt 5:21) and one said "whosoever is angry with his brother without a cause shall be in danger of the judgment" (Mt 5:22). The latter fits the spirit of verses like, "thou shalt not hate thy brother in thine heart" (Lev 19:17) and "whosoever hateth his brother is a murderer" (1Jo 3:15), so scripture can help us distinguish between the letter and the spirit. Jesus also showed "thou shalt not commit adultery" (Mt 5:27) meant "whosoever looketh on a woman to lust after her hath committed adultery with her already in his heart" (Mt 5:28). Here again, the issue is how we view God's commandments. One view raises the bar and seeks obedience from the heart, the other lowers the bar and this is why obeying the letter of the law does not work. We will look further into this in the chapter that follows the next case study.

When Romans 3:23 says, "all have sinned" this is talking about what people *have* done. It does not mean people "cannot cease from sin" (2Pt 2:14) because Peter indicated they can do so, and Jesus told at least two people to "sin no more" (Fourth gospel 5:14 & 8:11). "All have sinned" also is not saying no one can obey God, for the LORD said, "Abraham obeyed my voice, and kept my charge, my commandments, my statutes, and my laws" (Gen 26:5). Since we have an explicit statement that proves a human being can do this, we cannot say humans cannot do what Abraham did.

If we can exhibit faith as he did, then we can honor the LORD by obeying his voice as Abraham did. Members of the body of Christ also have the added advantage of the indwelling Holy Spirit, so obeying God cannot be harder for them than it was for Abraham.

Case Study: The Case of God's Gift

A Familiar Verse

This may be the most frequently quoted verse – "for God so loved the world, that he gave his only begotten Son, that whosoever believeth in him should not perish, but have everlasting life" (Fourth gospel 3:16). However, familiarity with a passage should not keep us from doing our due diligence. Even so, this is a temptation we are more likely to face when it comes to Bible verses we have heard many times.

Take a little time to read this verse in its context in your Bible and write down your thoughts on the principles this verse is teaching. Then come back to this study and see if scripture can show us how to get more out of God's word.

The Case of God's Gift

Unconditional?

"For God so loved the world, that he gave his only begotten Son, that whosoever believeth in him should not perish, but have everlasting life" (Fourth gospel 3:16). Some will characterize this verse by saying things like, *'this tells us God's love is unconditional,'* yet the plain words of the text actually teach precisely the opposite. "Whosoever believeth in him" is a condition! This is explicit, and since the verse is a conditional statement, it surely is not teaching unconditional love or universal acceptance. "Not perish, but have everlasting life" is not an unconditional blessing. It is only for those who meet the condition.

Whatever scripture may say elsewhere, we still need to be faithful in communicating this verse. It tells us the reason God gave his only begotten Son was that those who meet the condition should not perish. Since "believeth in him" is a necessary condition for everlasting life, unconditional love is not the subject of this verse.

Let Scripture Light the Way

In addition, the word "whosoever" is always linked to a condition. Thus, this word could not possibly imply the verse is for everyone without condition. Consider five verses where this word was used:

- "I [Aaron] said unto them, Whosoever hath any gold, let them break *it* off" (Ex 32:24),
- "speak unto Aaron, saying, Whosoever *he be* of thy seed in their generations that hath *any* blemish, let him not approach to offer the bread of his God" (Lev 21:17),
- "whosoever heareth these sayings of mine [Jesus], and doeth them, I will liken him unto a wise man, which built his house upon a rock" (Mt 7:24),
- "whosoever hath, to him shall be given; and whosoever hath not, from him shall be taken even that which he seemeth to have" (Lk 8:18),
- "whosoever shall confess that Jesus is the Son of God, God dwelleth in him, and he in God" (1Jo 4:15).

When seeking the meanings of words in scripture, we must not let our assumptions or the views of others prejudice our judgment. Rather, we should let scripture show us the meaning of the words, phrases, and word pictures in the Bible. If we do this for the word "whosoever," here is what the verses cited above can teach us:

- "whosoever hath any gold" [Here "whosoever" introduced a condition that defined a subset (those with "any gold")]
- "whosoever *he be* of thy seed" [Here the word introduced a condition that defined a set of men in Aaron's lineage]
- "whosoever heareth these sayings of mine, and doeth them" [Here "whosoever" refers only to those who meet the condition (i.e., hears Jesus' sayings and does them)]
- "whosoever hath... and whosoever hath not" [No one can be in both groups. Here two distinct conditions ("hath" and "hath not") were used to define two very different groups]
- "whosoever shall confess that Jesus is the Son of God" [Only those who "confess that Jesus is the Son of God" are in this subset].

The word "whosoever" introduces a condition. So, there is no way it could make any verse unconditional.

Besides this, similar terms like "whoso," "whomsoever," "soever," and "whatsoever" are also always tied to a condition:

- "whoso sheddeth man's blood, by man shall his blood be shed: for in the image of God made he man" (Gen 9:6),
- "he [Judas] that betrayed him [Jesus] gave them a sign, saying, Whomsoever I shall kiss, that same is he" (Mt 26:48),
- "he [Jesus] said unto them, In what place soever ye enter into a house, there abide till ye depart... " (Mk 6:10),
- "every beast, every creeping thing, and every fowl, *and* whatsoever creepeth upon the earth, after their kinds, went forth out of the ark" (Gen 8:19).

Such words define a subset based on some trait(s) or condition(s) that define who or what is included. Lastly, in the KJV the word "whosoever" appears 163 times and in every one of those verses, it introduces a condition or set of conditions.

So?

If we attach the wrong meaning to a word, we will misunderstand what scripture says. This occurs with the word "so" in the verse in question. The word "so" has various meanings and here are some of them:

- indicates a quantity – a large amount or extreme degree
  (He so loves the smell of coffee. / He has so much money.)
- indicates a quality – the way a thing is or was done
  (He takes his coffee like so. / It happened just so.)
- consequently, therefore
  (He had too much coffee, so he is unable to sleep.)
- in order that
  (He drinks coffee so he can stay awake.)
- indeed, certainly
  (He does so drink coffee.)

Here are four verses that use the word "so". In the first two, it refers to a quantity and in the second two verses it refers to a quality:

- "when Jesus heard *it,* he marveled, and said to them that followed, Verily I say unto you, I have not found <u>so great</u> faith, no, not in Israel" (Mt 8:10),
- "his disciples say unto him, Whence should we have <u>so much</u> bread in the wilderness, as to fill so great a multitude?" (Mt 15:33),
- "those things, which God before had showed by the mouth of all his prophets, that Christ should suffer, he hath **so fulfilled**" (Acts 3:18),
- "they which run in a race run all, but one receiveth the prize? **So run**, that ye may obtain" (1Cor 9:24).

Quantity and quality were expressed by different Greek words. Yet, in the verses above, the word "so" was used to translate both. But the Strong's number for these words gives us a way to know what meaning of the word "so" we need to have in mind.

Above, the phrase "so fulfilled" does not refer to the amount of fulfillment. It refers to the way those things were fulfilled.

Likewise, the phrase "so run" (1Cor 9:24) is not talking about a large quantity of running. It is about *how* one runs, and the writer used it to urge running in a way that resulted in victory. In these two verses, the word "so" translated Greek word number G3779 and this word always refers to a quality.

Other examples are "if then God so G3779 clothe the grass" (Lk 12:28) and "for so G3779 is the will of God" (1Pt 2:15). These verses talk about the quality of the design that is visible in nature and the quality of God's will.

Let Scripture Light the Way Once Again

"Let every one of you in particular so G3779 love his wife even as himself" (Eph 5:33). This is how a man should love his wife. It is not about the quantity of his love. Likewise, when we read "beloved, if God so G3779 loved us, we ought also to love one another" (1Jo 4:11) we can see this is *how* the brethren should love one another, not how much. Even if the context does not reveal the meaning of the word "so," there is no reason for us to be confused since we can verify whether the original word referred to quantity or quality. Look at scripture's use of word number G3779 in the first ten verses in the New Testament where this word was used:

- "the birth of Jesus Christ was on this wise G3779" (Mt 1:18),
- "thus G3779 it is written by the prophet" (Mt 2:5),
- "thus G3779 it becometh us to fulfill all righteousness" (Mt 3:15),
- "great *is* your reward in heaven: for so G3779 persecuted they the prophets" (Mt 5:12),
- "let your light so G3779 shine before men, that they may see your good works" (Mt 5:16),
- "whosoever therefore shall break one of these least commandments, and shall teach men so G3779" (Mt 5:19),
- "if ye salute your brethren only, what do ye more *than others*? do not even the publicans so G3779?" (Mt 5:47),
- "after this manner G3779 therefore pray ye" (Mt 6:9),
- "if God so G3779 clothe the grass of the field" (Mt 6:30),
- "whatsoever ye would that men should do to you, do ye even so G3779 to them" (Mt 7:12).

The way the writers of scripture used word number [G3779] proves this Greek word refers to a quality, not a quantity. It means "thus" or "in this manner."

The writers of scripture did use Greek words that refer to quantity or intensity, but none of them were used in the verse in question.

How Much? Or How?

The word "so" is a valid way to translate Greek word number [G3779], so the translators cannot be blamed if we misconstrue this word. When we attach a wrong meaning to the phrase "for God so loved the world," our choice keeps us from understanding the verse, so we need to get this right. Now, let us look at the verse in context:

"[14]as Moses lifted up the serpent in the wilderness, even so must the Son of man be lifted up: [15]That whosoever believeth in him should not perish, but have eternal life. [16]For God so loved the world, that he gave his only begotten Son, that whosoever believeth in him should not perish, but have everlasting life. [17]For God sent not his Son into the world to condemn the world; but that the world through him might be saved. [18]He that believeth on him is not condemned: but he that believeth not is condemned already, because he hath not believed in the name of the only begotten Son of God" (Fourth gospel 3:14-18).

The phrase "whosoever believeth in him" shows up in the verse before verse 16. Thus, the author meant to highlight this condition since he repeated it.

Verses 14 & 15 link how people got saved when "Moses lifted up the serpent in the wilderness" to how they get saved by "the Son of man" being "lifted up." In addition, in verse 17 the words, "that the world through him might be saved" refers to how the world "might be saved." So, this was stressed on both sides of verse 16. In verse 14, "so" refers to how "the Son of man" would "be lifted up" and the same Greek word is translated "so" in verse 16. Thus, the way this word was used in verse 14 shows it is wrong to think it was referring to how much God loved the world in verse 16.

We can test our view of a verse by looking for other passages on the same topic. Are there any other verses that indicate the words "God so loved" are about how God's love was expressed? Yes. For example, consider the passage below that taught the brethren the kind of love they ought to have for one another:

> "In this was manifested the love of God toward us, because that God sent his only begotten Son into the world, that we might live through him. Herein is love, not that we loved God, but that he loved us, and sent his Son *to be* the propitiation for our sins. Beloved, if God so loved us, we ought also to love one another" (1Jo 4:9-11).

How was the love of God expressed? "God sent his only begotten Son into the world." Why did he do it? "That **we** might live through him," and the context proves "we" refers to the "beloved" who are "of God."

The Focus of the Verse

When people are not open to correction, they will say things like, *'it's no big deal'* or *'what difference does it make'* so they can avoid having to change. But this dilutes the authority of scripture since it suggests staying true to God's word is sometimes unimportant.

If people think the word "so" in "for God so loved the world" refers to quantity and not quality does it make a difference? If scripture never says God loves all men unconditionally, but people are told scripture says he does, is this a big deal? A misrepresentation on "for God so loved the world... " is a big deal. It is easy to see why. If people say, *'the verse means God loves you so much that if you were the only person in the world he still would have sent his son to die for you'* where is the focus? It is on us. Yet, if we stick with the proper meaning of the words of scripture, where is the focus? It is on the gift!

"For God so loved the world, that he gave his only begotten Son" puts the focus on Jesus. He is the way God's love was expressed, and this fits with Jesus' words, "I am the way, the truth, and the life: no man cometh unto the Father, but by me" (Fourth gospel 14:6).

A right understanding of the phrase "God so loved the world" fits with the condition that is found in verses like, "he that believeth on the Son hath everlasting life: and he that believeth not the Son shall not see life" (Fourth gospel 3:36). However, this harmony is ruined if we say a conditional statement is unconditional or if the verse's focus is shifted from Jesus to us. If people say, *'the verse means God loves you, he always has and always will'* and we compare this to scripture, we would see their words are very different from the verse and we could notice the tense of a word was changed.

In scripture, the word is "loved," not *'loves'*. It is in the past tense because it referred to something that took place in the past, i.e., the time when God "gave his only begotten Son". The word "gave" is past tense, just like the word "loved," and we should not be rewording verses to make them support our beliefs. The benefits of God's gift are still available to those who satisfy the condition ("believeth in him"), but the verse used the past tense because it declared a love God had expressed through a gift already given. This also explains why the past tense was used in another verse. "In this was manifested the love of God toward us, because that God sent his only begotten Son into the world, that we might live through him" (1Jo 4:9). "Manifested" and "sent" are in the past tense because this manifestation occurred before the verse was written.

All of Us?

'God loves everybody' is a popular idea today. Yet, neither Jesus nor his apostles ever said *'God loves you'* to the various crowds who heard them! Thus, making indiscriminate and unconditional declarations of God's love for people is not in line with what Jesus and his apostles said in their public statements.

Moreover, they did not say this in private either. Jesus privately told his disciples, "if a man love me, he will keep my words: and my Father will love him" (Fourth gospel 14:23). The conditions specified by Jesus show all men are not automatically loved by the Father.

When Paul spoke to Felix and his wife about faith in Christ, it says, "as he reasoned of **righteousness, temperance, and judgment to come,** Felix trembled" (Acts 24:25).

The truth is a wake-up call and having to face up to his condition made Felix tremble. When people are confronted with the truth, some will repent, others will not. But there is no reason to think God would have preferred it if Paul had been more winsome and, instead of presenting the gospel, simply told Felix, God loved him.

Paul emphasized three points and he put Felix under conviction by talking about God's standards. Why did he do this? Because he wanted Felix to turn to God. In Romans 1:16 it says, "I am not ashamed of the gospel of Christ: for it is the power of God unto salvation to everyone that believeth." Then the next verse says, "therein is the righteousness of God revealed" (Rom 1:17). This links the gospel to God's righteousness and not simply his love alone. This is what Paul presented to Felix, and later we will discuss how faith comes to those who hear God's word.

What Does Scripture Say?

If scripture does not say God loves everyone, it is not compatible with God's word to *infer* this idea from what it does say.

In speaking of the LORD, Psalm 5:5 says, "thou hatest all workers of iniquity" and we cannot act as if verses like this do not exist. Did the LORD change his mind and decide he now loves workers of iniquity? Certainly not. Jesus declared he would tell one group, "I never knew you: depart from me, ye that work iniquity" (Mt 7:23), and this statement does not suggest he once loved those people, but they later fell out of favor with him.

So, if a person ignores what Jesus will say to those who he never knew and simply tells everyone, *'God has always loved you and he will continue to do so no matter what,'* does this honor Jesus?

When it says, "God commendeth his love toward us, in that, while we were yet sinners, Christ died for us" (Rom 5:8), we need to know who the word "us" refers to. In the same context, it says, "the love of God is shed abroad in our hearts by the Holy Ghost which is given unto us" (Rom 5:5). The word "us" referred to Jesus' followers in this verse. So, when verse 8 says, "God commendeth his love toward us… " the word "us" must also refer to the brethren.

In Romans 5, the word "us" refers to the subset of people who:

- "were reconciled to God by the death of his Son" (Rom 5:10a),
- "shall be saved by his life" (Rom 5:10b), and
- "have now received the atonement" (Rom 5:11).

Is God's Grace Universal?

A final word here about assuming God's grace, mercy, and love are unconditional. The LORD stated, "[I] will be gracious to whom I will be gracious, and will show mercy on whom I will show mercy" (Ex 33:19). To/on "whom I will" is a condition and Romans 9:15-18 cited this statement and confirmed this condition still applies.

Jesus said, "he that hath my commandments, and keepeth them, he it is that loveth me: and he that loveth me shall be loved of my Father, and I will love him, and will manifest myself to him" (Fourth gospel 14:21). Notice the condition Jesus stated here for people to be loved by him, "he that hath my commandments, and keepeth them... I will love him." Therefore, it is wrong for anyone to think Jesus' love is unconditional and applies to all men, even if they disregard his commandments.

The difference between who Jesus did and did not pray for also shows this distinction. When Jesus addressed the Father about his disciples he said, "I pray for them: I pray not for the world, but for them which thou hast given me" (Fourth gospel 17:9).

Jesus' concern was not merely for his followers who were alive in that day, for he then added, "neither pray I for these alone, but for them also which shall believe on me through their word" (Fourth gospel 17:20). So, all who have or will yet come to "believe on" him through the teachings of his disciples were included in his prayer. In this discussion with the Father about his followers, Jesus went on to say, "I have declared unto them thy name, and will declare *it*: that the love wherewith thou hast loved me may be in them, and I in them" (Fourth gospel 17:26).

Would his words lead anyone to conclude he meant he would be "in" everyone regardless of their respect for God? No.

Jesus said he would be in some people and they would also have God's love in them. Surely, this would include the future believers who he prayed for when he talked about those who would believe on him through the disciples' word. His prayer for this group links the love of the Father to a proper reverence for his authority. So, here is just one more fact that must be weighed as we think on the issue of God's love.

Scripture says, "the LORD taketh pleasure in them that fear him." (Ps 147:11) and also, "in the fear of the LORD *is* strong confidence" (Prv 19:27). Therefore, if the LORD is pleased when we fear him and strong confidence also results from this, then this is something we should cultivate. Conversely, if the LORD accepts everyone unconditionally, there is no reason to fear him – and if the fear of the LORD is neutralized, then people are cut-off from the benefits of the fear of the LORD.

The Conclusion to the Case of God's Gift

Think outside the box. This phrase is used to encourage thinking that is not limited by assumptions which may be wrong. This kind of thinking can help us to receive biblical correction since it will keep us open to having our assumptions challenged.

At the same time, if we want God's word to guide us, we must also think inside the book. Reading the Bible is the right place to start. But we must also train ourselves to judge according to scripture when we are considering biblical issues. That way, as we grow, our thinking will continue to be conformed to God's word.

We do not need to understand everything about a subject to know if an idea fails the test of scripture. We can ask questions like:

- Is the idea contrary to anything in God's word?
- Does it line up with the life and words of Jesus?
- Would it apply to the apostles and their teachings?

Doing this can help us cultivate a habit of relying on scripture as a litmus test for truth. The benefits of doing so and the problems that follow from not doing so are epitomized in this verse:

"Every word of God *is* pure: he *is* a shield unto them that put their trust in him. Add thou not unto his words, lest he reprove thee, and thou be found a liar" (Prv 30:5-6).

"For God so loved the world, that he gave his only begotten Son, that whosoever believeth in him should not perish, but have everlasting life" (Fourth gospel 3:16).

This tells us what God did ("gave his only begotten Son") and it tells us why God did it ("that whosoever believeth in him should not perish, but have everlasting life"). This verse puts the focus on the gift [Jesus] and so do we if we speak God's word faithfully.

The end of the Case of God's Gift

Chapter 9 – The Law of Liberty

When is someone no longer under the law? How can we do a spiritual self-assessment? What does it mean for us to walk as children of light? This chapter will look at these questions and will consider scripture's counsel on hearing and doing.

Hearers Versus Doers

Romans 2:13 says, "not the hearers of the law are just before God, but the doers of the law shall be justified." Romans 2:14 then talks about, "when the Gentiles, which have not the law, do by nature the things contained in the law... "

They did the things contained in the law even though they did not have the law. The Jews had the law but did not do what it said. How would the contrast in these verses have been received by most of the Jews? They likely would have taken offense at this.

One of the things that distinguished the descendants of Abraham was the practice of circumcision. This practice began 430 years before the law was given (cf. Gal 3:16-17). Surprisingly, the word "uncircumcision" appears in the Book of Romans as much as in all the rest of the Bible combined. It first shows up in Romans 2:25, "circumcision verily profiteth, if thou keep the law: but if thou be a breaker of the law, thy circumcision is made uncircumcision."

Then Romans 2:26 asks this question, "if the uncircumcision **keep the righteousness of the law**, shall not his uncircumcision be counted for circumcision?" So, men can keep the righteousness of the law and being uncircumcised is a state that can be changed without surgery! "Counted for circumcision" status did not require physically cutting-off part of the flesh. To "keep the righteousness of the law" we must cut off the lust of the flesh and do what is right. This is then counted for circumcision even if one is not physically circumcised. [Below, Romans 8:4 will show how the brethren can also fulfil the righteousness of the law.] Since God "shall justify the circumcision by faith, and uncircumcision through faith" (Rom 3:30), justification depends on faith, not on the physical status of a man's foreskin.

Romans 4:8-9 also contrasted circumcision and uncircumcision – "blessed *is* the man to whom the Lord will not impute sin" (Rom 4:8), and "*cometh* this blessedness then upon the circumcision *only*, or upon the uncircumcision also?" (Rom 4:9) God's blessing was not only for the Jews, and the passage went on to make this point:

"faith was reckoned to Abraham for righteousness. How was it then reckoned? when he was in circumcision, or in uncircumcision? Not in circumcision, but in uncircumcision. And he received the sign of circumcision, a seal of the righteousness of the faith which *he had yet* being uncircumcised: that he might be the father of all them that believe, though they be not circumcised" (Rom 4:9b-11).

"Faith was reckoned to Abraham for righteousness" when he was still "in uncircumcision." Circumcision came later and was a seal of what had occurred, but faith is what was reckoned to Abraham for righteousness, not circumcision. Being circumcised in the flesh will not be reckoned as righteousness apart from faith because circumcision served as "a seal of the righteousness **of the faith**." Faith is what made one a child of Abraham, not a physical surgery.

Moreover, scripture proves faith can be exercised by those who are not circumcised, for this is what happened in Abraham's case.

Romans 8:4 tells us, "the righteousness of the law" is fulfilled in those "who walk not after the flesh, but after the Spirit." So, when "the uncircumcision keep the righteousness of the law," this would indicate they were walking "not after the flesh, but after the Spirit." But how can "Gentiles, which have not the law, do by nature the things contained in the law?" (Rom 2:14) How would they know what to do, if they do not have the law?

The Handiwork of God

Scripture says, "the wrath of God is revealed from heaven against all ungodliness and unrighteousness of men, who hold the truth in unrighteousness" (Rom 1:18). Then it goes on to say: "that which may be known of God is manifest in them; for God hath showed *it* unto them" (Rom 1:19). This rebuke was continued in these verses:

"the invisible things of him [God] from the creation of the world are clearly seen, being understood by the things that are made, *even* his eternal power and Godhead; so that they are without excuse: Because that, when they knew God, they glorified *him* not as God, neither were thankful; but became vain in their imaginations, and their foolish heart was darkened" (Rom 1:20-21).

The attributes of God are seen and "understood by the things that are made." "They knew God." Yet, "they glorified *him* not as God, neither were thankful." The revelation of God that is mentioned in Romans 1:20 likely refers to the declaration of God's glory that is presented by his creation, as was noted earlier:

"The heavens declare the glory of God; and the firmament showeth his handiwork. Day unto day uttereth speech, and night unto night showeth knowledge. *There is* no speech nor language, *where* their voice is not heard. Their line is gone out through all the earth, and their words to the end of the world" (Ps 19:1-4).

If people choose to shut their ears to this "voice" and will not hear these "words" and refuse the "knowledge" that is communicated via "his handiwork," what will be the result? Romans 1:20-21 says those who refused the truth "became vain in their imaginations, and their foolish heart was darkened." Even worse, "professing themselves to be wise, they became fools" (v. 22), i.e., they were able to convince themselves they were right to do what they did.

When people hear the "voice" and conform to the "knowledge" noted in Psalm 19:1-4, they are acting as Abraham did when he responded to God's voice. He believed God, and it was counted unto him for righteousness. This is the case for all who honor God's call, like those who keep the righteousness of the law.

"Walk worthy of the Lord unto all pleasing, being fruitful in every good work, and increasing in the knowledge of God" (Col 1:10) was a goal put forth to the brethren. Given what Romans 1:24 tells us about those who "have not the law," we know people can begin this walk even if their knowledge of God is greatly lacking.

What is Required?

"All have sinned, and come short of the glory of God" (Rom 3:23). So, God commands all men everywhere to repent (cf. Acts 17:30). This is the way of escape for those who will obey this command. "This is the love of God, that we keep his commandments: and **his commandments are not grievous**" (1Jo 5:3) is a statement that connects obeying God to "the love of God." These things go hand in hand. Also, Jesus said of the Father, "his commandment is life everlasting" (Fourth gospel 12:50). Moreover, his commandments were not grievous when Moses asked Israel:

> "what doth the LORD thy God require of thee, but to fear the LORD thy God, to walk in all his ways, and to love him, and to serve the LORD thy God with all thy heart and with all thy soul, To keep the commandments of the LORD, and his statutes, which I command thee this day for thy good?" (Dt 10:12-13)

Micah 6:8 put it even more succinctly, "what doth the LORD require of thee, but to do justly, and to love mercy, and to walk humbly with thy God?" Can we say this requirement is too burdensome or rigid? Samuel said, "hath the LORD *as great* delight in burnt offerings and sacrifices, as in obeying the voice of the LORD? Behold, to obey is better than sacrifice, *and* to hearken than the fat of rams" (1Sa 15:22).

The LORD wants people to obey him, rather than disobey his will and then proceed to make offerings and sacrifices to atone for their misdeeds.

Them that Love God

1 Corinthians 2:9 says, "as it is written, Eye hath not seen, nor ear heard, neither have entered into the heart of man, the things which God hath prepared for them that love him."

Wait, it gets better. "We know that all things work together for good to them that love God, to them who are the called according to *his* purpose" (Rom 8:28). Not enough?

James 1:12 talks about "the crown of life, which the Lord hath promised to them that love him" and James 2:5 speaks of "the kingdom which he [God] hath promised to them that love him."

So, how can people today know if they are in this group?

In the fourth gospel, Jesus said some things on this subject on the night of his last Passover after Judas left. He told his disciples, "if ye love me, keep my commandments" (v. 14:15). He also stated, "he that hath my commandments, and keepeth them, he it is that loveth me" (v. 14:21).

In addition, he said, "if a man love me, he will keep my words: and my Father will love him, and we will come unto him, and make our abode with him" (v. 14:23). Jesus then put this idea in the negative and said, "he that loveth me not keepeth not my sayings" (v. 14:24).

After he and the disciples left the supper, he went on to tell them, "if ye keep my commandments, ye shall abide in my love; even as I have kept my Father's commandments, and abide in his love" (Fourth gospel 15:10).

Jesus set forth a clear standard in those verses. Yet, he also said, "my yoke *is* easy, and my burden is light" (Mt 11:30). So, who will say this standard is too hard?

The Gospel of Christ

The gospel of Christ "is the power of God unto salvation" (Rom 1:16).

But what does the phrase "unto salvation" mean? Is it becoming more like Jesus? Here is the verse in context:

"I am not ashamed of the gospel of Christ: for it is the power of God unto salvation to everyone that believeth; to the Jew first, and also to the Greek. For therein is the righteousness of God revealed from faith to faith: as it is written, The just shall live by faith. For the wrath of God is revealed from heaven against all ungodliness and unrighteousness of men, who hold the truth in unrighteousness" (Rom 1:16-18).

The salvation of the believers reveals "the righteousness of God." How so? "The just shall live by faith" and when they live this way (i.e., "serve in newness of spirit" (Rom 7:6), "walk as children of light" (Eph 5:8), etc.), their behavior is in line with God's goal. The goal is "that the righteousness of the law might be fulfilled in us, who walk not after the flesh, but after the Spirit" (Rom 8:4). Therefore, the difference in their behavior will be evident, since "they that are after the flesh do mind the things of the flesh; but they that are after the Spirit the things of the Spirit" (Rom 8:5).

The word "gospel" means good news. This does not mean we do not need to repent. Rather, it means we *can* do so. Those who are determined to justify their deeds regardless of what God says will always find a reason to dismiss God's righteous standard. However, scripture warns against doing so:

"Be not deceived; God is not mocked: for whatsoever a man soweth, that shall he also reap. For he that soweth to his flesh shall of the flesh reap corruption; but he that soweth to the Spirit shall of the Spirit reap life everlasting" (Gal 6:7-8).

The brethren were told, "if ye live after the flesh, ye shall die: but if ye through the Spirit do mortify the deeds of the body, ye shall live" (Rom 8:13). This is not how a person becomes justified. It is how justified people live their lives. They walk not after the flesh, but after the Spirit.

"Walk in the Spirit, and ye shall not fulfill the lust of the flesh. For the flesh lusteth against the Spirit, and the Spirit against the flesh: and these are contrary the one to the other: so that ye cannot do the things that ye would" (Gal 5:16-17).

"Ye cannot do the things that ye would" is a constraint. So, if they did not walk in the Spirit, what would they be doing?

"The works of the flesh are manifest, which are these; Adultery, fornication, uncleanness..." (Gal 5:19). But, "they which do such things shall not inherit the kingdom of God" (Gal 5:21).

Conversely, scripture indicates the brethren should act differently:

"the fruit of the Spirit is love, joy, peace, longsuffering, gentleness, goodness, faith, meekness, temperance: against such there is no law. And they that are Christ's have crucified the flesh with the affections and lusts. If we live in the Spirit, let us also walk in the Spirit" (Gal 5:22-25).

Free to Obey

"If ye then be risen with Christ, seek those things which are above, where Christ sitteth on the right hand of God. Set your affection on things above, not on things on the earth. For ye are dead, and your life is hid with Christ in God" (Col 3:1-3).

This is one of many admonitions directed to the brethren that we find in scripture. It also says, "where the Spirit of the Lord *is*, there *is* liberty" (2Cor 3:17). Jesus said, "the Spirit of the Lord *is* upon me, because he hath anointed me to preach the gospel to the poor; he hath sent me to heal the brokenhearted, to preach deliverance to the captives, and recovering of sight to the blind, to set at liberty them that are bruised" (Lk 4:18). The liberty offered by Jesus was not a freedom to sin. It was the freedom not to sin. The same idea is presented repeatedly in scripture in statements like:

- "sin shall not have dominion over you: for ye are not under the law, but under grace" (Rom 6:14),
- "being then made free from sin, ye became the servants of righteousness" (Rom 6:18),
- "being made free from sin, and become servants to God, ye have your fruit unto holiness" (Rom 6:22),
- "now we are delivered from the law, that being dead wherein we were held; that we should serve in newness of spirit" (Rom 7:6),
- "the law of the Spirit of life in Christ Jesus hath made me free from the law of sin and death" (Rom 8:2).

"Whosoever committeth sin is the servant of sin" (Fourth gospel 8:34) and "no man can serve two masters" (Mt 6:24). If "the law of the Spirit of life in Christ Jesus" sets us free, we are no longer slaves to sin. Those who are set free can repent and "become servants to God," have "fruit unto holiness," and "serve in newness of spirit."

"Be a vessel unto honor, sanctified, and meet for the master's use, *and* prepared unto every good work" (2Ti 2:21). The servants of sin cannot do this. A change must occur first.

Use the Law Lawfully

"A man is not justified by the works of the law, but by the faith of Jesus Christ... for by the works of the law shall no flesh be justified" (Gal 2:16). Even so, we are told "the law" is not the problem:

> "*Is* the law then against the promises of God? God forbid: for if there had been a law given which could have given life, verily righteousness should have been by the law. But the scripture hath concluded all under sin, that the promise by faith of Jesus Christ might be given to them that believe. But before faith came, we were kept under the law, shut up unto the faith which should afterwards be revealed. Wherefore <u>the law was our schoolmaster *to bring us* unto Christ, that we might be justified by faith</u>. But after that faith is come, we are no longer under a schoolmaster" (Gal 3:21-25).

Law cannot give life, otherwise "righteousness should have been by the law." But it was not, for "if righteousness *come* by the law, then Christ is dead in vain" (Gal 2:21). Righteousness does not come by the law, yet the law does show people that they need a savior. When people repent and become justified by faith, then they are no longer under this schoolmaster because, at that point, they are "children of God by faith in Christ Jesus" (Gal 3:26).

The law is not a bad thing. Rather, it depends on how it is used, since we are told "the law is good, if a man use it lawfully" (1Ti 1:8). How does one use the law lawfully?

Consider Romans 8:2 – "the law of the Spirit of life in Christ Jesus hath made me free from the law of sin and death." No one needs to be set free from the law of the Spirit of life in Christ Jesus, but we do need to be set free from the law of sin and death. If people see the law as God does, will this set them free from the bondage that is imposed by an unlawful use of the law? If so, then we know which use of the law reflects God's will for his children.

The idea of the law giving liberty may come as a surprise to some, but this is what happens when the law brings people to Christ and they become justified by faith.

Verses like, "the law of the LORD *is* perfect, converting the soul" (Ps 19:7) teach us the law is not our enemy. So how does the law of the LORD accomplish this converting of the soul? Consider this:

"Blessed *is* the man that walketh not in the counsel of the ungodly, nor standeth in the way of sinners, nor sitteth in the seat of the scornful. But his delight *is* in the law of the LORD; and in his law doth he meditate day and night" (Ps 1:1-2).

Might taking delight in the law of the LORD, and routinely thinking on what it says, have a positive impact on people and lead them to live a more God-honoring life? Of course.

Maintain Good Works

Romans 12:2 says, "be not conformed to this world: but be ye transformed by the renewing of your mind, that ye may prove what *is* that good, and acceptable, and perfect, will of God," and as we meditate on God's word it surely helps in this renewal process.

Following the words "humble yourselves in the sight of the Lord, and he shall lift you up" (Jas 4:10) is a warning. The next verse tells those who "speaketh evil of the law, and judgeth the law," "if thou judge the law, thou art not a doer of the law" (Jas 4:11).

So, people who assume they have the authority to judge the law, need to realize that judging the law is not compatible with the act of humbling ourselves in the sight of the Lord.

When a person obeys God's commandment to repent (cf. Acts 17:30) are they humbling themselves in the sight of the Lord? Yes, and if they join the body of Christ, then the words "he shall lift you up" will apply to them. "Lift you up" may refer to the resurrection. Or it might refer to what happens when a person is set free from the law of sin and death or to the change believers undergo that was detailed by Paul to Titus:

"For we ourselves also were sometimes foolish, disobedient, deceived, serving divers lusts and pleasures, living in malice and envy, hateful, *and* hating one another. But after that the kindness and love of God our Savior toward man appeared, Not by works of righteousness which we have done, but according to his mercy <u>he saved us, by the **washing** of regeneration, and **renewing** of the Holy Ghost</u>; Which he shed on us abundantly through Jesus Christ our Savior; That being justified by his grace, we should be made heirs according to the hope of eternal life. *This is* a faithful saying, and these things I will that thou affirm constantly, that they which have believed in God might be careful to maintain good works. These things are good and profitable unto men" (Titus 3:3-8).

If being "careful to maintain good works" is "good and profitable," then it is not burdensome or legalistic to do so. Do admonitions such as "put off all these; anger, wrath, malice, blasphemy, filthy communication out of your mouth" (Col 3:8) and "wherefore laying aside all malice, and all guile, and hypocrisies, and envies, and all evil speakings…" (1Pt 2:1) put Jesus' followers under bondage? No. They rightly encourage the brethren.

"By this we know that we love the children of God, when we love God, and keep his commandments" (1Jo 5:2). Thus, we show love to God's children when we love God and do what his word says. One of the things it says is:

"Love not the world, neither the things *that are* in the world. If any man love the world, the love of the Father is not in him. For all that *is* in the world, the lust of the flesh, and the lust of the eyes, and the pride of life, is not of the Father, but is of the world" (1Jo 2:15-16).

Obeying the above admonition is critically important because:

"every man is tempted, when he is drawn away of his own lust, and enticed. Then when lust hath conceived, it bringeth forth sin: and sin, when it is finished, bringeth forth death" (Jas 1:14-15).

Loving the world or the things that are in the world does not merely put a person on a slippery slope. It turns out to be more like getting trapped in quicksand.

The above passage describes a process that, unless it is stopped, inevitably leads to death. So, it is understandable why God's word presents many warnings against people playing around with lust, even if it is only in their minds.

With the internet, people can easily indulge in endless fantasies or rack up countless hours of wasted time. Even so, the brethren can conform their thoughts and deeds to the following admonition:

"lay apart all filthiness and superfluity of naughtiness, and receive with meekness the engrafted word, which is able to save your souls. But **be ye doers of the word**, and not hearers only, deceiving your own selves. For if any be a hearer of the word, and not a doer, he is like unto a man beholding his natural face in a glass: For he beholdeth himself, and goeth his way, and straightway forgetteth what manner of man he was. But whoso looketh into the perfect law of liberty, and continueth *therein*, he being not a forgetful hearer, but a doer of the work, this man shall be blessed in his deed" (Jas 1:21-25).

Self-Evaluation, By What Standard?

The passage above indicates we should judge ourselves by "the perfect law of liberty" if we want a true self-assessment.

The term law of liberty undoubtedly refers to the "law of the Spirit of life in Christ Jesus" that the writer of Romans said set him free "from the law of sin and death" (Rom 8:2).

We saw that Galatians 3:24 says, "the law was our schoolmaster *to bring us* unto Christ, that we might be justified by faith."

Similarly, looking into "the perfect law of liberty" gives us a way to honestly assess ourselves. This is good news because this helps a person to become a doer, rather than turn into a forgetful hearer.

The word gospel means good news. However, this good news will not produce a result on its own. The writer of Hebrews warned the brethren that hearing the gospel will not benefit people unless it is mixed with faith:

"Let us therefore fear, lest, a promise being left us of entering into his rest, any of you should seem to come short of it. For unto us was the gospel preached, as well as unto them: but the word preached did not profit them, not being mixed with faith in them that heard *it*" (Heb 4:1-2).

Here two groups were contrasted to show the gospel by itself is of no benefit. "Us" identified the brethren, while "them" referred to those who "came out of Egypt by Moses" (Heb 3:16) but later died in the wilderness because they "believed not" (Heb 3:18). This contrast reinforced the writer's point about the need to continue believing.

"Take heed, brethren, lest there be in any of you an evil heart of unbelief, in **departing from the living God**. But exhort one another daily, while it is called Today; lest any of you be hardened through the deceitfulness of sin. For we are made partakers of Christ, if we hold the beginning of our confidence stedfast unto the end" (Heb 3:12-14).

Is holding "the beginning of our confidence stedfast unto the end," too much for God to ask? No; but it is a process, not an experience that happens when one hears the gospel and responds with joy, as Jesus proved in the parable of the sower. In the next chapter we will consider this parable and see why faith is not a belief.

When James encouraged the brethren to be "doers of the word, and not hearers only," he said those who were "hearers only" were deceiving themselves. To help the brethren avoid falling prey to a double-minded approach, he used a word picture to warn against using a self-serving approach to handling the word of God:

"if any be a hearer of the word, and not a doer, he is like unto a man beholding his natural face in a glass: For he beholdeth himself, and goeth his way, and straightway forgetteth what manner of man he was" (Jas 1:23-24).

The word "glass" refers to a mirror (as in the term 'looking glass'). A mirror enables us to see ourselves from a different point of view. Looking into God's word lets us see if we are obeying him or not. Thus, we know if we are doing or merely hearing. Given the admonition "examine yourselves, whether ye be in the faith" (2Cor 13:5), it is not wise to *assume* we are doing God's will. We should look to see if we are in line with God's standard or not.

James and the writer of Hebrews did not give false assurance to the brethren and say, *'we are all growing believers.'* In fact, James suggested a believer will either become "a doer of the work" or "a forgetful hearer." He taught an ongoing regard for God's word is what matters when he said, "whoso looketh into the perfect law of liberty, and <u>continueth</u> *therein*, he being not a forgetful hearer, but a doer of the work, this man shall be blessed in his deed" (Jas 1:25).

Consume More of God's Word

One way to avoid becoming a forgetful hearer is to keep our mind saturated with scripture. Moses gave a lot of counsel about how people can honor God's word, including the following:

- "these words, which I command thee this day, shall be in thine heart: And thou shalt teach them diligently unto thy children, and shalt talk of them when thou sittest in thine house, and when thou walkest by the way, and when thou liest down, and when thou risest up" (Dt 6:6-7),
- "what thing soever I command you, observe to do it: thou shalt not add thereto, nor diminish from it" (Dt 12:32),
- "ye shall walk after the LORD your God, and fear him, and keep his commandments, and obey his voice, and ye shall serve him, and cleave unto him" (Dt 13:4).

These verses also speak to us, because "whatsoever things were written aforetime were written for our learning" (Rom 15:4).

The LORD said Abraham would "command his children and his household after him, and they shall keep the way of the LORD, to do justice and judgment; that the LORD may bring upon Abraham that which he hath spoken of him" (Gen 18:19).

This ought to have special significance for those in the faith, since "they which are of faith," "are the children of Abraham" (Gal 3:7). Also, God's word teaches the brethren to do justice and judgment when it says things like, "judge not according to the appearance, but judge righteous judgment" (Fourth gospel 7:24).

Commanded to Love?

"All the law is fulfilled in one word, *even* in this; Thou shalt love thy neighbor as thyself" (Gal 5:14). Doing this fulfills the law, but who will say urging people to do this equates to advocating legalism? The thought of people being commanded to love may seem to be a contradiction in terms. However, God expects people to obey these commandments and we find explicit statements that make this clear in both the Old Testament and the New Testament.

Moreover, Jesus indicated God's commandments regarding love are what upholds the rest of scripture when he said:

"Thou shalt love the Lord thy God with all thy heart, and with all thy soul, and with all thy mind. This is the first and great commandment. And the second is like unto it, Thou shalt love thy neighbor as thyself. On these two commandments hang all the law and the prophets" (Mt 22:37-40).

He did not mean 'these two commandments summarize the law,' because the word "hang" did not mean sum up. Rather, he was pointing out that if we will not obey these two commandments, "the law and the prophets" have nothing to hang on.

A balance must hang on a fixed point to work. Likewise, doing what is right in God's eyes and understanding his word starts with keeping these two commandments in mind as we diligently seek to honor the whole counsel of God's word consistently.

Chapter 10 – In Conclusion

When is love not good? By what standard can we distinguish truth from error? How can we renew our minds, know the will of the Lord, and grow in grace and knowledge? These issues and key points noted earlier herein will be brought together in this final chapter to leave the reader with a firm foundation.

Counsel from Psalm 119

Psalm 119:1 says, "blessed *are* the undefiled in the way, who walk in the law of the LORD." So, we know some people can do this. Verse 2 tells us, "blessed *are* they that keep his testimonies, *and* that seek him with the whole heart." Thus, it is not impossible for people to do these things either. Then in verse 3 it says, "they also do no iniquity: they walk in his ways." Here again, we see at least some human beings are able to do this too.

Psalm 119 offers an extended discussion of the LORD's word, and what it says about the law and the commandments is still relevant. This book cannot weigh all 176 verses of this Psalm, but here are some key verses for your consideration. The psalmist noted his reliance upon scripture and said, "I will meditate in thy precepts, and have respect unto thy ways" (v. 15), "I will delight myself in thy statutes: I will not forget thy word" (v. 16), and "thy testimonies also *are* my delight *and* my counselors" (v. 24).

He then asked the LORD for help. "Make me to understand the way of thy precepts: so shall I talk of thy wondrous works" (v. 27). "Give me understanding, and I shall keep thy law; yea, I shall observe it with *my* whole heart" (v. 34). This last verse lets us know understanding from the LORD can enable people to keep his law.

He said, "I will delight myself in thy commandments, which I have loved" (v. 47). So, he did not see the commandments of the LORD as burdensome. In saying, "I thought on my ways, and turned my feet unto thy testimonies" (v. 59), he was saying he subjected his ways to the test and took his direction from the testimonies of the LORD. Moreover, he did not do this grudgingly or drag his feet. "I made haste, and delayed not to keep thy commandments" (v. 60).

The psalmist also indicated his fear of the LORD was not unique. "I *am* a companion of all *them* that fear thee, and of them that keep thy precepts" (v. 63). Thus, others did this too.

He went on to write, "teach me good judgment and knowledge: for I have believed thy commandments" (v. 66). This implies there is a link between having respect for the commandments of the LORD and learning good judgment and knowledge.

In addition, he made statements like, "all thy commandments are faithful" (v. 86), and "I will never forget thy precepts" (v. 93). But notice that absent from his words is any esteem for the teachings of men.

He declared, "O how love I thy law! it is my meditation all the day" (v. 97). He learned from the LORD; "I have more understanding than all my teachers: for thy testimonies *are* my meditation" (v. 99) and said, "through thy precepts I get understanding: therefore I hate every false way" (v. 104).

"Thy word is a lamp unto my feet, and a light unto my path" (v. 105), "I love thy commandments above gold" (v. 127), "thy testimonies *are* wonderful: therefore doth my soul keep them" (v. 129) are all verses that further show his esteem for what the LORD had said.

Instead of seeking to justify himself, the psalmist was willing to subject himself to the LORD's standard. This was shown when he said, "righteous *art* thou, O LORD, and upright *are* thy judgments" (v. 137) and "thy righteousness is an everlasting righteousness, and thy law is the truth" (v. 142).

His theme was consistent – "thy word *is* true *from* the beginning: and every one of thy righteous judgments *endureth* forever" (v. 160), "great peace have they which love thy law" (v. 165), "I have kept thy precepts and thy testimonies" (v. 168), and "my tongue shall speak of thy word: for all thy commandments *are* righteousness" (v. 172).

The psalmist repeatedly declared his respect for the LORD's word, yet this did not guarantee he could not go wrong. We know this for the Psalm ends, "I have gone astray like a lost sheep; seek thy servant; for I do not forget thy commandments" (v. 176).

Understanding the Lord's Will

"Be ye not unwise, but understanding what the will of the Lord *is*" (Eph 5:17). This was written to "the faithful in Christ Jesus" (Eph 1:1), so the will of the Lord is something we should seek to understand. Psalm 119 indicates his will is for us to keep his testimonies, seek him with the whole heart, do no iniquity, and walk in his ways (cf. Ps 119:2-3). Still, some say, *'the law was given to show no one can obey the law,'* even though Psalm 119 and many other passages teach otherwise.

Does Psalm 119 present an impossible standard? No. But if we believe God's commandments are impossible to keep, then they become null and void to us, for no one is obliged to do something they are unable to do. To ask a blind person to identify the color of an object or to require a deaf person to distinguish between audible sounds raises an impossible standard. Does God do this? Sometimes people quote portions of scripture that can make it seem so. Isaiah 55:8-9 says:

"[8]my thoughts *are* not your thoughts, neither *are* your ways my ways, saith the LORD. [9]For *as* the heavens are higher than the earth, so are my ways higher than your ways, and my thoughts than your thoughts."

Did the LORD mean human beings are unable to follow his ways or understand his thoughts? No. Psalm 119:3 speaks of those who "walk in his ways." In addition, scripture lets us know people can keep the commandments of Jesus, walk in the law of the LORD, and obey God from the heart (cf. Fourth gospel 14:15, Ps 119:1, Rom 6:17).

So, what is meant in Isaiah 55:8-9? Look at Isaiah 55:6-8 and see how the context of this passage casts the words in another light:

"[6]Seek ye the LORD while he may be found, call ye upon him while he is near: [7]Let the wicked forsake his way, and the unrighteous man his thoughts: and let him return unto the LORD, and he will have mercy upon him; and to our God, for he will abundantly pardon. [8]For my thoughts *are* not your thoughts, neither *are* your ways my ways, saith the LORD."

The LORD called for a change. "Let the wicked **forsake** his way, and the unrighteous man his thoughts: and let him **return** unto the LORD." The wicked and unrighteous had to change because their thoughts and ways did not conform to the LORD's thoughts and ways. This was their condition, not the state of all men.

Mercy and pardon were listed as two benefits for those who would forsake their way and "return unto the LORD," i.e., repent. But this would mean submitting to the LORD's authority and, if they did this, then his ways and thoughts would govern their lives.

"My thoughts *are* not your thoughts, neither *are* your ways my ways" was a rebuke to the thinking and the behavior of the wicked and the unrighteous. This verse was not describing Abel, Noah, Abraham, Moses, etc., because when the LORD said this, he was not comparing himself to all men. He was contrasting his ways with the way of the wicked and his thoughts with the thoughts of the unrighteous.

The brethren can "live in the Spirit" and "walk in the Spirit" (Gal 5:25), can understand "the will of the Lord" (Eph 5:17), and can "have the mind of Christ" (1Cor 2:16). If they do this, their ways and thoughts would be in line with the LORD's ways and his thoughts.

When Jesus told people to "sin no more" (Fourth gospel 5:14 & 8:11) could they do it? When Peter quoted God saying, "be ye holy; for I am holy" (1Pt 1:16), did he raise an impossible standard or was he urging his readers to live in a way that honors God?

Love, By What Standard?

Some people judge themselves to be good and assume God will ignore their disobedience because scripture says, "God is love" (1Jo 4:8). But this defines love by their standard, not God's standard. As we saw earlier, a similar distortion of scripture occurs when people say things like, *'God is not willing that any should perish'* or *'God loves everyone unconditionally,'* which falsely imply God has low or no standards. Still, such ideas are popular because they lower the bar by suggesting everyone is good with God (and if this is true, then those who disobey God do not need to repent).

The words "God is love" appear twice in scripture (1Jo 4:8 & 16), but men are wrong to think their definition of "love" determines who God is. For example, if people think, *'God loves you just the way you are'* accurately represents God's word, it shows they are not judging by his word, since scripture does not say this. It says, "whom the Lord loveth he chasteneth" (Heb 12:6). He chastens them to get them to change, so he does not love them the way they are. Parents of drug-addicts do not love their children the way they are – they hate the way their children are, and they want their children to change because they love their children and they want what is best for them.

Does the LORD want what is best for those of his children who are addicted to sin? Yes. This is why he corrects his children. "Whom the LORD loveth he correcteth" (Prv 3:12). Saying *'God loves people just as they are'* is a far different matter, since that makes people feel good about themselves, whether or not they are an evildoer.

Saying God's love is universal and/or without condition comforts all who "will not endure sound doctrine," but "after their own lusts," "heap to themselves teachers" (2Ti 4:3) and "turn away *their* ears from the truth" (2Ti 4:4). People like this seek out teachers, but they do not want sound doctrine or truth. Scripture has many warnings for such people. One of them is, "thus saith the LORD; Cursed *be* the man that trusteth in man, and maketh flesh his arm, and whose heart departeth from the LORD" (Jer 17:5). Two verses later scripture gives a better option. "Blessed *is* the man that trusteth in the LORD, and whose hope the LORD is" (Jer 17:7).

By This We Know

"The word of God *is* quick, and powerful, and sharper than any two-edged sword, piercing even to the dividing asunder of soul and spirit, and of the joints and marrow, and *is* a discerner of the thoughts and intents of the heart" (Heb 4:12). This discernment will challenge people who are doing things they should not be doing. Such people tend to seek out teachers who assure them they can have life without obeying God. But verses like, "we know that we have passed from death unto life, because we love the brethren" (1Jo 3:14) give us a reliable measure. Also, earlier we looked at the verses below on how we can know if we are loving the brethren:

"By this we know that we love the children of God, when we love God, and keep his commandments. For this is the love of God, that we keep his commandments: and his commandments are not grievous" (1Jo 5:2-3).

While Jesus said, "whosoever shall do the will of God, the same is my brother, and my sister, and mother" (Mk 3:35), he did not mean doing God's will *for one moment in time* makes one a child of God. Consider what Jesus told his disciples about the need for them to continue in his love:

"As the Father hath loved me, so have I loved you: **continue** ye in my love. If ye **keep** my commandments, ye shall **abide** in my love; even as I have kept my Father's commandments, and abide in his love" (Fourth gospel 15:9-10).

In the verses above, God's love is linked to his commandments, so no one should think his commandments were set aside. When Jesus told his disciples, "continue ye in my love," those words also implied that it was possible for a man to <u>not</u> continue in his love. Examples of this might be when "many of his disciples went back, and walked no more with him" (Fourth gospel 6:66) or when some men stopped following Jesus in this verse, "they went out from us, but they were not of us; for if they had been of us, they would *no doubt* have continued with us" (1Jo 2:19).

How do followers of Jesus abide in his love? Jesus' counsel was clear. "If ye keep my commandments, ye shall abide in my love." Can people keep the commandments of God? It seems they can, because the following words indicate this is what the brethren do:

"we keep his commandments, and do those things that are pleasing in his sight. And this is his commandment, That we should believe on the name of his Son Jesus Christ, and love one another, as he gave us commandment. And he that keepeth his commandments dwelleth in him, and he in him" (1Jo 3:22-24).

On the night Jesus was arrested, he told his disciples:

"I am the vine, ye *are* the branches: **He that abideth in me**, and I in him, the same bringeth forth much fruit: for without me ye can do nothing. **If a man abide not in me**, he is cast forth as a branch, and is withered; and men gather them, and cast *them* into the fire, and they are burned" (Fourth gospel 15:4-6).

Is the phrase "if a man abide not in me" describing someone who once followed Jesus but stopped doing so? If it does, then being attached to Jesus at some point does not guarantee a person who is following him will continue to do so. Those who love God submit to his standard of right and wrong, and they continue to do so.

Ungodly Love?

Loving is not a virtue in and of itself. This point was made by Jesus when he told his disciples, "if ye love them which love you, what thank have ye? for sinners also love those that love them" (Lk 6:32). He also said, "no man can serve two masters: for either he will hate the one, and love the other; or else he will hold to the one, and despise the other. Ye cannot serve God and mammon" (Mt 6:24). Loving mammon is not good, so love is not always virtuous.

Micah 3:2 speaks of those "who hate the good, and love the evil." This shows both love and hate can serve an ungodly agenda. Conversely, the LORD told the house of Israel to "hate the evil, and love the good" (Amo 5:15).

Psalm 97:10 says, "ye that love the LORD, hate evil" (Ps 97:10) and Proverbs 8:13 says, "the fear of the LORD *is* to hate evil." So, it is wrong to assume hate is always bad. If a person says Jesus never hated anything, point them to scripture. To the angel of the church of Ephesus, Jesus said, "thou hatest the deeds of the Nicolaitans, which I also hate" (Rv 2:6). His message to the angel of the church in Smyrna said, "so hast thou also them that hold the doctrine of the Nicolaitans, which thing I hate" (Rv 2:15).

The Book of Hebrews also had this to say about Jesus, "thou hast loved righteousness, and hated iniquity" (Heb 1:9) and this fits what is said in this verse, "the LORD trieth the righteous: but the wicked and him that loveth violence his soul hateth" (Ps 11:5).

Strait and Narrow

Scripture states, "the haters of the LORD should have submitted themselves unto him" (Ps 81:15). Repentance was the remedy, but many people go a different way. We see this in Matthew 7:13-14 when Jesus told his disciples:

"Enter ye in at the strait gate: for wide *is* the gate, and broad *is* the way, that leadeth to destruction, and many there be which go in there at: Because strait *is* the gate, and narrow *is* the way, which leadeth unto life, and few there be that find it."

Jesus contrasted two options, a "wide" versus a "strait" gate and a "broad" versus a "narrow" way. Then he followed this with an ominous warning, "beware of false prophets, which come to you in sheep's clothing, but inwardly they are ravening wolves" (Mt 7:15).

After giving his disciples a directive about entering the right way, he immediately followed it with a warning for them to be on guard against false teaching. Why? Was he warning against falling for ideas that turn people away from the strait gate and narrow way? The sheep's clothing indicates false prophets outwardly seem like followers of Jesus. So, their talk will be cloaked in scriptural terms, but it will not accurately reflect God's word.

His next words were, "ye shall know them by their fruits. Do men gather grapes of thorns, or figs of thistles?" (Mt 7:16) In posing this rhetorical question, Jesus both taught his disciples how to identify false prophets and showed no one should go to them to be fed.

Can phrases such as "God so loved the world" (Fourth gospel 3:16), "the truth shall make you free" (Fourth gospel 8:32), "God is love" (1Jo 4:8), and "the Lord is… not willing that any should perish" (2Pt 3:9), be used in a way that makes it appear as if the gate is wide and the way is broad? Yes. Some try to make God more appealing to the largest number of people by acting as if the New Testament was meant to be a loving, affirming, and tolerant replacement for the Old Testament, which they see as authoritarian and intolerant. The New Testament, however, lets us know the Old Testament is backed by the same authority (cf. 2Ti 3:16, Jas 2:11, et al.).

By dividing God's word against itself it makes the broad way look like the right way. Nevertheless, the following passage indicates the brethren have received "the spirit which is of God" and this enables them to recognize the things that come from God:

"we have received, not the spirit **of the world**, but the spirit which is **of God**; that we might know the things that are freely given to us of God. Which things also we speak, not in the words which man's wisdom teacheth, but which the Holy Ghost teacheth; comparing spiritual things with spiritual. But the natural man receiveth not the things of the Spirit of God: for they are foolishness unto him: neither can he know *them*, because they are spiritually discerned" (1Cor 2:12-14).

Here two spirits are contrasted, one is "of the world" and the other is "of God." The brethren receive the second one, not the first, and the spirit which is of God enables them to know things they would not know otherwise. Two teaching methods are also contrasted. It said, "we speak, not in the words which man's wisdom teacheth." Instead, they spoke the things "which the Holy Ghost teacheth; comparing spiritual things with spiritual." These two methods are not compatible, yet many people still go ahead and put confidence in the words which man's wisdom teacheth.

Mixing the teachings of men and teaching of God is also contrary to this idea, "be ye not unequally yoked together with unbelievers: for what fellowship hath righteousness with unrighteousness? and what communion hath light with darkness?" (2Cor 6:14) Some see this in terms of marriage between believers and unbelievers, but it turns out the words husband, wife, and marriage do not appear anywhere in this passage. In fact, the passage is warning against combining incompatible things! The next verse shows this, as it then goes on to list more things that ought not to be mixed. "What concord hath Christ with Belial? or what part hath he that believeth with an infidel? (2Cor 6:15)

The reason these incompatible things should not be joined, i.e., "yoked together," is that doing so inhibits the process of adoption. This is the point that was stressed in 2 Corinthians 6:17-18 when the passage went on to call for a separation:

"Wherefore come out from among them, and be ye separate, saith the Lord, and touch not the unclean *thing*; and I will receive you, And will be a Father unto you, and ye shall be my sons and daughters, saith the Lord Almighty."

To urge unity, without giving due regard to the counsel of scripture on the need to separate, is to disregard what is right in the sight of the LORD.

When truth causes division or if God's word calls on his children to be separate from people or things that would cause them to be unclean, this is not something a child of God should grieve over or seek to avoid.

Separation and Sanctification

The brethren were told, "God hath from the beginning chosen you to salvation through sanctification of the Spirit and belief of the truth" (2Th 2:13). They were also told:

"this is the will of God, *even* your sanctification, that ye should abstain from fornication: That every one of you should know how to possess his vessel in sanctification and honor" (1Th 4:3-4).

"Dearly beloved, let us cleanse ourselves from all filthiness of the flesh and spirit, perfecting holiness in the fear of God" (2Cor 7:1).

"God hath not called us unto uncleanness, but unto holiness" (1Th 4:7).

"He that soweth to his flesh shall of the flesh reap corruption; but he that soweth to the Spirit shall of the Spirit reap life everlasting" (Gal 6:8).

"Blessed *is* every one that feareth the LORD; that walketh in his ways" (Ps 128:1).

These and many other verses make one point clear; those who have been set free from sin are obliged to obey God.

Romans 8:1 says, "*there is* therefore now no condemnation to them which are in Christ Jesus, who walk not after the flesh, but after the Spirit." So, would this mean there is no condemnation for those who say they believe in Jesus or does the no condemnation promise apply only to people who do what the verse says?

"They that are after the flesh do mind the things of the flesh; but they that are after the Spirit the things of the Spirit" (Rom 8:5).

Minding "the things of the flesh" will lead to behaviors that have dire consequences:

"the works of the flesh are manifest, which are *these*; Adultery, fornication, uncleanness, lasciviousness, idolatry, witchcraft, hatred, variance, emulations, wrath, strife, seditions, heresies, envyings, murders, drunkenness, revellings, and such like: of the which I tell you before, as I have also told *you* in time past, that they which do such things shall not inherit the kingdom of God" (Gal 5:19-21).

Ephesians 5:5 provides a similar warning: "No whoremonger, nor unclean person, nor covetous man, who is an idolater, hath any inheritance in the kingdom of Christ and of God."

On the other hand, the brethren who heard God and were "taught by him" (Eph 4:21) were told, "put on the new man, which after God is created in righteousness and true holiness" (Eph 4:24).

Similar counsel is found in other passages such as this:

"as Christ hath suffered for us in the flesh, arm yourselves likewise with the same mind: for he that hath suffered in the flesh hath ceased from sin; That he no longer should live the rest of *his* time in the flesh to the lusts of men, but to the will of God" (1Pt 4:1-2).

This was written to those "who by him [Jesus] do believe in God, that raised him up from the dead" (1Pt 1:21). This group was also told, "seeing **ye have purified your souls in obeying the truth** through the Spirit unto unfeigned love of the brethren, *see that ye* love one another with a pure heart fervently" (1Pt 1:22).

If people purify their soul in obeying the truth through the Spirit, it leads to unfeigned love of the brethren. But loving "one another" requires discrimination, for if we are going to love "the brethren," we must distinguish between who is in this group and who is not.

Does the term "one another" mean all men or some? After Judas departed from the group at Jesus' last Passover supper (Fourth gospel 13:31), Jesus told his disciples, "a new commandment I give unto you, That ye love one another; as I have loved you, that ye also love one another" (v. 34). A little later, he told them, "this is my commandment, That ye love one another, as I have loved you" (Fourth gospel 15:12) and he said, "greater love hath no man than this, that a man lay down his life for his friends" (v. 15:13). Many know he said this but do not realize he went on to say, "ye are my friends, if ye do whatsoever I command you" (v. 15:14). Should we conclude he laid down his life for everyone, even the workers of iniquity who he said he never knew? (cf. Mt 7:23) Or did he lay down his life for those who are his friends?

How can a person know if Jesus counts them as a friend? He said, "ye are my friends, if ye do whatsoever I command you" (v. 15:14). So, an honest self-assessment according to the scriptures is what is needed if people want to know if they are a friend of Jesus.

The Household of Faith

In Acts 11:27-28, a prophet from Jerusalem went to Antioch and he told the disciples in that city about a coming famine that would be throughout all the world. This caused the disciples to take up a collection and "every man according to his ability, determined to send relief unto the brethren which dwelt in Judea" (Acts 11:29). Did they send relief to be indiscriminately shared with everyone in Judea? Or did they think it right to discriminate in their giving and designate the brethren as the recipients of this relief effort? Many today send donations for people in need to organizations that allocate those funds without regard to what is right in the sight of the LORD or, worse yet, even openly support ungodly people and practices. When we give would it not be better if we focus on the brethren, groups that seek to honor God, and people in need who we personally interact with as we go through our daily lives?

Consider two verses, "he [Jesus] laid down his life for us: and we ought to lay down *our* lives for the brethren" (1Jo 3:16) and "beloved, if God so loved us, we ought also to love one another" (1Jo 4:11). Are these telling us how to relate to the brethren or to every man? Scripture tells the brethren how to view their ties to one another, "ye are the body of Christ, and members in particular" (1Cor 12:27). In Ephesians 5:29-30, the bar was set even higher:

"no man ever yet hated his own flesh; but nourisheth and cherisheth it, even as the Lord the church: For we are members of his body, of his flesh, and of his bones."

Verses such as, "if any man have not the Spirit of Christ, he is none of his" (Rom 8:9), let us know every person is not in the body of Christ. This is not to say we should not do good to those who are not counted among the brethren, for Galatians 6:9-10 says:

"let us not be weary in well doing: for in due season we shall reap, if we faint not. As we have therefore opportunity, let us do good unto all *men*, especially unto them who are of the household of faith" (Gal 6:9-10).

This contrast between "all" and "them who are of the household of faith" lets us know we should do good to anyone when we have the opportunity, but it is also right to treat the brethren differently.

This aligns with a key identifying feature of the disciples of Jesus. He told his disciples, "by this shall all *men* know that ye are my disciples, if ye have love **one to another**" (Fourth gospel 13:35). Notice, he did not say, all will know you are my disciples if you love them.

So, people should be able to identify his disciples by the distinctive love his disciples exhibit toward each other. But if people want to experience this love, they need to become a disciple of Jesus. Thus, the unique love between the members of the body of Christ also acts as a witness against those who reject the gospel.

One of the most notable examples of this love in the body of Christ happened following the events on the day of Pentecost. This was said of those who responded to Peter's message on that day:

"they that gladly received his word were baptized: and the same day there were added *unto them* about three thousand souls. And they continued stedfastly in the apostles' doctrine and fellowship, and in breaking of bread, and in prayers. And fear came upon every soul: and many wonders and signs were done by the apostles. And all that believed were together, and had all things common; And sold their possessions and goods, and parted them to all *men*, as every man had need. And they, continuing daily with one accord in the temple, and breaking bread from house to house, did eat their meat with gladness and singleness of heart, Praising God, and having favor with all the people. And the Lord added to the church daily such as should be saved" (Acts 2:41-47).

Notice, the word "all" was used of two different groups. It was used of "all that believed" and the passage indicates the believer's care for one another caused them to have "favor with all the people." Unbelievers recognized the love the believers had for one another just as Jesus had said! Here is another example of this love:

"the multitude of them that believed were of one heart and of one soul: neither said any of them that ought of the things which he possessed was his own; but they had all things common. And with great power gave the apostles witness of the resurrection of the Lord Jesus: and great grace was upon them all. Neither was there any among them that lacked: for as many as were possessors of lands or houses sold them, and brought the prices of the things that were sold, And laid them down at the apostles' feet: and distribution was made unto every man according as he had need" (Acts 4:32-35).

None of the believers "lacked" because those who had real estate sold it and this money was shared with other believers according to each one's need. The love the brethren showed to one another was not how they treated everyone. [In 2 Chronicles 19:2 there is a rhetorical question that asks, "shouldest thou help the ungodly, and love them that hate the LORD?" and the one who had done so was then told, "therefore is wrath upon thee from before the LORD." This shows the need to discriminate according to his standards.]

For the Brethren

The distinction between believers and non-believers is also seen in Acts 5:1-10. This tells us about Ananias and Sapphira who were killed by God after they falsely represented themselves. Then the passage goes on to say:

"great fear came upon all the church, and upon as many as heard these things. And by the hands of the apostles were many signs and wonders wrought among the people; (and they were all with one accord in Solomon's porch. And of the rest durst no man join himself to them: but the people magnified them. And believers were the more added to the Lord, multitudes both of men and women.)" (Acts 5:11-14)

"Of the rest" no man dared "join himself to them." This was not a call to join the church. It was a separation between people who submit to God's authority and those who do not. This also caused people not to join themselves to the church, since it carried a risk.

This was said in the context of the death of Ananias and Sapphira, so it may be those two had done this. Did they *join themselves to* the church? If a branch does not graft itself into a tree, why would we conclude it is up to people to join themselves to the church?

Acts 2:47 tells us, "the Lord added to the church daily such as should be saved." Was this the Lord's doing or theirs? Acts 16:14 tells of a woman "whose heart the Lord opened, that she attended unto the things which were spoken of Paul." Did the Lord also open the hearts of those in the household of Cornelius? In Peter's report on this, he said, "as I began to speak, the Holy Ghost fell on them" and he asked, "what was I, that I could withstand God?" (Acts 11:15 & 17) (So, who should we conclude is building the church? See Matthew 16:28, where Jesus said, "I will build my church... ")

The words, "have fervent charity [love] among yourselves" (1Pt 4:8) reminded the brethren about the kind of love they should show for others who are in the body of Christ. "Among yourselves" was not a reference to all human beings. Nevertheless, we are still obliged to "do good unto all" (Gal 6:10), as was noted earlier.

"*Be* kindly affectioned one to another with brotherly love; in honor preferring one another" (Rom 12:10) urges those in the body of Christ to treat each other this way. Similarly, 1 John 3:16-19 has counsel regarding caring for the brethren using this world's good:

"he [Jesus] laid down his life for us: and we ought to lay down *our* lives for the brethren. But whoso hath this world's good, and seeth his brother have need, and shutteth up his bowels *of* compassion from him, how dwelleth the love of God in him? My little children, let us not love in word, neither in tongue; but in deed and in truth. And hereby we know that we are of the truth, and shall assure our hearts before him."

Believers can know they "are of the truth" and assure their hearts by loving one another "in deed and in truth." This is where we see scripture teaching a standard of assurance. It encourages a love of the brethren but not for an organization that calls itself a church.

Jesus "loved the church" (Eph 5:25) but he did not tell his followers to do so because they are the church. Rather, people in the body of Christ were told to love "one another." Scripture also indicates our love of God is linked to our love of the brethren:

"he that loveth not his brother whom he hath seen, how can he love God whom he hath not seen? And this commandment have we from him, That he who loveth God love his brother also" (1Jo 4:20-21).

The foregoing discussion has shown that terms like "yourselves" or "one another," and sometimes "every man" or "all," were used to refer to a group of people that included everyone in the group, but not all human beings. It is wrong to assume words such as us, we, men, all, none, etc., have to be referring to every living person because scripture's use of a term must shape our understanding of a word, such as when these terms are used of the brethren.

[Do the words "love your enemies" (Mt 5:44) mean the brethren and enemies should be treated as if they are the same? "The devil" is an "enemy" (Mt 13:39) but is not to be loved. So, how does scripture reconcile these matters? This question is left for your self-study.]

A Call to Separation

Peter's last words on the day of Pentecost were, "save yourselves from this untoward generation" (Acts 2:40). He gave a similar warning later when he wrote about separating from things that can lead people to live the rest of their "time in the flesh to the lusts of men" rather than "to the will of God" (1Pt 4:2). Such things keep us from being renewed in the spirit of our mind. Jesus told a man who said he wanted to follow him, "no man, having put his hand to the plow, and looking back, is fit for the kingdom of God" (Lk 9:62). Men cannot go in two directions at once. Likewise, we cannot love the things of the world and love the Father (cf. 1Jo 2:15-16).

Separating from people or behaviors that are part of our life can be painful and costly. So, Jesus told people to count the cost of following him, to see if they are able to make it to the end with him:

"there went great multitudes with him [Jesus]: and he turned, and said unto them, If any *man* come to me, and hate not his father, and mother, and wife, and children, and brethren, and sisters, yea, and his own life also, he cannot be my disciple. And whosoever doth not bear his cross, and come after me, cannot be my disciple. For which of you, intending to build a tower, sitteth not down first, and counteth the cost, whether he have *sufficient* to finish *it*? (Lk 14:25-28)

Then he succinctly put it this way, "whosoever he be of you that forsaketh not all that he hath, he cannot be my disciple" (Lk 14:33).

If a man prays, "teach me to do thy will; for thou *art* my God: thy spirit *is* good; lead me into the land of uprightness" (Ps 143:10) is it alright for him to go on filling his mind with things of the world that will keep him from having this prayer answered? Speaking to God as if he is our authority while refusing to separate ourselves from the things of the world, is the equivalent of *talking* after the spirit while *walking* after the flesh.

"They that are after the flesh do mind the things of the flesh; but they that are after the Spirit the things of the Spirit" (Rom 8:5). Thus, the way we walk is linked to what we occupy our minds with.

Avoid Entanglements

We need to avoid entanglements with things of the world, for they work to cut people off from God's blessings. If we associate with people who are ungodly or fill our minds with ideas that come via the entertainment, reporting, and educational systems controlled by those who are ungodly, how will this work out?

Peter warned of people who "allure through the lusts of the flesh... those that were clean escaped from them who live in error" (2Pt 2:18). He said, "while they promise them liberty, they themselves are the servants of corruption: for of whom a man is overcome, of the same is he brought in bondage" (2Pt 2:19). Although servants of corruption do not have liberty, they used the lusts of the flesh and a promise of liberty to lure those who had escaped and bring them back into bondage. Is the same thing still going on today? Surely.

Jesus said, "whosoever committeth sin is the servant of sin" (Fourth gospel 8:34). Romans 6:16 asks, "know ye not, that to whom ye yield yourselves servants to obey, his servants ye are to whom ye obey; whether of sin unto death, or of obedience unto righteousness?" Therefore, we must do what it takes to avoid being influenced by servants of corruption. Their idea of liberty seems to amount to the freedom to associate with them and to not have to obey God. What happens to those who fall for their message? Peter said, "of whom a man is overcome, of the same is he brought in bondage." This warning was written to believers. We know the servants of corruption were seeking to allure the followers of Jesus because Peter went on to say:

"For if after they have escaped the pollutions of the world through the knowledge of the Lord and Savior Jesus Christ, they are again entangled therein, and overcome, the latter end is worse with them than the beginning. For it had been better for them not to have known the way of righteousness, than, after they have known *it,* to turn from the holy commandment delivered unto them. But it is happened unto them according to the true proverb, The dog is turned to his own vomit again; and the sow that was washed to her wallowing in the mire" (2Pt 2:20-22).

So, a false promise of liberty can get people who had "escaped" "through the knowledge of the Lord and Savior Jesus Christ" to turn from the holy commandment. This would mean they end up exchanging this knowledge for a lie.

Those who allowed the servants of corruption to influence them were made to think they are not free unless they are free to do what they want. If we give our minds to programming produced by those who allure through the lusts of the flesh, then it is being programmed by servants of corruption. In Peter's day, those who had "escaped from them who live in error" fell for such allurements and got entangled again in "the pollutions of the world." In our day, the lusts of the flesh are still in operation, so let us be forewarned.

God's Word Versus Man's Opinions

"Keep thy heart with all diligence; for out of it are the issues of life" (Prv 4:23). Scripture repeatedly urges those who seek to honor God to guard their heart and to avoid being influenced by those who follow the ways of the world. Here is another such passage:

"Blessed is the man that walketh not in the counsel of the ungodly, nor standeth in the way of sinners, nor sitteth in the seat of the scornful. But his delight is in the law of the LORD; and in his law doth he meditate day and night" (Ps 1:1-2).

The servants of corruption who allure through the lusts of the flesh would undoubtedly fall into the bad categories listed in this Psalm, thus we must not follow their lead. Those who want to honor God need to avoid the influence of messages, personalities, and things that disregard God's standard because they can lead people away from God. While this would include things like images of people engaging in fornication (simulated or otherwise), it involves more than this. How else might programs, books, articles, ads, etc., appeal to the lusts of the flesh and promise liberty? How about by undermining the authority of God's word regarding creation?

"In the beginning God created the heaven and the earth" (Gen 1:1) and "thus the heavens and the earth were finished, and all the host of them" (Gen 2:1) lead off the Bible's testimony on this topic.

"By the word of the LORD were the heavens made; and all the host of them by the breath of his mouth" (Ps 33:6). We find confirmation of this testimony in Paul's reference to "God that made the world and all things therein" (Acts 17:24) and in many other passages like:

- "the LORD God formed man of the dust *of* the ground, and breathed into his nostrils the breath of life; and man became a living soul" (Gen 2:7),
- "*in* six days the LORD made heaven and earth, the sea, and all that in them *is*" (Ex 20:11),
- "Lord GOD! behold, thou hast made the heaven and the earth by thy great power and stretched out arm" (Jer 32:17).

Genesis 2:21-22 also says this about the creation of Adam's wife:

"the LORD God caused a deep sleep to fall upon Adam, and he slept: and he took one of his ribs, and closed up the flesh instead thereof; And the rib, which the LORD God had taken from man, made he a woman, and brought her unto the man."

Scripture does not say non-living material accidentally turned into living things over eons of time. So, it cannot be good for those who believe God's word to subject their mind to educational institutions and media that push the idea of creation by unguided processes.

Those who hold to this accidental origin of the universe viewpoint deem their conclusions to be 'scientific,' while data that does not fit their belief is ignored and views that align with the testimony of scripture are called 'unscientific.' This practice has helped to bully many people into accepting the random evolution viewpoint. But merely calling a view 'science' or 'accepted belief' does not mean it is true or consistent with all of the available evidence.

When data first began to show handwashing between operations would save lives, doctors refused to acknowledge this evidence until decades later. The same thing occurs today as the believers in the idea of an unplanned creation ignore evidence like DNA that proves non-living things do not turn into living things by accident. Information and programming require a mind. They do not arise from matter and energy randomly interacting.

How does a random creation idea fuel the lusts of the flesh? If God was not the creator as scripture says, scripture has no authority to define right behavior. Without God's standard, people are free to indulge themselves in catering to "the lust of the flesh, the lust of the eyes, and the pride of life" (1Jo 2:16). But if it is good to obey admonitions such as "keep thy heart with all diligence" (Prv 4:23), then verses like "come out from among them, and be ye separate" (2Cor 6:17) have a very broad application in this modern media age.

The Righteousness of the Law

Scripture tells us, "all things work together for good to them that love God, to them who are the called according to *his* purpose" (Rom 8:28). The verse is conditional, so it only applies to people who meet the condition and not everyone loves God. But those who God has chosen "to salvation through sanctification of the Spirit and belief of the truth" (2Th 2:13) do love God. So, the whole process of salvation through sanctification is one of the things that work for their good. This is true even when the call to change their life, be separate, and avoid uncleanness makes them uncomfortable.

If we want to obey the admonition, "be not conformed to this world: but be ye transformed by the renewing of your mind" (Rom 12:12), how can we do this? Here is how we can do it – "whatsoever things are true, whatsoever things *are* honest, whatsoever things *are* just, whatsoever things *are* pure, whatsoever things *are* lovely, whatsoever things *are* of good report; if *there be* any virtue, and if *there be* any praise, **think on these things**" (Phl 4:8). If we want to guard our heart, we must avoid engaging in things that cater to the lusts of the flesh, even if those things hold out the promise of entertaining or informing us.

In describing man's condition, Jesus said, "the things which come out of him, those are they that defile the man" (Mk 7:15). So, a change on the inside is needed, i.e., a circumcision of the heart is required (cf. Deu 10:16). As was noted earlier, this is picturing the cutting off of the lust of the flesh. How can someone do this? Scripture tells us, if a man keeps "the righteousness of the law," this is "counted for circumcision" (Rom 2:26). While some may think no one can keep the righteousness of the law, scripture tells us this can be done.

Galatians 3:6 says, "Abraham believed God, and it was accounted to him for righteousness." "They which are of faith" (Gal 3:7) obtain this righteousness in the same way, and this result was also linked to the law because the brethren were told "through faith" is how "we establish the law" (Rom 3:31).

The Gospel Includes Sanctification

"Man looketh on the outward appearance, but the LORD looketh on the heart" (1Sa 16:7). This is why we cannot ignore the fact that the gospel includes a call to sanctification:

"God hath from the beginning chosen you to salvation through sanctification of the Spirit and belief of the truth: Whereunto he called you by our gospel, to the obtaining of the glory of our Lord Jesus Christ" (2Th 2:13-14).

The idea of "salvation through sanctification" was always central to the gospel. Peter told the men of Israel, "God, having raised up his Son Jesus, sent him to bless you, in turning away every one of you from his iniquities" (Acts 3:26). Peter said similar words on the day of Pentecost. "Repent, and be baptized every one of you in the name of Jesus Christ for the remission of sins, and ye shall receive the gift of the Holy Ghost" (Acts 2:38). The word translated "remission" here meant a release from bondage, and it was also translated as forgiveness, liberty, and deliverance. It is the idea of being set free from sin that we find in verses like, "to him [Jesus] give all the prophets witness, that through his name whosoever believeth in him shall receive remission of sins" (Acts 10:43).

Forgiveness, By What Standard?

Consider the standard of forgiveness that is in this famous prayer:

"Our Father which art in heaven, Hallowed be thy name. Thy kingdom come. Thy will be done in earth, as *it is* in heaven. Give us this day our daily bread. And forgive us our debts, as we forgive our debtors. And lead us not into temptation, but deliver us from evil: For thine is the kingdom, and the power, and the glory, for ever. Amen" (Mt 6:9-13).

Notice, when we say this prayer, we are asking God to hold us to a standard for forgiveness. "Forgive us our debts, as we forgive our debtors" (Mt 6:12). This request is for conditional forgiveness!

This principle was even made more explicit in what Jesus said when he went on to contrast "if ye forgive" and "if ye forgive not" in the verses following that model prayer:

"if ye forgive men their trespasses, your heavenly Father will also forgive you: But if ye forgive not men their trespasses, neither will your Father forgive your trespasses" (Mt 6:14-15).

Jesus also taught conditional forgiveness in the following parable:

"the kingdom of heaven likened unto a certain king, which would take account of his servants. And when he had begun to reckon, one was brought unto him, which owed him ten thousand talents. But forasmuch as he had not to pay, his lord commanded him to be sold, and his wife, and children, and all that he had, and payment to be made. The servant therefore fell down, and worshipped him, saying, Lord, have patience with me, and I will pay thee all. Then the lord of that servant was moved with compassion, and loosed him, and forgave him the debt. But the same servant went out, and found one of his fellow servants, which owed him an hundred pence: and he laid hands on him, and took *him* by the throat, saying, Pay me that thou owest. And his fellowservant fell down at his feet, and besought him, saying, Have patience with me, and I will pay thee all. And he would not: but went and cast him into prison, till he should pay the debt. So, when his fellow servants saw what was done, they were very sorry, and came and told unto their lord all that was done. Then his lord, after that he had called him, said unto him, O thou wicked servant, I forgave thee all that debt, because thou desiredst me: Shouldest not thou also have had compassion on thy fellowservant, even as I had pity on thee? And his lord was wroth, and delivered him to the tormentors, till he should pay all that was due unto him. So, likewise shall my heavenly Father do also unto you, if ye from your hearts forgive not everyone his brother their trespasses" (Mt 18:23-35).

Jesus compared the judgment of his Father to a king who had pity on a man who asked to have the judgment against him postponed. It says, the king "forgave ^{G863} him the debt" but the word translated as "forgave" merely means to leave it alone or let it go. So, this did not erase the debt. Rather, the king granted the man's request and deferred enforcement of the judgment. Later, the man was asked to defer enforcement against someone else, yet he refused and ordered immediate enforcement. (He had a double standard.)

This led the king to call him a wicked servant because he wanted mercy but was unwilling to show mercy when he was in a position to do so. Disrespect for the king's gift of mercy caused the man to forfeit the mercy that was withholding enforcement against him.

What did Jesus want people to learn from this? Did he want them to think being forgiven by God meant a person has a get out of jail free card that allows them to ignore God's standards of behavior? Or was he letting them know we cannot accept God's standard when it benefits us and disrespect his standard when it costs us?

The king set an example for the man when he showed him mercy. But this did not lead to a corresponding thankfulness and respect for the ways of the king in the heart of that man.

When that man had the opportunity to show mercy, he refused to extend to another person the same mercy he had asked for and had received. He had a different standard when it came to others.

The king's mercy did not mean the debt was paid. It merely meant the demand for payment at that time was not going to be enforced. When this wicked servant refused to do as the king had done, he proved he was not worthy of the mercy the king had shown to him.

When Paul and Barnabas presented the word of God to a group who did not respond to it, they told them, "ye put it from you, and judge yourselves unworthy of everlasting life" (Acts 13:46).

In his refusal to show mercy, the wicked servant judged himself unworthy of mercy. There is another teaching that shows mercy does not make God's standard void and it is found in this passage:

"the scribes and Pharisees brought unto him [Jesus] a woman taken in adultery; and when they had set her in the midst, They say unto him, Master, this woman was taken in adultery, in the very act. Now Moses in the law commanded us, that such should be stoned: but what sayest thou? This they said, tempting him, that they might have to accuse him. But Jesus stooped down, and with his finger wrote on the ground, *as though he heard them not.* So, when they continued asking him, he lifted up himself, and said unto them, He that is without sin among you, let him first cast a stone at her. And again, he stooped down and wrote on the ground. And they which heard *it,* being convicted by *their own* conscience, went out one by one, beginning at the eldest, *even* unto the last: and Jesus was left alone, and the woman standing in the midst. When Jesus had lifted up himself, and saw none but the woman, he said unto her, Woman, where are those thine accusers? hath no man condemned thee? She said, No man, Lord. And Jesus said unto her, Neither do I condemn thee: go, and sin no more" (Fourth gospel 8:3-11).

Jesus showed mercy unto her but he also called on her to change. Likewise, being forgiven by God does not remove God's standard.

Would there have been thieves and prostitutes among those who confessed their sins and were baptized by John the Baptist? Yes. Did confessing and being baptized mean they were now set free to continue doing those things? No. John told "the multitude that came forth to be baptized of him" (Lk 3:7), "bring forth therefore fruits worthy of repentance, and begin not to say within yourselves, We have Abraham to *our* father" (Lk 3:8). This indicates he anticipated this kind of self-talk was likely to occur. Nevertheless, his words show being linked to Abraham did not relieve people of having to produce fruits worthy of repentance.

"They which are of faith, the same are the children of Abraham" (Gal 3:7). Yet, faith is not the end. Those who are of faith must grow and be fruitful. 2 Peter 1:5-8 shows this [but as you read, note that the word "charity" in this passage is translating a Greek word (G26) that was far more often translated as "love"]:

"**add to your faith** virtue; and to virtue knowledge; And to knowledge temperance; and to temperance patience; and to patience godliness; And to godliness brotherly kindness; and to brotherly kindness charity. For if these things be in you, and abound, they make you that *ye shall* neither *be* barren nor unfruitful in the knowledge of our Lord Jesus Christ."

The New Covenant/Testament

At his last Passover, Jesus said, "this cup is the new testament [G1242] in my blood" (Lk 22:20). The word "testament" in this verse is translating a word that was also translated as "covenant(s)." Thus, even though this idea is expressed by just one Greek word ([G1242]), we see two different English words. In our Bible, Jesus is called both "the mediator of the new testament [G1242]" and "the mediator of the new covenant [G1242]" (Heb 9:15 & 12:24). The same Greek word was used in both verses, so we know the writer was expressing the same concept in both instances.

The new covenant is a key idea, but it does not mean God's law has been set aside as some people think. Consider this passage:

"This *is* the covenant that I will make with them after those days, saith the Lord, I will put my laws into their hearts, and in their minds will I write them; And their sins and iniquities will I remember no more" (Heb 10:16-17).

If his laws are internalized in this new covenant, how could anyone think Jesus frees us *from* these laws? Are people under bondage when God's laws are in their hearts and minds? No. Moreover, the new covenant is an Old Testament idea! The passage above actually cited Jeremiah 31:33-34 – and this told of a future change, so people are not this way to begin with. <u>The new covenant exists when God's laws reside in the hearts and minds of people</u>. Is this why Jesus told the woman who was taken in adultery, "go, and sin no more," rather than stop at "neither do I condemn thee" and leave it at that? (Fourth gospel 8:3-11) Jesus' words prove this woman did not have to be like those who "cannot cease from sin" (2Pt 2:14). Instead, she could be like those who are "made free from sin" and become "the servants of righteousness" (Rom 6:18).

This same call to live in a way that honors God is seen in verses like, "as ye have yielded your members servants to uncleanness and to iniquity unto iniquity; even so now yield your members servants to righteousness unto holiness" (Rom 6:19). This change is also called for in other passages like, "be ye reconciled to God" (2Cor 5:20) and "we beseech you, brethren, and exhort *you* by the Lord Jesus, that as ye have received of us how ye ought to walk and to please God, *so* ye would abound more and more" (1Th 4:1).

James 4:8 says, "draw nigh to God, and he will draw nigh to you. Cleanse your hands, *ye* sinners; and purify *your* hearts, *ye* double minded." This lets us know people need to change on the inside. Does the term, "double minded" indicate that a double standard is linked to having dirty hands and an impure heart? If so, then anyone who seeks to "draw nigh to God" must be diligent to hold to a single standard (i.e., what is right in the sight of the LORD, and this parallels what Isaiah 55:6-7 says about seeking the LORD).

Colossians 3:8-10 also calls for a similar change in behavior:

"put off all these; anger, wrath, malice, blasphemy, filthy communication out of your mouth. Lie not one to another, seeing that you have put off the old man with his deeds; and have put on the new *man* which is renewed in knowledge after the image of him that created him."

Doing Right Makes A Difference

Daniel told the king to "break off thy sins by righteousness, and thine iniquities by showing mercy to the poor" (Dan 4:27). The LORD told Cain, "if thou doest well, shalt thou not be accepted?" (Gen 4:7)

Proverbs 16:6 says, "by mercy and truth iniquity is purged; and by the fear of the LORD *men* depart from evil." "He that covereth his sins shall not prosper: but whoso confesseth and forsaketh *them* shall have mercy" (Prv 23:13). Why does doing this get them mercy? Because "the sacrifices of God *are* a broken spirit: a broken and contrite heart, O God, thou will not despise" (Ps 51:17). "The LORD *is* nigh unto them that are of a broken heart; and saveth such as be of a contrite spirit" (Ps 34:18).

"God is no respecter of persons" (Acts 10:34). Unlike what the world says is right, God does not respect *people* – or else he would have to respect evildoers. Instead, he deals with people based on what they do, as the next verse says, "but in every nation he that feareth him, and worketh righteousness, is accepted with him" (Acts 10:35). This principle is further clarified in Romans 2:5-11 where it says this about "the righteous judgment of God:"

> "Who will render to every man according to his deeds: To them who by patient continuance in well doing seek for glory and honor and immortality, eternal life: But unto them that are contentious, and do not obey the truth, but obey unrighteousness, indignation and wrath. Tribulation and anguish, <u>upon every soul of man that doeth evil</u>... But glory, honor, and peace, <u>to every man that worketh good</u>... For there is no respect of persons with God."

God "will render to every man according to his deeds" is an idea that is confirmed in verses like, "as righteousness *tendeth* to life: so he that pursueth evil *pursueth it* to his own death" (Prv 11:19), and "unto thee, O Lord, *belongeth* mercy: for thou renderest to every man according to his work" (Prv 62:12).

Scripture lets us know, "every man shall receive his own reward according to his own labor" (1Cor 3:8). Jesus said, "the Son of man" will "reward every man according to his works" (Mt 16:27) and when "the dead, small and great, stand before God" in Revelation 20:12, it says they will be judged "according to their works."

Belief is a Thought, Faith is an Action

Jesus was asked, "what shall we do, that we might work the works of God?" (Fourth gospel 6:28) and he said, "this is the work of God, that ye believe on him whom he hath sent" (v. 29). (This must continue as will be shown.) Belief is not faith. "Faith *cometh* by hearing, and hearing by the word of God" (Rom 10:17) When God's word is heard by people who believe and understand it, then they will act in faith, as we see when Jesus explained the parable of the sower. He pictured this process as the seed of God's word taking root in good soil and yielding fruit:

"Hear ye therefore the parable of the sower. When any one heareth the word of the kingdom, and understandeth *it* not, then cometh the wicked *one*, and catcheth away that which was sown in his heart. This is he which received seed by the wayside. But he that received the seed into stony places, the same is he that heareth the word, and anon [instantly] with joy receiveth it; Yet hath he not root in himself, but dureth for a while: for when tribulation or persecution ariseth because of the word, by and by he is offended. He also that received seed among the thorns is he that heareth the word; and the care of this world, and the deceitfulness of riches, choke the word, and he becometh unfruitful. But he that received seed into the good ground is he that heareth the word, and understandeth *it*; which also beareth fruit, and bringeth forth, some a hundredfold, some sixty, some thirty" (Mt 13:18-23).

When Jesus explained this parable to the disciples, he told them, "the seed is the word of God" (Lk 8:11). His explanation concluded with this statement, "but that on the good ground are they, which in an honest and good heart, having heard the word, **keep** *it,* **and bring forth fruit with patience**" (Lk 8:15).

[The word "patience" is letting us know bringing forth fruit is not a speedy process. It is something that happens over a longer term.]

"Faith is the **substance** of things hoped for, the **evidence** of things not seen" (Heb 11:1). Unlike thoughts or beliefs that cannot be seen, actions can be seen. Behaviors serve as evidence of what people are thinking, since our actions are dictated by our thoughts.

Mark 2:5 says, "Jesus saw their faith... " and what he saw was their deeds. Their behavior was evidence of their belief. Faith is not an idea; faith is belief in action. This is why "faith without works is dead" (Jas 2:26). Faith can only exist when those who trust in God are acting on their belief. If a man says he believes in God and he continues to commit fornication what is the evidence of his belief, his words or his deeds? What we do follows from what goes on in our mind, so our actions say something about our thought process and what we really believe.

The faith of those who continue to believe on Jesus can be seen because it shows in their lives, since "they that are Christ's have crucified the flesh with the affections and lusts" (Gal 5:24). "The just shall live by faith" (Rom 1:17), so their lives conform to God's word. [The context shows this is what "live by faith" refers to because the verse is all about "the righteousness of God" being "revealed." The verse before notes "the gospel of Christ" is "the power of God" that brings people to "salvation." After "the righteousness of God" and "the just" living by faith are linked in verse 17, then verse 18 presents a contrast with the "ungodliness and unrighteousness of men who hold the truth in unrighteousness."] But God-honoring behavior is not something that happens automatically for followers of Jesus.

"If ye live after the flesh, ye shall die: but if ye through the Spirit do mortify the deeds of the body, ye shall live" (Rom 8:13) warns us about the need to live a life that honors God. We know people are able to do this because verses like "walk in the Spirit, and ye shall not fulfill the lust of the flesh" (Gal 5:16) show how this can be done.

Grace Initiates, Faith Carries On

Paul wrote these words to the faithful in Christ Jesus, "**by grace are ye saved through faith**; and that not of yourselves: it is the gift of God" (Eph 2:8). Being saved happens because of God's grace, while faith is the vehicle. So, this is the why and the how.

Those who are thankful for God's grace and this gift of God, do have choices to make. However, they do not initiate the process. The words "not of yourselves" show men are not saved merely by their choice to choose God or receive Christ (cf. Fourth gospel 1:13).

Being saved by grace is "the gift of God" and this gift is not given based on the will of man. Furthermore, grace precedes faith, so this lets us know phrases like, "thy faith hath saved thee" (Lk 7:50) incorporate an unexpressed condition – God's grace came first. Faith is necessary, for "without faith it is impossible to please *him* [God]" (Heb 11:6). But scripture indicates God's grace, not our faith, is what causes people who were dead in trespasses and sins to be saved, as can be seen from the following passage:

"you *hath he quickened,* who were dead in trespasses and sins; Wherein in time past ye walked according to the course of this world, according to the prince of the power of the air, the spirit that now worketh in the children of disobedience: Among whom also we all had our conversation in times past in the lusts of our flesh, fulfilling the desires of the flesh and of the mind; and were by nature the children of wrath, even as others. But God, who is rich in mercy, for his great love wherewith he loved us, Even when we were dead in sins, hath quickened us together with Christ, (by grace ye are saved;)" (Eph 2:1-5).

Believing God and having faith are required for salvation, and men who are dead in sins do not believe God or exhibit faith. The word "dead" described their status, until God "quickened" them and this offered a way of escape. It says, "by grace ye are saved" because those who are dead cannot make the first move.

Continue to Believe

Merely accepting an idea will not yield salvation. James 2:19 says, "thou believest that there is one God; thou doest well: the devils also believe, and tremble." So, belief in God's existence does not mean God will be honored. Moreover, Jesus spoke of "the Spirit, which they that believe on ^{G1519} him should receive" (Fourth gospel 7:39). Here, the word "on" is translating Greek word ^{G1519}. It appears over 1700 times in scripture. The top three ways it was translated are: into, to, and unto. It refers to moving toward something. If this process stops, then one stops believing "on" Jesus at that point. Some people who "believed on ^{G1519} him" later stopped doing so (cf. Fourth gospel 8:30 & 45), thus, believing "on" him at a moment in time is not the point. Rather, scripture teaches us to see believing as an ongoing process. This continues to move people toward Jesus because it keeps them submitted to God and makes them fruitful.

This aligns with what Jesus said in other verses such as, "I am the vine, ye *are* the branches: He that abideth in me, and I in him, the same bringeth forth much fruit" (Fourth gospel 15:4). Abiding is an ongoing process – a branch must stay connected to the vine and continue to be nourished by it in order to live.

The brethren are told to "grow in grace, and in the knowledge of our Lord and Savior Jesus Christ" (2Pt 3:18). God wants them to be "conformed to the image of his Son" (Rom 8:29). This is the process that God's word indicates should show up in the lives of those who continue to believe "on" Jesus.

Peter wrote this to the beloved, "I stir up your pure minds by way of remembrance" (2Pt 3:1). He also pointed them to a higher calling, "what manner *of persons* ought ye to be in *all* holy conversation and godliness" (2Pt 3:11). As has been noted, the word conversation meant lifestyle, not merely talking. Urging others to honor God in their lives is not imposing legalism, nor does it set the bar too high. Jesus told his disciples, "let your light so shine before men, that they may see your good works, and glorify your Father which is in heaven" (Mt 5:16). If seeing the followers of Jesus do "good works" causes men to glorify God, then we should seek to live in a way that produces this result.

Living a life that honors God does not seem easy, given the many verses on correction such as, "brethren, if a man be overtaken in a fault, ye which are spiritual, restore such a one in the spirit of meekness; considering thyself, lest thou also be tempted" (Gal 6:1). If people are disobeying God, reminding them of God's standard is likely to make them feel guilty or ashamed. Even so, calling on people to obey what is said in God's word can help those who have been "overtaken in a fault" to turn their life around.

The brethren were told, "let us consider one another to provoke unto love and to good works" (Heb 10:24). This book aims to do this and there is no reason we who live today should do anything less.

Submit to the King's Authority

Scripture talks of "the invisible God" (Col 1:15), so is this also true of his kingdom? "The kingdom of God is not meat and drink; but righteousness, and peace, and joy in the Holy Ghost" (Rom 14:17). So, his kingdom is of a different quality. An eye can see an action, but the thoughts in our mind are what determine how we perceive and judge that behavior. "The things which are seen *are* temporal; but the things which are not seen are eternal" (2Cor 4:18).

If God's kingdom is eternal, we should not be looking for it with physical eyes. Peter saw miracles with his eyes and he talked about hearing God speak from out of heaven in 2 Peter 1:16-18. But then he said, "we have also a more sure word of prophecy; whereunto ye do well that ye take heed, as unto a light that shineth in a dark place" (2Pt 1:19). Notice, he indicated scripture was "more sure" than things he experienced through his eyes and ears of flesh. So, miracles are not more important than God's word.

Jesus said this to the Jews, "search the scriptures; for in them ye think ye have eternal life: and they are they which testify of me" (Fourth gospel 5:39). Scripture was not the problem. The problem was a refusal to submit themselves to God's rule. God's word says, "the goodness of God leadeth thee to repentance" (Rom 2:4). Thus, those who see God as their king and themselves as loyal subjects should be willing to do what it takes to change their ways and conform to his standards.

Jesus was asked, "what shall I do to inherit eternal life?" by a man who was "very rich" (Lk 18:18 & 23) and this is how it went from there:

"Thou knowest the commandments, Do not commit adultery, Do not kill, Do not steal, Do not bear false witness, Honor thy father and thy mother. And he said, All these have I kept from my youth up. Now when Jesus heard these things, he said unto him, Yet lackest thou one thing: sell all that thou hast, and distribute unto the poor, and thou shalt have treasure in heaven: and come, follow me" (Lk 18:20-22).

Those who choose earthly riches over treasure in heaven are not judging by God's standard. The parallel passage in Matthew says, "he went away sorrowful: for he had great possessions" (Mt 19:22). This also suggests his claim regarding those five commandments was based on the letter of the law, not the spirit of it (as per 2Cor 3:6). Scripture does say, "blessed *are* they that do his commandments, that they may have right to the tree of life" (Rv 22:14). But to assume either the letter of the law or five out of ten qualifies is a risky idea.

Jesus said, "my kingdom is not of this world" (Fourth gospel 18:36), so it is not based on what can be perceived with physical eyes.

Scripture declares, "a scepter of righteousness *is* the scepter of thy [Jesus'] kingdom" (Heb 1:8). This speaks of how he rules. It is not an object in his hand. Believers were told God "delivered us from the power of darkness, and hath translated *us* into the kingdom of his dear Son" (Col 1:13). Ignorance, rebellion, stealing God's word, etc., are the types of darkness that keep people in bondage to sin (not a lack of visible light). In verses like, "let not sin therefore <u>reign</u> in your mortal body," "sin shall not have <u>dominion</u> over you," and "to whom ye yield yourselves <u>servants</u> to obey, his servants ye are to whom ye obey" (Rom 6:12, 14, & 16), kingdom terms continued to be applied to those who God was bringing into his realm.

When the disciples heard Jesus tell them, "blessed are your eyes, for they see: and your ears, for they hear" (Mt 13:16), he was talking about what it takes to perceive the truths of God (cf. v. 17). Contrast this with his response to the Pharisees. They asked him when "the kingdom of God should come" and he said, "the kingdom of God cometh **not with observation**" (Lk 17:20). Their question exposed their inability to see. Jesus represented God's kingdom, so it had already come near to them through Jesus and his message.

Since they judged based on physical sight, they likely envisioned a kingdom with a king on a physical great white throne like the one they read about in their scriptures. In terms of this world's wealth, Solomon was the most prosperous king in their history, and he made himself a great ivory throne. Ivory is white, so undoubtedly the "great white throne" of Revelation 20:11 was picturing a better, more God-honoring throne than the one Solomon sat on when he "made a great throne of ivory, and overlaid it with pure gold" (2Chr 9:17). While sitting on this throne, he "loved many strange women," "sacrificed unto their gods," and "did evil in the sight of the LORD" (1Kgs 11:1, 6, & 8), and the LORD took the kingdom away from Solomon because of all this (1Kgs 11:11-13). In worldly terms, the kingdom was at its high point under Solomon, but "the wisdom of this world is foolishness with God" (1Cor 3:19). So, judging spiritual issues using worldly standards is not a wise thing to do.

Solomon judged himself worthy of such a throne, yet his judgment also led him to take 700 wives, commit idolatry, and give the LORD who had blessed him only a half-hearted commitment (cf. 1Kgs 11:6).

Jesus' followers are subject to his authority. In Matthew 6:19-34 he taught his disciples to have a single standard (cf. v. 22) and to keep God's kingdom first – "seek ye first the kingdom of God, **and his righteousness**" (Mt 6:33). In this context, he told them not to let their thinking be distracted by cares about other things (cf. v. 24-32). Seeking first "the kingdom of God, and his righteousness" meant their time should be spent thinking on these things, and if we keep respect for God and his word at the forefront of our mind, we honor this principle. Furthermore, the LORD said, "he that hath my word, let him speak my word faithfully" (Jer 23:28). Doing this will preserve the power and authority of his word. Yet, many people tend to add their views to scripture when they are discussing what it says.

If a man says, *'those who are born again cannot sin and like it,'* did he speak God's word faithfully? The Bible says, "whosoever is born of God doth not commit sin; for his seed remaineth in him: and he cannot sin, because he is born of God" (1Jn 3:9). But unless we spend time meditating on the word of God to put it in our mind, how can it guard our heart and help us to recognize when people add their view to God's word or take scripture out of context?

The LORD told Joshua, "this book of the law shall not depart out of thy mouth; but thou shalt meditate therein day and night, that thou mayest observe to do according to all that is written therein: for then thou shalt make thy way prosperous, and then thou shalt have good success" (Jos 1:8). This was said to Joshua, but would this principle also apply to us? Since the New Testament indicates the things in the Old Testament were written "for our admonition" (1Cor 10:11) and "for our learning" (Rom 15:4), the answer is yes.

Thinking on God's word day and night and seeking to do as it says might seem like a high bar, but let us keep in mind Jesus' words, "unto whomsoever much is given, of him shall be much required" (Lk 12:48). Grace is a great gift, so all who have been given this gift have a standard to live up to, just as the king himself has said.

God gives various talents and callings to people. Yet, no matter where people may be on this spectrum, whatever time a person puts into his or her own study of scripture will yield better results if they get in the habit of using the method modeled in this book.

In Closing

As members of the body of Christ grow in their understanding of God's word, they will be better equipped to provoke one another "unto love and to good works" (Heb 10:24). Receiving and sharing biblical correction plays a part in this process. Proverbs 3:12 says, "whom the LORD loveth he correcteth," so when we are corrected it should encourage us, as this is an expression of the LORD's love. If we would want people to offer us biblical correction when we are in error, then the words "love thy neighbor as thyself" (Lev 19:18) tell us how we ought to deal with those who we know are in error.

"Grace and truth came by Jesus Christ" (Fourth gospel 1:17). Grace is not shown by ignoring truth or tolerating falsehood, for grace and truth go together. "Speaking the truth in love" is how the brethren "grow up into him [Christ]" (Eph 4:15). Growth takes time and it often happens in spurts. So, while correction benefits the body of Christ, the process is not always quick. We can "hate every false way" like the psalmist did (Ps 119:104) and still show grace to those who are in error by showing patience. In any case, agreement among the brethren is not needed for God to advance his kingdom.

In Philippians 1:15 Paul wrote, "some indeed preach Christ even of envy and strife; and some also of good will." "Envy and strife" are not the optimal way to present the message of Jesus, yet Paul did not say those who did so should be stopped. Just the opposite. He said, "whether in pretense, or in truth, Christ is preached; and I therein do rejoice" (Phl 1:18). Christ being preached "in pretense" rather than "in truth" was not the best situation, but Paul said he could "rejoice" even in this because Christ was being preached.

Conflict between church members is not a good thing, but what Paul wrote shows such infighting does not mean Christ is not being preached by one side or the other. However, *whether* Christ is being preached or not is a different question, for Paul would not rejoice in false teaching. But if the truth about Christ is taught, then the message is what matters and any conflicts with the messenger should not sway our judgment. In such cases, it would be best to follow this counsel that was offered to the brethren, "let every man be swift to hear, slow to speak, slow to wrath" (Jas 1:19).

The brethren were also warned about two kinds of wisdom, one is "not from above" and one "is from above" (Jas 3:15 & 17). The wisdom that is "not from above" is "earthly, sensual, devilish" (Jas 3:15), "but the wisdom that is from above is first pure, then peaceable, gentle, *and* easy to be intreated, full of mercy and good fruits" (Jas 3:17). So, this lets us know the brethren can fall prey to earthly wisdom, and we need to act in accord with "the wisdom that is from above" if we want to get better results.

A common story in church circles shows how earthly wisdom can lead people to misunderstand the word of God. It is about a man who seeks to know God's will for his life by flipping Bible pages and pointing a finger at random selections. First, he hit the verse that says Judas "went and hanged himself," next he saw "go, and do thou likewise," and lastly he hit on "that thou doest, do quickly" (Mt 27:5, Lk 10:37, & Fourth gospel 13:27). This aims to make the point that taking portions of scripture out of context is a dangerous practice, and it is. But while an example like this might make the point, it can also give people a false sense of assurance. How?

First off, they may believe the one who tells them this knows better and would never quote scripture out of context. Second, if people think it is easy to tell when scripture is being taken out of context, they will be less likely to watch for this and might think they could never make this mistake. But consider a question that was asked by Jesus, "why beholdest thou the mote that is in thy brother's eye, but perceivest not the beam that is in thine own eye?" (Lk 6:41) His question indicates people can notice a flaw in others even as they fail to notice when they do the same thing or worse. So, if we see people misapply scripture, before critiquing them, we should look to see if we might be making the same mistake in some way or on some issue. Doing so would be in line with Jesus' counsel, "cast out first the beam out of thine own eye, and then shalt thou see clearly to pull out the mote that is in thy brother's eye" (Lk 6:42).

For example, Jeremiah 29:11 says this, "I know the thoughts that I think toward you, saith the LORD, thoughts of peace, and not of evil, to give you an expected end." If a man claims this is a promise for him today, he ignores the fact that in the KJV "you" is plural, and the group who this referred to is defined in the context.

The LORD said, "after seventy years be accomplished at Babylon I will visit **you**, and perform my good word toward **you**, in causing **you** to return to this place" (Jer 29:10). This was one verse prior, and the LORD went on to say, "I will turn away your captivity, and I will gather you from all the nations, and from all the places whither I have driven you" (Jer 29:14). So, verse 11 was said to those who had been "carried away from Jerusalem unto Babylon" (Jer 29:4). Is it okay to ignore this? Lifting the verse out of context is the only way people can say verse 11 is a personal promise to them. But since the verse does not say God has thoughts of peace to all men, this treats scripture like it was treated in the page-flipping story above.

Claiming a verse as a personal promise is based on preference, for no one claims, "the LORD will rejoice over you to destroy you" (Dt 28:63). We find God's will for the brethren in numerous verses including, "all things work together for good to them that love God, to them who are the called according to *his* purpose" (Rom 8:28), "this is the love of God, that we keep his commandments" (1 Jo 5:3), and "by humility *and* the fear of the LORD *are* riches, and honor, and life" (Prv 22:4). But these verses have conditions, so the words of an out-of-context, unconditional Jeremiah 29:11 will appeal to more people. However, scripture's authority is lost in the process, just as it is when any part of scripture is used contrary to the whole counsel of God. Whenever we are applying biblical principles or quoting scripture, it is up to us to represent scripture accurately.

As has been shown, if we lean on our own understanding, we will fall prey to mistakes that can be avoided if we honestly judge both our beliefs and the words of others by the standard of scripture. Here is a review of some key points that were made in this book:

- Our approach to separating truth from error must conform to the whole counsel of God if it is going to consistently produce results that honor God.
- A method of assessing Bible truth which leads someone to accept a false view in one area will be likely to have the same effect when it comes to other Bible passages.
- Groups and teachers often cite the teachings of men as if they are biblical authorities, but we see Jesus refute ideas that were believed by those who put confidence in man.
- Neither our own understanding nor the teachings of men can replace the words of scripture as a measure of truth.

We should not be intimidated when men's views are cited to justify a belief, because **"the fear of man** bringeth a snare: but whoso putteth his **trust in the LORD** shall be safe" (Prv 29:25).

Here is a final example of how God's word can teach us. One time when Jesus was rebuking the Pharisees, he told them, "ye tithe mint and rue and all manner of herbs" and then he went on to say, "these ought ye to have done" (Lk 11:42). Since he mentioned tithing, this verse along with verses on offerings may lead people to give money to support the efforts of a minister, church, denomination, or group. But who teaches on giving and tells people how to give and get an amazing blessing at the same time? Jesus did.

One verse before the verse on the tithe, Jesus said, "give alms of such things as ye have; and, behold, all things are clean unto you" (Lk 11:41). Did their tithe make "all things clean unto" them? No. But if they had given alms in accord with Jesus' words, this would have been the result! Giving, as Jesus said here, did something to bless the almsgiver in a way that other types of giving did not. Alms can refer to money (cf. Acts 3:2-6), but would giving food in a famine or taking the time to help people in need also qualify? What in the Old Testament would equate to almsgiving? Does giving alms as Jesus indicated yield this benefit for us today, or was it only for those who he said this to back then? Did this apply to Cornelius? For readers who have not considered this topic, it is hoped that the opportunity to search the scriptures on this will challenge the readers to put the method they learned in this book into practice as they continue thinking on God's word.

Thank you for taking the time to weigh the biblical evidence that was presented herein. The aim of this book was to show it is better to trust scripture to teach us and to answer our Bible questions. Thus, it is fitting to leave the followers of Jesus with this statement of Paul from Acts 20:32, "now, brethren, I commend you to God, and to the word of his grace, which is able to build you up, and to give you an inheritance among all them which are sanctified."

Both eBook and print versions of books in the Better Bible Study Method series, along with answers to frequent questions, contact information, and links to free Bible software and Bible study tools can be found online at ABetterBibleStudyMethod.com (or ABBSM.com).

Postscript

"Every word of God *is* pure: he *is* a shield unto them that put their trust in him. Add thou not unto his words, lest he reprove thee, and thou be found a liar" (Prv 30:5-6).

"Thou shalt not bear false witness" (Mt 19:18).

"Blessed is that man that maketh the LORD his trust, and respecteth not the proud, nor such as turn aside to lies" (Ps 40:4).

"There is a way which seemeth right unto a man, but the end thereof *are* the ways of death" (Prv 14:12).

"Every way of a man *is* right in his own eyes" (Prv 21:2).

"He that trusteth in his own heart is a fool: but whoso walketh wisely, he shall be delivered" (Prv 28:26).

"The fear of the LORD *is* the beginning of knowledge: *but* fools despise wisdom and instruction" (Prv 1:7).

"Hear instruction, and be wise, and refuse it not" (Prv 8:33).

"The ear that heareth the reproof of life abideth among the wise. He that refuseth instruction despiseth his own soul: but he that heareth reproof getteth understanding" (Prv 15:31-32).

"Prove all things; hold fast that which is good" (1Th 5:21).

"Judge not according to the appearance, but judge righteous judgment" (Fourth gospel 7:24).

"The heart of the righteous studieth to answer" (Prv 15:28).

"The heart of the prudent getteth knowledge; and the ear of the wise seeketh knowledge" (Prv 18:15).

"Trust in the LORD with all thine heart; and lean not unto thine own understanding. In all thy ways acknowledge him, and he shall direct thy paths" (Prv 3:5-6).

Index

A

Abraham, 42, 47, 84-5, 152, 156-7, 162, 166, 179, 180-1, 191-2, 196, 214, 217

Apostles, the, 71, 73, 75, 89-93, 95, 100, 104, 112, 144, 158, 162, 174, 177, 206-7

B

Bathsheba, 18, 22-5, 27-9

Better Bible study method, a, 6-7, 14-5, 43, 112, 169, 227, 230

Bible, the (scripture), 5-10, 14, 16-8, 22-7, 29, 31-3, 36, 38-9, 40, 43-4, 46-9, 52, 55, 57, 59, 61, 63-6, 68-74, 81, 86-9, 91-2, 95, 97, 101-4, 107-8, 110-13, 115-17, 119-20, 122-3, 126, 129-30, 132-8, 143-4, 148, 154, 157, 161-2, 168-9, 171-4, 177, 184-6, 190, 195-7, 199-200, 205, 208, 211, 213, 217-18, 222-5, 227, 231

  according to, 5, 24, 32, 59, 72, 103-4, 108, 113-4, 121, 157, 188, 204, 210, 223

  as evidence, 5, 16, 23, 28, 61, 95, 119, 125, 169

  authority of, 26, 76, 90, 98, 101, 107, 110, 113, 119, 127, 154, 161-2, 164, 171, 182-3, 227

  counsel of, the, 25, 98, 102, 105, 114, 202, 230

  inspired by God, 4, 7, 97, 108, 116, 130, 135-6

  measure of truth, the, 6, 22, 38, 99, 100, 110-11, 113-5, 120, 138, 140, 143-4, 177

word of God, the, 5-10, 12, 14-16, 21-3, 26, 30, 32-3, 37-8, 41, 51, 56, 62, 67-70, 73, 75, 77-8, 84, 87, 89, 92, 97, 99-106, 108, 110-22, 128-30, 132-5, 137-9, 140, 143, 146, 148-9, 155-6, 167, 173-5, 177-8, 187, 189-95, 200-02, 211-12, 216, 220-25, 227-8, 230-32

Born again, 60, 62-70, 77, 116

C

Cain, 131, 142, 149, 219

Cornelius, 82-6, 162, 207

Cretians, 144-5

D

David, 5-6, 17-30, 39, 72-3, 154

  his mighty men, 25, 27-9

  killed Uriah, 19, 21, 26

  took Bathsheba, 18, 20-6, 28-9

Disciples. See Jesus, disciples of.

Double standard, 137, 140, 143, 148, 216, 219

Drink blood, 5-6, 38

F

Faith, 5, 31-2, 46, 54, 68, 88, 111, 114, 127-30, 137-9, 142, 145, 157-8, 160, 170, 179-80, 183-6, 189-91, 205, 217-8, 220-3

  so great, 126

False prophets, 104-5, 200

Fear of the LORD/of God, 4, 25, 82-5, 112, 157, 164, 177, 190, 194, 199, 202, 220, 230, 232

G

God, 5-8, 16-17, 21, 23, 25-6, 29,
31-3, 36-41, 44-7, 49-51, 53, 55-
64, 66-78, 81-90, 92-3, 95, 97-9,
101-4, 106-10, 112-22, 124, 127-
44, 146, 148-9, 152-8, 160-91,
195-203, 205-15, 217-27, 231
  authority of, 26, 55, 58, 62-3,
  101, 103, 107, 108, 110, 119,
  128, 132, 135, 137, 146, 196, 211
  counsel of, 53, 56, 110, 192,
  195, 224, 230
  glory of, 87, 164, 181-82
  grace of, 85, 102, 133, 154, 176,
  185, 188, 206, 222-4, 228
  honor from, 102, 121, 230
  kingdom of, 57-60, 62-8, 70, 75,
  184, 203, 209, 215, 224-7
  showing honor to, 85, 87-8, 97,
  99, 120, 128, 181, 190, 199,
  211, 222, 224, 230
  will of, the, 72, 158, 161, 171,
  190, 195-6, 198, 202-4, 209,
  229, 230
  so loved the world, 167-8, 172-4,
  178, 200
Gospel, the, 51, 54, 68, 82, 103-4,
121, 157, 174, 183, 190, 205, 214

J

Jesus, 5-6, 8, 17, 23-5, 29, 31-3, 35,
37-40, 42-69, 71-81, 84-95, 98-101,
103-4, 106-7, 110, 111-20, 123-30,
132, 134-5, 138-9, 143-4, 146-58,
160-3, 166, 168-71, 173-5, 177,
183, 185-6, 188-9, 191, 195-6,
198-200, 203-6, 208-11, 214,
216-20, 222, 224-5, 227-8, 230

abide in/believe on/continue in,
  9, 49, 151-2, 156, 183, 198, 222-4
  blood of, 5, 38, 78, 218
  caused division, 48-9, 107, 151-3,
  202
  disciples of, 9, 45-6, 48, 67, 91-5,
  98, 101, 113, 124-5, 127-8, 151,
  156, 170, 183, 198
  only begotten Son, the, 167-8,
  172-4, 178
  raised a widow's son, 45-6
  raised Lazarus, 46, 125, 127, 130
  resurrection of, 46, 50, 71-4,
  85, 89, 90-95, 99, 101, 104,
  109-10, 163, 203, 206, 214
  wept, 123-6, 128-30
John the Baptist, 43-6, 48, 51, 53,
  56, 70, 110-11, 120, 158, 162, 217
  his question, 43, 46-7, 51-2
  no greater prophet than, 46, 50

L

Law, the
  of God, 148, 165-6, 191, 218
  of Moses, 150, 282, 302-3
  of sin and death, 185-7, 189
  of the LORD, 187, 193, 195, 211
  of the Spirit, 185-6
Lazarus, 46, 124-5, 127, 130
Lord, the, 6-7, 17, 20-27, 30, 41, 45,
  47, 50, 68, 74, 83, 88, 90, 91-4,
  101-2, 104-9, 112, 114-15, 118,
  120-21, 124, 126-30, 141, 156,
  159-60, 163, 166, 175-6, 178, 182,
  191-2, 197, 199, 207, 227-8, 231-2
  reason together with, 33, 34
Love of the truth, 85, 152-4, 156,
  178

Love thy neighbor, 86, 191, 228
Lusts of the flesh, 210-11, 213, 222

M

Martha, Lazarus' sister, 123-5, 128
Mary, Lazarus' sister 123-5, 128
Matthias, 90-95
Miracles, 43, 49, 51, 56-8, 60-63, 74-5, 125, 127-8, 130, 154, 225, 227
Moses, 8, 47, 49-50, 88, 91, 98, 100, 103-4, 119, 172, 182, 190, 196, 217, 227. *See also* Prophet like Moses

N

Nathan the prophet, 20-23, 27, 29-30, 39
Nicodemus, 16, 53, 60-70

P

Paul, 8, 17, 44, 54, 86, 90-92, 95, 98-100, 103-4, 109, 114-15, 121, 131-2, 144, 158, 160-62, 165, 187, 207, 216, 222
Pentecost, 71, 92-3, 144, 205, 209, 214
Peter, 24, 50, 71-7, 80, 82-6, 90-93, 102, 121, 133, 158-9, 161, 166, 196, 205, 210, 214, 224-5
Pharisees, 16, 32, 48-9, 53, 56, 60, 62, 70, 98, 101, 110-11, 113, 117, 133-4, 158, 217, 226
Priests, chief, 32, 56, 63, 98, 117, 133
Prophet like Moses, the, 47-52

R

Repentance, 26, 50, 73-6, 85, 109, 158-60, 165, 182, 184-5, 187, 196, 214, 217, 223, 225
Replacement for Judas, 91, 92, 94
Rewards, 87-8, 165, 171
Righteousness, 7, 70, 84-5, 120, 133, 142, 157, 160, 162, 171, 176-7, 179, 180-81, 183-6, 188, 194, 196, 199, 201, 203, 210, 213, 218-19, 220, 222, 224, 226

S

Sadducees, 32, 98, 101, 133
Samaritan, the good, 146-8, 150
Samaritans, 16, 33, 36, 39, 40-42, 147-8
Sanctification/sanctified/sanctify, 69, 107, 116, 161, 163, 186, 202, 213-14
Scripture(s). *See* Bible, the
Spirit of truth, the, 107
Spirit of unity, a, 106-7
Standard of truth. *See* Bible, the; measure of truth, the

T

Taught by God, 77-8, 81, 87, 107, 115-16, 122, 139
Teachings/traditions of men, the, 7, 14, 56, 100-02, 104, 108, 112-14, 116, 133-5, 137, 143-5, 173, 176, 194, 201, 231
Thomas, 89, 94, 95
Twelve, the, 45, 89-94
Two masters, 107-8, 114, 152, 185, 199

U

Unconditional love, 141, 155, 168-9, 173-8, 196-7

Ungodly counsel, 51, 187, 211

Unity of the Spirit, 107

Understanding, 4, 9, 16, 40, 64, 118, 127, 133, 135-36, 139-41

Uriah the Hittite, 17, 18-28

Uriah's wife. *See* Bathsheba

W

Weightier issues, 111, 137-9

Well of Bethlehem, 6

Whosoever, 24, 34, 36, 46, 51, 97-8, 118, 137, 139, 158, 167-9, 172, 178, 185, 198, 209-10, 214

Wisdom,
justified of her children, 174, 177-8, 245, 279
of God, 81, 160
of this world, 9, 81, 102-4, 116, 160, 178, 191, 269

Wise counsel, 114-15, 118

Woman at Jacob's well, the, 33, 36, 42, 147
had five husbands, 34-5, 37-41

Word numbers, 64-5, 170-172

Word pictures, 5-6, 15, 20, 23, 38-41, 54, 68-70, 102, 131, 133, 149, 169, 190

Writers of scripture, the, 64, 78, 92, 93, 129, 133, 155, 172, 189

The eBook version is available from ABetterBibleStudyMethod.com
The electronic text can also be searched to find passages in this book

"Blessed *is* every one that feareth the LORD; that walketh in his ways"
(Ps 128:1).